THE MAGICAL MELTING POT™

PRAIRIE VIEW MIDDLE SCHOOL
MEDIA CENTER
TINLEY PARK, IL 60477

THE MAGICAL MELTING POT ™

America's Leading Chefs Share Childhood Memories and Favorite Foods

Michelle Greenwald

CHEF ILLUSTRATIONS
Alvina Kwong

MAP ILLUSTRATIONS
Linda Jo Russell

CHERRY PRESS
CALIFORNIA

**To order individual copies or larger quantities for premiums,
sales promotions, fund-raising, or educational use,
please visit our website at
www.magicalmeltingpot.com
Special editions or book excerpts can also be created to specifications.**

Copyright© 2003 by Michelle Greenwald

All rights reserved. No portion of this book may be reproduced—
mechanically, electronically,
or by any other means, including photocopying—
without written permission of the publisher.

The Magical Melting Pot™:The All-Family Cookbook That Celebrates America's Diversity

Published by Cherry Press, a division of The Magical Melting Pot LLC

Library of Congress Control Number: 2003092161

ISBN 0-9717565-0-3

Cover Design/Photography and Interior Design:
Koechel Peterson & Associates, Inc.
Minneapolis, Minnesota
www.koechelpeterson.com
Interior Concept Design: Kathy Herlihy-Paoli
Michelle Greenwald
Chef Illustrations by Alvina Kwong
Map Illustrations by Linda Jo Russell

Manufactured in Hong Kong

First Printing October 2003
10 9 8 7 6 5 4 3 2 1

DEDICATION

Dedicated to my parents Florence and Irving,

who inspired in me a love of travel,

a fascination with other cultures,

and a passion for adventurous eating

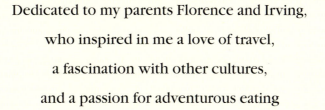

ACKNOWLEDGEMENTS

I'd first like to thank all the chefs in the book for allowing me to interview them and for sharing their stories. They taught me a great deal about their cultures and cuisines, and also about the importance of having a vision and the determination to see it through.

I'd also like to thank Alvina Kwong, my illustrator, for her perpetual good cheer and for her tremendous talent. When I began this project I was discouraged from working with an illustrator so young, who lacked professional experience. After working with Alvina, for the past few years, however, I can't think of anyone I would have enjoyed working with more. I loved Alvina's style and creativity, her ability to deliver what I was looking for, and her sense of responsibility.

A special thank you to Kathy Hurlihy-Paoli for her brilliant interior design. It captured the friendly, accessible, inviting look I was after. I thank her also for her patience and tremendous professionalism. Thanks to David Koechel and Heather Rohm for their dynamic and distinctive cover and their terrific refinement and execution of the book's interior. Thanks to both for their endless patience, honest opinions, and great taste. Thanks to Linda Jo Russell for stepping in and creating and illustrating such charming and informative maps. Thanks to Tom Maakstad for taking such a special interest in this project, and for providing help and input far above and beyond what a printer normally does.

Thanks to Joyce Bromberg, my daughters' former 5th grade teacher, for her help in editing the book. She is one of the best grammarians I know. Thanks to Jessee Silver for encouraging me to use the best people I could find to design and execute my book and for encouraging me not to settle for mediocrity given the amazing group of chefs, the strength of the concept, and the quality of Alvina's illustrations.

Thanks to my three children Adam, Rachel, and Becky for letting me drag them all over on food adventures for all these years, for their willingness to try my kitchen experiments, and for listening to me talk incessantly about the book. My deep appreciation to Rachel for letting me know how proud she was of what I was doing, and to Becky for taking such genuine interest in all aspects of the book and for always being there for me. I'll never forget it. Thanks to Adam for photographing several of the chefs.

Thanks to my sister Wendy and my friend Faye Strumpf for being such terrific resources and for their interest in my frequent progress reports. Thanks to the libraries, librarians, bookstores, and coffee shops for providing me with a nice environment to work in.

Lastly, thanks to my parents, Florence and Irving Kram, who took us with them on their travels abroad, and by example taught us to love the adventure of discovering open air markets, new foods, cultures, and customs. It has so enriched my life and now enriches the lives of my children.

The Garden of Humanity

The garden of humanity is beautiful because of its magnificent variety.

The splendor of each rose does not compete with

or diminish that of the tulip, geranium or orchid.

Each human being, different and special in color and culture,

is necessary for the beauty of the whole.

TINA ANDREWS

TABLE OF CONTENTS

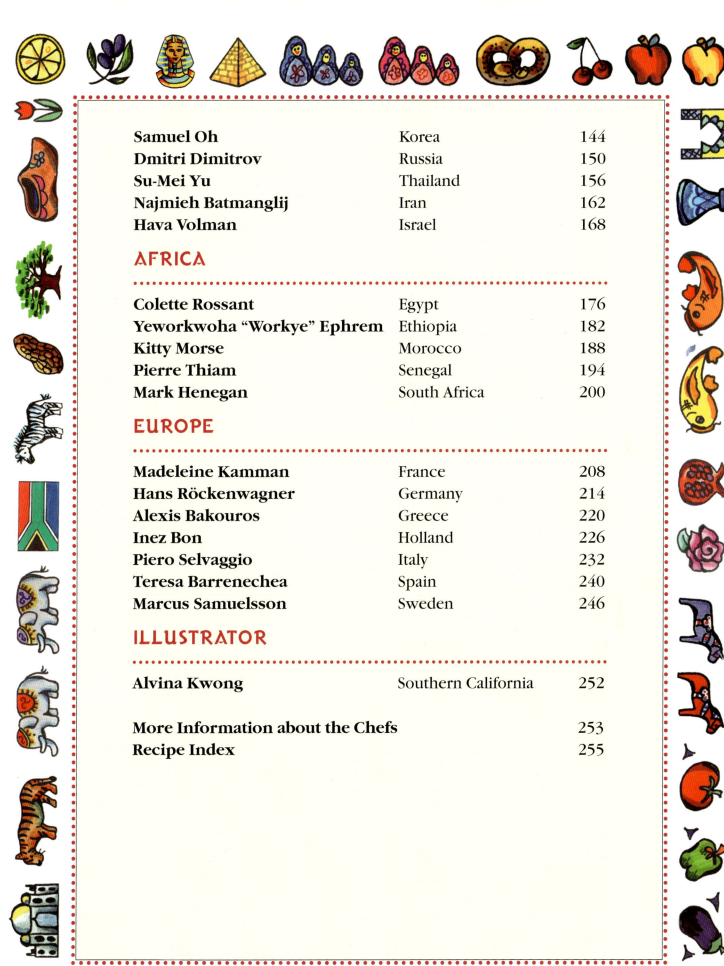

INTRODUCTION

I've wanted to write this book for years and finally decided "to do it". I thought the stories about the foods and traditions of different cultures would be extremely interesting. While that has proven to be the case, what have also been both fascinating and tremendously inspiring, are the stories of each of the chefs, restaurant owners, cookbook authors, and other food professionals featured in the book. A number of these individuals came to America from other countries at a young age to seek a better life. In some cases they came with very little. With hard work, a goal, and determination, they succeeded in realizing their dreams.

I have great respect and admiration for the chefs and restaurant owners because they possess so many different types of skills. They are chemists who almost magically transform ingredients into delicious foods. They're often artists who make dishes that are beautiful to look at. They're inventors and innovators, often adapting the foods of their countries by finding and using the best available, local ingredients. They're goodwill ambassadors who share their native cultures, make their guests feel at home, and create good relations with their communities. They're leaders, directing and guiding their employees to create food, service, and an environment their customers will enjoy. Last, but not least, they are good business people who know they must earn a profit to survive.

America is both a "*Magical Melting Pot*" and a colorful mosaic. We're becoming even stronger as a nation because we're learning not just to tolerate our differences, but to appreciate and enjoy them. What better or more pleasurable way to learn about each other than by sharing the foods and customs of the different countries represented in our population! Food is fun and comforting. It reflects traditions, history, religion, celebrations, and family. Both the rapid growth of different types of ethnic restaurants across the United States, and the dramatic increase in ethnic foods carried by grocery stores, are evidence of Americans' growing interests in sampling other cultures.

Every day we're becoming a more and more ethnically diverse country. According to the United States Census Bureau, in 1950, 90% of Americans were Caucasian and only 10% were "minorities". By 2050, the Census Bureau projects that the percent of Caucasians will comprise only 53% of the U.S. population. By around 2060, "minorities" will be the majority of Americans.

For a long time I've wanted to write a cookbook about foods from different countries that kids especially love to eat and make. Cooking is a way that adults and kids can spend fun, quality time together and learn in the process. Cooking reinforces concepts of math, chemistry, physics, precision, process order, and even art. It encourages creativity; and the result, good food, creates feelings of satisfaction and accomplishment.

I thought it would be fun to ask some of the best chefs, restaurant owners, cooking teachers, food writers, and cookbook authors in America, with a broad range of cultural and ethnic backgrounds, to think back to when they were children. I asked them what their favorite dishes were to eat or help prepare, and why those dishes were so special, both to their cultures and to them personally. I wanted to know how they decided to pursue a career in food, what steps they took along the way, and what obstacles they had to overcome in order to succeed. I wanted the book to go beyond just providing recipes, to include a context of world geography, culture, customs, and a bit of history.

Recipes were selected that we thought both kids and adults would enjoy. In many cases the recipes were also chosen because they're fun for kids to help make. You, the supervising adult, are the best judge of those kitchen steps you feel your children are capable of safely handling. We've tried to use ingredients that are available in most major supermarkets, as well as utensils and equipment that most Americans already have in their kitchens. On a few occasions, a unique kitchen implement or an unusual ingredient is used. Whenever possible, a more commonly available (though less authentic) substitute is provided as an alternative. The *Magical Melting Pot*™ website: www.magicalmeltingpot.com will list sources for hard to find utensils and ingredients, plus other information.

Learning about the foods of other countries is a fun way to develop an adventurous spirit and gain a greater appreciation of our differences.

Have fun cooking and eating!

KITCHEN MATH

3 teaspoons = 1 tablespoon

1 tablespoon = ½ fluid ounce

2 tablespoons = 1 fluid ounce

4 tablespoons = ¼ cup

5 ⅓ tablespoons = ⅓ cup

8 tablespoons = ½ cup

10 ⅔ tablespoons = ⅔ cup

12 tablespoons = ¾ cup

16 tablespoons = 1 cup

1 cup = 8 fluid ounces

1 cup = ½ pint

2 cups = 1 pint

4 cups = 1 quart

2 pints = 1 quart

4 quarts = 1 gallon

16 ounces = 1 pound

Butter

1 stick = 4 ounces = ½ cup

Sugar

Granulated:

   1 pound = 2 ½ cups

Brown:

   1 pound = 2 ⅓ cups packed

White Flour

   1 pound = 4 cups

Potatoes

1 pound = 3 medium

   or 2 ⅓ cups sliced

Eggs

2 large = 3 small

8-10 large egg whites = 1 cup

12-14 large egg yolks = 1 cup

1 large egg = ¼ cup

Lemon

1 medium lemon yields

   3 tablespoons juice

1 medium lemon yields

   1 tablespoon grated rind

Tomatoes

1 pound = 3 medium

LESSONS LEARNED

I've made my fair share of cooking mistakes over the years and have learned a number of lessons I wanted to share with you.

1. Don't try too many new dishes at one time, especially for a party. I'm often overly ambitious and plan to make more dishes than I can comfortably handle. Inevitably I "peter out" and never get to the last few dishes, even though I've shopped for the ingredients, because I run out of time.

2. Read through the recipe and place all the ingredients on your counter before you start. I often forget to add an ingredient because I accidentally failed to read a step. Having all the ingredients out on your counter will increase the likelihood that even if you do forget a step, you'll realize it when you see the ingredient sitting on your counter. Hopefully it won't be too late.

3. Follow the recipe instructions as closely as you can the first time you prepare the dish. After that, feel free to improvise. Once you try a recipe, you'll often think of ways that you can improve upon it, or make it more to your liking. It's good to see the way the cook book author envisions the dish by following the directions the first time, but don't be afraid to experiment and make it your own after that.

4. Feel free to combine dishes from different cultures within the same meal. Feel free to plan a menu that might, for example, include a side dish from Latin America with a meat dish from Africa and a dessert from Europe. Combinations can work extremely well.

5. Don't be afraid your family won't like a change from their normal food routines. I've found that the more I get my family used to trying new and different foods, the more they like it when I prepare something they've never tasted. They enjoy the surprise element and invariably like the dishes. They've also become more adventurous when dining out, and when eating at the homes of friends from different cultural backgrounds.

6. Encourage your family to help with the preparation and the cleanup. Cooking together is a fun, creative, and bonding experience. Enlisting help with the cleanup instills in family members the habit of keeping a kitchen clean. Importantly, it also makes the task of cooking far more enjoyable for you, so you'll feel like doing it more often.

NORTH AMERICA

Alan Wong

Hawaii

Alice Waters

Northern California

Sam Choy

Hawaii

Thomas Keller

Northern California

Norma Jean Darden

New York

Loretta Barrett Oden

Oklahoma

Ella Brennan

New Orleans

Patrick O'Connell

Virginia

Marion Cunningham

Northern California

Michelle Greenwald

Southern California

Zarela Martinez

Mexico

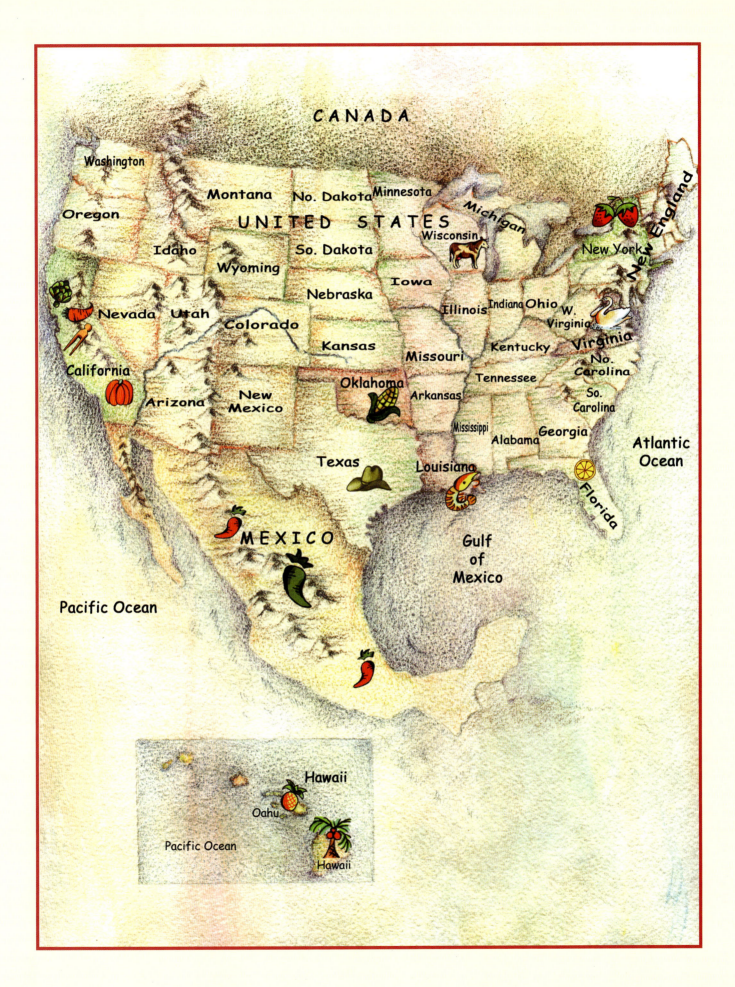

Alan Wong

Hawaii

Above: Alan Wong, 4 years old, cutting cucumbers.
Left: Chef Alan Wong.

As Alan Wong will tell you, no one has been more surprised at what a successful chef he's become than his mother, because as a child he was such a picky eater. Alan, who has a great sense of humor, made me laugh when he described his childhood eating habits. He hated all vegetables with the exception of corn, peas and tomatoes. They made him gag and he just couldn't swallow them.

Alan related how in 4th grade his teacher would inspect his tray at lunch to make sure he'd eaten his vegetables. He tried to convince her that he was allergic to vegetables. When that didn't work, he came up with the bright idea of stuffing them into his empty milk cartons. One day his teacher discovered what he was up to, so he developed a new plan: he'd stuff the vegetables into the pockets of his shorts or pants. After lunch came recess, at the end of which he'd have big wet patches around his pockets. The worst were from soft, mushy vegetables like creamed spinach, coleslaw, and red beets that stained. His mom, who did his laundry every day, particularly dreaded creamed spinach day. Eventually

Alan outgrew his aversion to vegetables, and today he can eat anything.

If you asked Alan when he was a kid what he'd be when he grew up, he would have told you a baseball coach. He loved baseball so much that he slept with his baseball and mitt.

Alan was born in Japan, to a Hawaiian Chinese father and a Japanese mother. When he was 5, his parents decided to move back to the Hawaiian Island of Oahu. When Alan was 9, he developed asthma, and his family moved out of the city to an area near the pineapple fields where the air would be cleaner. As a kid, he spent most summers working in the pineapple fields to earn extra money.

One of Alan's first cooking experiments was a fiasco that looking back, makes him laugh. When he was 13 years old, he tried to cook a hot dog. He boiled it and boiled it until it exploded and the hot dog skin popped off. It looked like a giant meatball.

Alan grew up surrounded by good cooks. Both his Chinese grandfather, who enjoyed cooking for large parties, and his Japanese mother, who was an excellent cook, taught him the importance of good tasting food, and how to distinguish good food from bad. He also grew up knowing the tastes of a variety of ingredients such as ginger, wasabi, and miso, so he later felt comfortable experimenting with them. Family get-togethers were usually potluck parties on the beach where all his relatives, who had different ethnic backgrounds, would try to outdo each other with the different dishes they'd bring. Today Alan's mom cooks at his restaurant on weekends, and she sometimes cooks the staff meals.

Alan attributes some of his success to his curiosity. He was born in the Chinese year of the monkey and he said that growing up he was a lot like Curious George, always wanting to learn more. He first became interested in food preparation when his friend, who was a chef at a hotel, taught him how to carve ice and vegetables. His first restaurant job, when he was 15, was washing dishes in a hotel in Hawaii. He went on to work at ten different jobs in that hotel: including busboy, waiter, host, cashier, front desk, and manager.

Alan then decided to go to cooking school to learn more about how good food was prepared. As he says, prior to that point, he thought that bread came out of a package and salad dressing came out of a bottle. In culinary school he found that the more he learned, the more he wanted to learn; and he began to try foods he'd never eaten before. For the most part, he liked them. One of the first "real" dishes Alan made was a great tasting banana cream pie. It was a

Pineapples

Columbus discovered pineapple when he visited the West Indies. The Spanish brought it back to Spain along with the Indian custom of placing pineapples on their doors or roofs to indicate that strangers were welcome. That's how pineapples came to signify hospitality.

Pineapples are ripe when slightly soft to the touch and golden yellow in color. It's one of the few fruits that don't ripen after picking. They should not be too green (under ripe) or evidence decay at the base (over ripe). Hibiscus is the state flower of Hawaii.

revelation to realize just how much he was capable of creating.

After culinary school, Alan set about learning as much as possible about fine food from the best teachers he could find. He worked for several years at the grand, world famous Greenbrier Hotel in West Virginia. Next he worked at Lutèce in New York City, the best French restaurant in America at the time, under the legendary, French born chef, Andre Soultner. After three years at Lutèce, Alan decided to return to Hawaii, where he was able to combine his classical training with the wonderful ingredients and dishes that were native to Hawaii.

Back in Hawaii, Alan worked in the restaurants of several fine hotels and then decided to open his own restaurant in 1995. His restaurant, Alan Wong's in Honolulu, is so extraordinary, that it's been voted Hawaii's favorite restaurant every year since 1996. Gourmet Magazine just rated his restaurant the 6th best restaurant of any kind in the United States. His food celebrates the melting pot of different cultures that live in Hawaii.

Part of the restaurant's success is due to Alan's creativity. Besides coming up with unusual new ingredient combinations, he has fun names for many of his dishes, like "Ultimate Wontons", "Poky Pines", and "Loco Moco". In addition, he uses fun presentations, like serving coleslaw in shave ice cups, and a seafood dish in what looks like Jiffy Pop foil. The symbol for his restaurant is a golden pineapple. Pineapples have traditionally been a symbol of hospitality. The restaurant's pineapple logo represents the hospitality he wants his guests to enjoy, and it has personal significance because it reminds Alan of the pineapple fields he lived near and worked in as a boy.

Alan shares his recipes for Pineapple granita, a refreshing, light dessert, and for the Hoisin Baby Back Ribs he developed to recreate the flavors he enjoyed as a kid at family hibachi barbecues in his backyard or at the beach.

Alan loves to teach people who are interested in becoming chefs how to cook. He has a way of encouraging his students to stretch themselves. He's very supportive and delights when his students and staff succeed. Alan is a great coach who teaches the importance of teamwork. In his spare time he enjoys night fishing and diving and singing karaoke.

ASIAN SLAW

(makes 6-8 servings)

1 cup red cabbage, thinly sliced
4 cups Chinese cabbage, thinly sliced
1 cup snow peas, julienned
1 cup carrots, julienned
8 won-ton wrappers, julienned and deep fried until crispy

1. Combine all the vegetables and won-ton wrappers in a large bowl.

2. Toss with the soy vinaigrette below.

Vinaigrette

¼ cup water
½ cup soy sauce
¼ cup vegetable oil
¼ cup rice wine vinegar
¼ cup mirin (rice wine)

2 cloves garlic, crushed
2 tablespoons minced ginger
¼ teaspoon sesame oil
2 tablespoons lime juice
1 serrano chile, minced

1. Combine the ingredients in a bowl.

2. Refrigerate for at least 30 minutes to allow the flavors to marry.

3. Strain and stir before pouring over the slaw ingredients above.

ADAPTED FROM ALAN WONG

ROASTED GARLIC SMASHED POTATOES

(makes 4 servings)

1 ½ pounds potatoes, peeled
2 ounces (½ stick) butter
6 ounces half-and-half cream, warmed

2 heads garlic, roasted
Salt and pepper to taste

1. Cut off the tops of both heads of garlic. Wrap each head in foil and bake in a preheated 350° oven about 45 minutes, or until soft when pierced with a fork.

2. Steam peeled potatoes for around 40 minutes, or until fully cooked. Mash the potatoes while they're still warm, and place in a medium bowl.

3. Cut the butter in pieces and add it to the warm potatoes. Stir until the butter is melted. Add the cream.

4. Remove the foil from the garlic and squeeze the soft garlic from each clove into the mashed potato mixture.

5. Mix well and season with salt and pepper to taste.

ADAPTED FROM ALAN WONG

Magical Melting Pot

HOISIN BABY BACK RIBS

(makes 6 servings)

These ribs are unusually good. If you have extra sauce, you can keep it in the refrigerator for up to a week and use it on chicken. The ribs (and chicken) are best when allowed to marinate in the sauce all day or overnight.

¾ cup hoisin sauce

1 cup ketchup

½ cup honey

5 tablespoons soy sauce

5 tablespoons dry sherry

¼ cup plus 2 tablespoons white wine vinegar

¼ cup white sesame seeds, toasted

2 tablespoons plus 2 teaspoons curry powder

2 tablespoons plus 2 teaspoons dark sesame oil

2 tablespoons grated orange zest

2 tablespoons fermented black beans (available in Asian section of grocery)

2 tablespoons minced garlic

1 tablespoon minced red serrano chiles with seeds, or 1 tablespoon chile sauce with garlic (available in Asian section of grocery)

3 pounds pork baby back ribs

Salt and pepper to taste

1. Combine the ingredients above to make the sauce.

2. Divide the ribs and place in two baking dishes. Reserve half the sauce and refrigerate separately. Spread the remaining sauce over the ribs. Refrigerate eight hours or overnight.

3. Heat the grill. Remove the sauce and sprinkle the ribs with salt and pepper.

4. Preheat the oven to 375°.

5. Grill the ribs for 15 minutes, turning frequently.

6. Transfer the ribs to a roasting pan. Add 1 inch of water, brush with ½ the remaining sauce, and cover with foil.

7. Bake in the oven for about 2 hours or until fork-tender. Cut into individual ribs and transfer them to a serving platter.

8. Simmer the remaining sauce until heated through. Transfer to a small bowl with a ladle, and pass the sauce separately.

ADAPTED FROM ALAN WONG

PINEAPPLE GRANITA

(makes 12 servings)

Granita comes from the Italian word for granular or grainy. It's a coarse form of sorbet that's made with the clear juice of the fruit and it doesn't contain any milk or cream. An ice cream maker is not used to make granita.

**1 whole pineapple, skin
and core removed**

**1 ½ cups sugar
Enough water to make 1 gallon**

1. Purée half the pineapple in a food processor, adding enough water to make a loose purée. Strain it through a fine sieve. Repeat with the other pineapple half. The purée will be a beautiful golden yellow color. Discard the pulp that remains in the sieve.

2. Dissolve the sugar in 1 quart of water in a saucepan over low heat, until the sugar is totally dissolved.

3. Add the strained pineapple juice to the sugar water solution and add enough water to make one gallon.

4. Pour into a large metal bowl and place in the freezer.

5. After about 45 minutes, use a wire whisk to beat the granita throughout. Return to the freezer and whisk approximately every 20 minutes until it's nearly frozen. Transfer to a glass Pyrex baking pan and freeze completely.

6. When ready to serve, use the tines of a fork to scrape out the ice crystals into individual size portions.

ADAPTED FROM ALAN WONG

Hawiian/English Translations

aloha	love, hello	mahalo	thank you
kaukau	food	lei	garland of flowers
kai	sea	pua	flower, garden
kahuna	priest, someone skilled	keiki	child
tsunami	tidal wave	wai	water

Sam Choy

Hawaii

Above: Sam at age 4.
Left: Sam Choy at a Luau.
Photo by Douglas Peebles.

The mayor of the island of Hawaii named Sam Choy Hawaii's culinary ambassador, and others have called him the ambassador of Hawaii's "soul food". In Hawaii he's a celebrity. When people see him, everyone says hi and wants an autograph, a handshake, or a hug. Sam is known for popularizing Hawaiian "comfort food" which is characterized by fresh fish and vegetables, and generous helpings of rice and Spam. Spam is a canned mixture of pork shoulder and ham that's extremely popular in Hawaii and is usually eaten in slices or cut up in chunks.

Sam grew up in a little fishing village called Laie on the north shore of the island of Oahu. His mother was part German and part Hawaiian and his father was 3rd generation Chinese. His father's family were taro root (a potato-like root) farmers, and his grandmother routinely cooked for all the workers on the farm. Sam's dad learned to cook from his mom, and Sam in turn learned from his dad. He loved watching his dad neatly cut vegetables into strips for stir-fries. Sam's dad impressed upon him the importance of making the food look good going into the pot, so it would come out of the pot looking good, and he also stressed that attractive presentation was key.

Later in life, Sam's father opened his own restaurant, and on week-ends started the first large luaus for tourists and locals on Oahu. As many as 800 people would attend each luau. A luau is a traditional outdoor feast with a wide variety of beautifully presented Hawaiian dishes. It always includes a pig that's been roasted in charcoals in the ground for hours until it becomes tasty, soft, and tender. Luau guests are often given a lei necklace made of fresh, local flower blossoms. Sam, his brother, and sisters would take turns cooking at home during the week and helping his father prepare the luaus on weekends.

Sam's mother was also an excellent cook, though her cooking style was very different. As a result of her German heritage, she made wonderful roasted meats and stews.

One of Sam's favorite food memories was his family's traditional Halloween meal that he still makes every year for his own children. It includes creamed chicken, Harvard beets, and mashed potatoes. When Sam was young, he used to play with the food on his plate. He always mixed his peas and corn into his mashed potatoes. He still likes his mashed potatoes that way, and figured others would as well, so he turned it into a popular side dish that's now served in his restaurants.

Sam worked in hotel kitchens for more than 20 years, before opening his own restaurant. Even though he'd attended a local cooking school and had plenty of experience cooking both at home for his family and at his dad's large luaus, he still had to start from the bottom up as a dishwasher. Gradually, however, he impressed people; and he worked his way into more responsible positions at hotels like the Waldorf Astoria in New York City and the Kona Hilton in Hawaii.

Sam first became famous when he went out on his own and opened a tiny restaurant in an industrial park on the island of Hawaii. The food was so good, the portions so huge, and the prices so reasonable, that the restaurant became a big hit. Today the restaurant has t-shirts for sale that say "Yup-No Small Portions" and "Never Trust a Skinny Chef". The cooking is home-style, local cooking. Everything is very fresh, and whenever possible, Sam uses "Island fresh" local products: the fish he serves comes right off the boats each day and the lettuce for salads comes from gardens that grow near the lava line. As Sam puts it best: "I cook the comfort foods from when I grew up. I think of my cuisine as a melting pot that gathers the freshest ingredients from every culture on these islands. What we like to offer and what Hawaii is all about—is Aloha: welcome, warmth, open your doors, come in and share."

Today Sam is an extremely busy man! He currently has eight restaurants; he's written ten cookbooks; he's the host of the popular Hawaiian TV show "Sam Choy's Kitchen"; and he has his own line of frozen foods.

As busy as he is, Sam still finds time to head a program for kids called "Let's Forget About Crime. Let's Learn to Cook and Grind." He believes kids will learn to become adventurous eaters if they're taught to help in the kitchen. In the process they learn about foods and cooking, ask questions, and train their taste buds. Sam is also involved in the Big Brothers and Big Sisters Program and he's helped create a new Children's Discovery Center in Hawaii. What follows are some of the recipes that kids enjoy when they dine at Sam's restaurants.

CHICKEN LONG RICE

(makes 6 servings)

Chicken long rice is a comforting chicken noodle soup with a subtle ginger and garlic flavor. The long rice is really clear noodles called cellophane noodles, made from mung beans.

1 pound boneless, skinless
  chicken thighs
2 quarts water
1 teaspoon salt
2 cloves garlic, crushed
1 tablespoon canola oil
¼ cup fresh ginger root,
  sliced

4 ounces long rice
  (Cellophane noodles, also
  called glass noodles or
  mung bean threads are
  available in the Asian foods
  section of grocery stores.)
½ cup chopped green onions
Soy sauce (optional)

TO PRE-COOK CHICKEN AND BROTH

1. In a large pot, sauté chicken thighs in oil over medium-high heat until brown.

2. Add garlic and sauté until garlic begins to turn light brown.

3. Add water and fresh ginger. Bring liquid to a boil.

4. Lower heat and simmer for about 40 minutes, or until chicken is tender.

5. Remove pot from heat. When chicken is cool enough to handle, carefully move to a plate. Reserve the broth in the pot.

TO PREPARE DISH

1. Add long rice (cellophane noodles) to the reserved broth and let stand for 20 minutes.

2. Meanwhile, tear or cut chicken into bite-size pieces. Set aside.

3. Remove long rice with a slotted spoon, again reserving the broth.

4. Cut strands of long rice into 4-inch lengths using a knife or kitchen shears.

5. Return the chicken and long rice to the reserved broth and heat for another 5 to 10 minutes, or until the long rice is clear in color.

6. Serve in individual bowls and sprinkle with chopped green onions. If you'd like, you can stir in a little soy sauce to taste.

ADAPTED FROM SAM CHOY

SLOPPY DOGS WITH BEANS

(makes 4 servings)

1 can (15 ounces) pork and beans
2 tablespoons brown sugar
2 tablespoons ketchup
1 teaspoon prepared mustard

2 hot dogs (frankfurters)
4 hot dog buns
¼ cup shredded Cheddar cheese

1. Place pork and beans into a medium-size pot and cook over medium heat, partially covered until small bubbles appear. Add brown sugar, ketchup, and mustard and stir.

2. Meanwhile, slice hot dogs into thin slices. Add to beans and stir. Heat until thoroughly cooked (about 5 minutes).

3. Place open buns on plates and top with bean mixture. Sprinkle shredded cheese over top and serve. (It's probably easiest to eat this with a knife and fork.)

ADAPTED FROM SAM CHOY

SOMEN SALAD

(makes 4-6 servings)

This is a delicious and hearty pasta salad with a light, slightly sweet dressing. Somen is a type of egg noodle that looks like curly spaghetti and comes from Japan. It's available in the Asian section of grocery stores. If you can't find it, substitute 9 ounces of regular spaghetti.

1 package (9 ounces) somen noodles
   (Look in Asian section of grocery.)
Water for boiling pasta
1 tablespoon vegetable oil
   (for pasta pot)
½ head iceberg lettuce, shredded

1 cup thinly sliced ham,
   cut in ¼-inch strips
1 hard boiled egg, diced
1 small cucumber, cut into
   thin strips

SOMEN SALAD DRESSING
3 tablespoons rice vinegar
2 teaspoons vegetable oil
2 teaspoons toasted sesame oil
3 tablespoons soy sauce
2 tablespoons granulated sugar
1 tablespoons sesame seeds

1. Combine all the salad dressing ingredients in a small bowl and whisk them together.

TO PREPARE SALAD

1. Boil 2 quarts water with 1 teaspoon salt and 1 tablespoon vegetable oil in a large pot. Add somen noodles and cook until they start to soften. Drain and set aside. When noodles are cool, cut them into 2-inch lengths.

2. In a large bowl toss together the lettuce, ham, diced egg, cucumber, and somen noodles.

3. Toss with Somen Salad Dressing and serve.

ADAPTED FROM SAM CHOY

PINEAPPLE-COCONUT YUM YUM

(makes 24 bars)

This dessert is rich, delicious, and very Hawaiian.

BOTTOM CRUST
2 sticks (½ pound) butter, softened
1 tablespoon butter to grease the pan
⅔ cup granulated sugar
½ teaspoon vanilla extract
1 ½ cups all-purpose flour
1 cup macadamia nuts, chopped

1. Preheat oven to 350°.

2. Cream the butter and sugar together until light and fluffy. Add the vanilla.

3. Add the flour and macadamia nuts.

4. Press into the bottom of a greased 9 x 13-inch pan and bake for 15 minutes.

FILLING

1 cup sugar
1 tablespoon cornstarch
1 20-ounce can crushed pineapple with juice (2 ½ cups)
½ cup shredded coconut

1. Combine the sugar and cornstarch in a small saucepan.

2. Add the crushed pineapple with juice.

3. Cook over medium heat until thickened.

4. Add the coconut and pour over the crust.

TOPPING

½ cup granulated sugar
¼ cup all-purpose flour
8 tablespoons (1 stick) cold butter, cut into 8 pieces
2 cups rolled oats

1. Combine the sugar, flour, and butter in a bowl.

2. With a pastry cutter or 2 knives, blend the mixture until the butter is the size of peas. Stir in the oatmeal.

3. Sprinkle the topping evenly over the filling and pat down firmly.

4. Bake for about 35 minutes, or until lightly browned.

5. Cut into bars and serve plain or with vanilla ice cream.

ADAPTED FROM SAM CHOY

Coconut

The coconut palm is considered the most useful tree there is. The liquid inside is a beverage. The coconut meat is a food ingredient. Oil can be extracted from the coconut meat for cooking or as ingredient in soap. The leftover pulp is used as animal feed.

Wood, Fronds, and Shells

The wood from coconut trees is used to make furniture. The fronds or leaves can be woven into hats, mats and baskets. The coconut shells can be used to make bowls and cooking and serving implements.

Norma Jean Darden

New York

Above: Norma Jean with her mom and sister, Carole.
Left: Norma Jean in New York.

Norma Jean Darden has enjoyed a wide variety of fun and interesting careers. As a top runway model, she experienced the thrill of showcasing the clothes of the most famous designers in the world; and she appeared in all the leading American and European fashion magazines. She's been an actress, appearing in numerous TV commercials over the years; and she's been a successful author too. Norma Jean has written articles on beauty, fashion, and food for magazines and newspapers; and, together with her sister, she's written the popular cookbook, *Spoonbread and Strawberry Wine*. Today she owns a very successful catering company in New York City, as well as two wonderful restaurants. The path that led her to the catering and restaurant business is an interesting and happy story.

Ever since they were little girls, Norma and her sister, Carole, enjoyed cooking together and giving parties. At one of their parties they mentioned that they were one hundred percent American because their grandfather had been a slave and their great-grandmother

was a Cherokee Indian. The guest asked them if they had any recipes that had been passed down from their ancestors. The question aroused their curiosity because as kids they'd visited relatives in different parts of the country and each family had their own special dishes. They decided to go back to many of the places they'd visited to try and find out more about their relatives and their traditions, and to see if they would share some of their best recipes. Carole and Norma Jean's search took them to Virginia, North Carolina, Alabama, and Ohio.

The recipes they discovered included fruit wines, preserves, breads, candy, ice cream, and even homemade cosmetics. The recipes were wonderful, and their relatives' stories were incredibly inspiring because they were so talented and hardworking, and they had accomplished so much. Norma and Carole were so moved and impressed, that they decided to turn the stories and recipes into a cookbook. They called it *Spoonbread and Strawberry Wine: Recipes and Reminiscences of a Family*.

Spoonbread was a favorite dish that their grandmother prepared often. She lived on a dairy farm and many of the dishes she made used milk and cream. Spoonbread is a custard-like pudding made with milk, eggs, and cornmeal that's eaten as a side dish with the main meal.

Their grandfather, Papa Darden, who was freed from slavery as a young boy, had opened a store where he sold the fruits and vegetables he grew, as well as fresh, hot roasted peanuts. He learned to make wines out of fruits like strawberries, peaches, grapes, and watermelon, and these he sold at his store. The strawberry wine was Norma Jean's favorite. She's still crazy about strawberries. Her restaurants today are decorated with strawberry curtains. Papa Darden and his wife,

Strawberries

Strawberries are actually a member of the rose family. They're also the only fruit that has its seeds on the outside and fleshy fruit inside. Strawberries are an excellent source of vitamin C.

Strawberries are the quintessential American fruit. They're evocative of the 4th of July, strawberry shortcake, and summer.

Dianah, went on to raise ten children who became doctors, lawyers, teachers, and a pharmacist.

Norma Jean and Carole's cookbook was such a success, that people started asking them to cater their parties. Little by little the catering business grew and became very well-known. They specialized in soul food and some African and Caribbean dishes. Norma Jean's company, Spoonbread Catering, has catered parties for famous people like Whitney Houston, Bill Cosby, Mike Tyson, and former New York City Mayor David Dinkins. Their food was featured in Eddie Murphy's movie *Boomerang*. They've even cooked in Africa for the African Culture Festival. The success of her catering business led Norma to open two cheerful restaurants in the Harlem section of New York City, where all her specialties are served in big, hearty portions.

Norma Jean spent most of her childhood growing up in New Jersey, where her dad was a doctor. One of her fondest memories was the family tradition that her dad started: a backyard bar-b-cue every 4th of July. His special fried chicken was one of the highlights. It was crispy and lightly spiced on the outside and very juicy inside. Aunt Annie's candied yams were also a

treat. The yams were tossed with brown sugar, lemon rind, orange juice, butter, cinnamon, and nutmeg, and then baked in the oven. Both are served at Norma Jean's restaurants today.

Every summer her family would travel to the South to visit relatives. Norma Jean remembers helping her aunts and uncles in Wilson, North Carolina make fresh, homemade ice cream on hot summer days. They'd use an old-fashioned ice cream maker with ice (and salt to make the ice even colder). The kids would take turns cranking the machine by hand until the liquid mixture was transformed into frozen ice cream. Norma Jean's two favorite flavors were peach and vanilla.

Another happy memory was making home-made lollipops with her best friend, Dotty Savoy. They'd have a sleepover date on a Friday night, stay up late watching the roller derby competition on TV, and then make cherry and lemon flavored lollipops. With the lollipop sticks they made a grid like a tic-tac-toe board. Then they'd boil the candy syrup until it hardened when dropped into ice water. When it was ready, they poured the syrup in between the squares, and, before the candy had a chance to harden, they'd insert the lollipop sticks standing upright. After the grid sticks were removed, they had square lollipops. The same recipe can be used to make candied apples.

Winters were filled with fun memories too. On the first big snow of the year, their mother would make what they called "nature's ice cream". She'd collect fresh snow in a big pan, add sugar, heavy cream, and vanilla extract, and then mix it all up. It had to be eaten quickly before the snow melted. Boy was it good!

What follows are some of Norma Jean's favorite childhood recipes.

MOM SAMPSON'S SPOONBREAD

(makes 8 servings)

1 cup yellow cornmeal	**1 teaspoon salt**
2 cups boiling water	**3 eggs, well beaten**
2 tablespoons butter	**1 cup milk**

1. Preheat oven to 375°.

2. Grease a 2-quart casserole.

3. Place cornmeal in a medium-size bowl. Add the boiling water, stirring constantly until thick and smooth. Add butter and salt, and cool to lukewarm.

4. Add the eggs and milk, and beat for 2 minutes. Pour into casserole.

5. Bake for 35 minutes, or until golden brown.

6. Serve while still hot and pass the butter!

ADAPTED FROM NORMA JEAN DARDEN

FRIED CHICKEN

(makes 4 servings)

This fried chicken is not heavy or greasy. It has a very light, crunchy crust.

One 2 ½ to 3-pound chicken,
  cut into eighths
One 3-pound can solid vegetable
  shortening or enough vegetable
  oil to reach 1 ½-2 inches up the
  side of a Dutch oven or large
  skillet

1 cup flour
1 ½ teaspoons paprika
1 ½ teaspoons dry mustard
1 teaspoon grated nutmeg
1 teaspoon garlic powder
1 ¼ teaspoons salt
¼ teaspoon black pepper

1. Combine the dry ingredients above in a sturdy plastic bag.

2. Wash the chicken pieces in cold water, leaving some moisture.

3. Place a few pieces of chicken at a time in bag and shake until evenly coated. Set on a plate and coat the rest.

4. Melt the vegetable shortening or heat the vegetable oil in the Dutch oven or large skillet until the fat sizzles when a drop of water hits it.

5. Place half the coated chicken pieces in the hot oil. Do not crowd or place pieces on top of each other. Fry until golden brown on both sides. Drain on paper towels. Repeat to cook the rest.

ADAPTED FROM NORMA JEAN DARDEN

MATTIE'S BAKED MACARONI WITH CHEESE

(makes 8 servings)

This is by far the best macaroni and cheese I've ever had. It's light, fluffy, cheesy and delicious, and extremely easy to make. My biggest regret is that I didn't discover this recipe 25 years ago.

1 tablespoon salt
2 cups uncooked elbow macaroni
½ stick (¼ cup) melted butter
  or margarine
12 ounces (3 cups) cheddar cheese,
  grated

2 eggs, lightly beaten
1 ½ cups (a 12-ounce can)
  evaporated milk
Paprika (optional)

1. Preheat oven to 375°.

2. Fill a 3-quart saucepan with water and place over a high flame. When the water comes to a rapid boil, add salt and gradually add the elbow macaroni so the water does not stop boiling.

3. Cook, uncovered, for 8 to 9 minutes, until the pasta is cooked, but still a little bit firm.

4. Remove from stove, pour into a colander to drain, and rinse with cold water for a few seconds.

5. In a large bowl combine the macaroni, melted butter or margarine, 2 cups of the grated cheese, the eggs, and the milk. Mix gently.

6. Pour into a greased, 2-quart casserole. Sprinkle the remaining cheese over the top and dust with paprika.

7. Bake for 30 minutes.

ADAPTED FROM NORMA JEAN DARDEN

LOLLIPOPS OR CANDY APPLES

(makes 2 dozen lollipops or 4 large candied apples)

2 cups sugar
¾ cup clear corn syrup
1 cup water
2 teaspoons fruit-flavored extract,
  such as cherry, lemon, or orange

¼ teaspoon food coloring
Lollipop sticks

1. Grease 2 large cookie sheets.

2. Combine the sugar, corn syrup, water, and salt in a medium-size saucepan.

3. Cook over medium heat stirring constantly, until the hard crack point of 300° is reached on a candy thermometer, or a drop of the mixture placed in a cup of cold water turns into a brittle ball. If you remove the candy too soon, you will end up with clear, chewy taffy on a stick, which you don't want.

4. Promptly remove the candy from the heat and stir in the extract and food coloring. Work fast as the candy hardens quickly.

5. Pour little circles of candy on the cookie sheet and leave enough room for the sticks, which you must push in immediately, making sure that ½-inch of the end is well covered with candy.

6. When the lollipops are cool, jiggle loose from cookie sheet and wrap in wax paper. If lollipop sticks are unavailable, Dixie cup spoons split in two work well. Without a stick, you will still have delicious hard candy.

7. To make candy apples, insert Popsicle sticks into 4 large apples and dip them in the mixture to coat all around. Let cool.

ADAPTED FROM NORMA JEAN DARDEN

SNOW ICE CREAM

(makes 1 serving)

One cup of freshly fallen snow
1 tablespoon sugar (or more
    to taste)

½ teaspoon vanilla extract
⅓ cup heavy cream or half-
    and-half

1. For each serving, use the proportions listed above. In a small bowl, combine the fresh, clean snow, sugar, cream, and vanilla.

2. Mix well, and add more cream and sugar to taste.

3. As a variation you can substitute 2 tablespoons real maple syrup per serving for the sugar and vanilla.

ADAPTED FROM NORMA JEAN DARDEN

Ella Brennan

New Orleans

Ella Brennan, the Queen of Creole cooking.

Ella Brennan is known as the Queen of New Orleans cooking, perhaps the most distinctive of all the American cooking styles. The Cajun and Creole cooking of New Orleans is famous around the world and it goes back hundreds of years. Both cooking styles combine the influences of the many different peoples who settled Louisiana: The French, the Native American Indians, the Spanish, the Africans, and the Acadian settlers.

The French began colonizing Louisiana in 1698. When they arrived, the Native American Indians taught them about local ingredients such as corn, squash, beans, and sassafras, a tree whose ground leaves were used to thicken and flavor stews. The port city of New Orleans, became known as the Paris of the New World. The African slaves who cooked for the French aristocrats combined the cooking techniques they learned from the French with the foods they had brought from Africa such as garlic, yams, eggplant, okra, rice, and kidney beans.

In 1755 a group of French colonists who lived in an area known as Acadia (now Nova Scotia and New Brunswick in Canada and Maine) were expelled by the British who ruled the area because they refused to pledge allegiance to England. They found their way to the Mississippi River and headed south until they came to a swampy, marshy area west of New Orleans, where they were given free homes by the Spanish governor who wanted them to help colonize Louisiana. This area was known for its web of waterways called bayous that were filled with alligators. Because the bayous were hard for people unfamiliar with the area to navigate, this group kept their separate and distinct ways. Over time, their name changed from Acadians to Cajuns.

The Cajuns loved to celebrate and party. They liked spicy dishes and seafood such as shrimp, crab, crayfish (tiny lobsters), and redfish from the local waters and the Gulf of Mexico. This country cooking style wasn't fancy looking, but it was packed with flavor, and many of the dishes, such as gumbos or jambalayas (spicy stews) combined lots of ingredients in one big pot.

In 1762 Louisiana was turned over by France to Spain, and the Spanish began to influence the more European, yet local, Creole cuisine. They introduced spicy, red cayenne pepper and tomatoes, which the French had thought were poisonous. The word Creole was coined by the Spanish. They called all residents of European heritage as well as African Americans "Criollo". Creole cooking was more elegant than Cajun cooking. It had more subtle sauces, more delicate desserts, and fancier looking food presentation.

Ella Brennan grew up in a large family with six kids, and food was the center of activities. Ella's mom was a great cook and her uncles used to bring home fish and game they caught, such as wild duck and crabs, for her mom to prepare. The kids would gather around the kitchen table talking and watching their mom cook. Ella

remembers sitting and listening to the radio while she helped her mom clean the snap beans and remove the shells from the fresh, locally grown pecans. The nuts would later be made into pecan pies and sugar-coated, pecan praline candies. Ella was crazy about her mom's fried oysters and shrimp. Her favorite dish of all was a very simple comfort food: soft scrambled eggs served with bananas sautéed with sugar and butter.

Ella's mom only used the best and freshest local ingredients, a philosophy her daughter has always stood by. Holidays like Christmas, Thanksgiving, New Year's, and Mardi Gras (Fat Tuesday) were festive celebrations with special foods for each. Mardi Gras occurs just before the start of the 40-day Lent fast prior to Easter. Nowhere in the United States is this holiday a bigger celebration than in New Orleans where for several days there are parties all over town, parades with floats and fun costumes, and dancing in the street.

When Ella was 19 her dad and older brother bought their own restaurant, which they named Brennan's. As the restaurant began to grow, Ella and the rest of her family started to help out. Sundays when the restaurant was closed, the head chef would come in to make the soup stock or broth that cooked down for a long time to be used as a base for sauces. In the morning he would make the kids different egg dishes which they loved. Years later the restaurant became well known for its wonderful brunch and its many unusual egg dishes.

As the restaurant grew, Ella and her brothers wanted to learn more about how to create the best restaurant they could: a restaurant that was elegant, festive and comfortable for guests, and that featured the best of New Orleans cooking. They started by reading and collecting cookbooks. Then they traveled to Europe, New York,

and San Francisco to see how the finest restaurants prepared meals and treated their guests.

In 1969 her family bought Commander's Palace which had been a restaurant for almost 100 years. It was in New Orleans' fashionable Garden District, known for its beautiful southern mansions like in the movie *Gone with the Wind*. The restaurant, which at one time had been elegant and grand, had become dark and dreary. To restore its cheerfulness and give it personality, they painted the outside turquoise blue (which was a bit shocking to the neighbors). The Brennan's made the inside light and welcoming, and created an upstairs room with large glass windows that looked out onto a giant oak tree in the courtyard, thereby creating the feeling of being in a tree house. They also created a kitchen that guests could walk through and watch the chefs in action.

Ella and her sister worked for years at the Sophie Wright School in New Orleans, tutoring kids and teaching them about the restaurant business. For years she's also trained many of the employees at Commander's Palace including some of the country's most famous chefs such as Paul Prudhomme, Emeril Lagasse, and Jamie Shannon. In addition to being a wonderful teacher, Ella is known for her sense of humor, her attention to details, and her warmth and hospitality. In 1996 Commander's Palace was named the best restaurant in the United States, which made the whole family and all its employees extremely proud. Ella is fortunate because in addition to having a job she loves that brings pleasure to many, she's surrounded by her wonderful family. Her daughter, niece, and nephew run Commander's Palace on a day to day basis.

What follows are some of Ella's favorite childhood recipes and recipes kids enjoy when they dine at Commander's Palace.

COCONUT SHRIMP WITH SWEET AND TANGY DIPPING SAUCE

(makes 6 servings)

COCONUT SHRIMP

4 eggs, lightly beaten
1 cup beer
3 ½ teaspoons Creole Seafood
  Seasoning
1 ¼ cups all-purpose flour
2 tablespoons baking powder

48 large shrimp (about 2 pounds),
  peeled but with tails on, deveined
1 ½ to 2 cups shredded coconut,
  fresh or moist pack
Vegetable oil for deep frying

SWEET AND TANGY DIPPING SAUCE

2 cups orange marmalade
¼ cup Creole or Dijon mustard

3 tablespoons bottled white
  horseradish

1. Combine eggs, beer, 1 teaspoon seafood seasoning, flour, and baking powder in a medium-size bowl. Blend well.

2. Season shrimp with remaining seafood seasoning.

3. Place shredded coconut in a large flat bottomed dish or pie plate.

4. Dip the shrimp in beer batter and roll in coconut.

5. Heat oil to 350° in a deep-fat fryer, wok, or deep saucepan. The oil should be at least 1½ inches deep. Drop in the shrimp, a few at a time, and fry until golden brown. Remove and drain on paper towels.

6. Warm the dipping sauce ingredients in a small saucepan over low heat until the marmalade melts and the ingredients blend together.

7. Serve shrimp with dipping sauce on the side.

ADAPTED FROM ELLA BRENNAN

SCRAMBLED EGGS WITH BROWN SUGAR SAUTÉED BANANAS

(makes 2 servings)

The sautéed bananas also taste great over ice cream with 2 tablespoons of banana liquor and 3 ounces of rum added to the sauce. This famous dessert called Bananas Foster, was created by the Brennan family.

SCRAMBLED EGGS
5 eggs, beaten
1 tablespoon butter

SAUTEED BANANAS
4 tablespoons (½ stick)
  unsalted butter
4 tablespoons brown sugar
2 ripe bananas, peeled and
  sliced lengthwise
½ teaspoon cinnamon

1. To sauté bananas, melt butter in a large skillet. Add the brown sugar and cinnamon and stir until the brown sugar is dissolved and incorporated into the butter. Add the bananas and sauté until tender, about 3 minutes on each side.

2. To scramble eggs, melt butter in another large skillet. Pour in eggs. Scramble until cooked to your liking.

3. To serve, place half the eggs in the center of each plate. Place a banana half on each side of the eggs. Pour sauce over the bananas, not on the eggs.

4. Season individually with salt.

ADAPTED FROM ELLA BRENNAN

Magical Melting Pot

BREAD PUDDING WITH CLEAR RUM SAUCE

(makes 6 servings)

1 cup sugar
4 tablespoons (½ stick) butter,
    softened
5 eggs, beaten
1 pint (2 cups) half-and-half cream

¼ teaspoon cinnamon
1 tablespoon vanilla extract
¼ cup raisins
12 slices, each 1-inch thick,
    of fresh or stale French bread

·1. Preheat oven to 350°.

2. In a large bowl cream together the sugar and butter. Add eggs, cream, cinnamon, vanilla, and raisins, and mix well. Pour into a 8 x 12-inch pan, at least 1¾ inches deep.

3. Arrange the bread slices flat in the egg mixture and let stand for 5 minutes to soak up some of the liquid. Turn bread over and let stand for

10 minutes longer. Then push bread down so that most of it is covered by the egg mixture. Do not break the bread.

4. Set the pan in a larger pan filled with water to ½ inch from the top. Cover with aluminum foil. Bake for 45 to 50 minutes, uncovering the bread pudding for the last 10 minutes to brown. When done, the custard should still be soft, not firm.

RUM SAUCE

1 cup sugar
2 ½ cups water
1 cinnamon stick or 1 teaspoon
    ground cinnamon

1 tablespoon unsalted butter
½ teaspoon cornstarch
1 tablespoon light or dark rum

1. In a medium-size saucepan, combine sugar, 2 cups water, cinnamon, and butter and bring to a boil.

2. Stir in cornstarch blended with remaining ½ cup water, and simmer, stirring, until sauce is clear (just a few minutes).

3. Remove from heat and add rum. Sauce will be thin.

4. Serve sauce on the side for each person to add their own.

ADAPTED FROM ELLA BRENNAN

PECAN PIE

(makes one 8 or 9-inch pie)

My husband, whose favorite dessert in the world is pecan pie, thinks this is the best one he's ever eaten. It's rich, but not overly sweet, full of nuts, and it looks beautiful.

PIE CRUST
1 ¼ cups all-purpose flour
¼ teaspoon salt
½ teaspoon sugar

8 tablespoons (1 stick) unsalted butter
¼ cup vegetable shortening
  or margarine
3 to 4 tablespoons ice water

1. Preheat oven to 375°.

2. Sift flour, salt, and sugar into a mixing bowl or food processor bowl. Cut the butter and shortening with a pastry blender, two knives, or the chopping blade of the food processor until the mixture resembles coarse cornmeal.

3. Add water and mix with a fork until dough holds together.

4. Shape into a ball, wrap in wax paper, and chill for 30 minutes. (If not using right away, the dough can be wrapped and refrigerated for several days or it can be frozen.)

5. Roll dough on a floured surface into a circle 2 inches in diameter wider than the pie plate, and ⅛-inch thick. Transfer to pan by rolling dough onto the rolling pin and unrolling it over the pan. Ease gently into the pan, trim the edge, and crimp with a fork. This will help keep the crust from shrinking.

6. Prick bottom and sides with a fork and bake for 10 minutes, or until light golden brown. Do not turn oven off.

FILLING
⅓ cup butter
¾ cup firmly packed light brown
  sugar
½ cup light corn syrup

3 eggs
1 cup chopped pecans
1 teaspoon vanilla extract
¼ teaspoon salt
¾ cup pecan halves (for the top)

1. Cream together butter and brown sugar. Beat in eggs, one at a time. Stir in corn syrup, pecans, vanilla extract, and salt.

2. Fill baked pie shell and decorate the top with pecan halves. I like a pattern with concentric circles.

3. Bake for 30 minutes, or until the filling no longer appears loose.

ADAPTED FROM ELLA BRENNAN

Marion Cunningham

Northern California

Marion Cunningham is someone I respect and admire tremendously for many reasons. After her children were grown she had the courage and energy to start a whole new exciting career as a cooking teacher and food writer. She spent nine years revising *The Fannie Farmer Cookbook* which contains nearly 2000 recipes that were all tested and retested by Marion. *The Fannie Farmer Cookbook* was one of the earliest American cookbooks ever published. Fannie Merritt Farmer published it in 1896 as the *Boston Cooking School Cookbook*. She was the first person to stress the importance of precisely measuring ingredients in recipes. For over one hundred years the book has taught Americans how to cook. Marion updated and modernized the book in the 1970's, 80's, and 90's by including ethnic influences such as Mediterranean, Asian and Moroccan, all of which have become common in American cooking, and by adding sections on grilling, and microwave and vegetarian cooking.

Marion has authored seven other cookbooks, and she's still writing more. Today she

also contributes articles to food magazines such as *Gourmet*, *Bon Appetit*, and *Saveur* as well as the *San Francisco Chronicle* and *Los Angeles Times* newspapers.

Another reason I admire Marion is because she was able to overcome her fears. Marion has always loved to cook and has taught cooking lessons in her home from time to time. For years she had heard about James Beard, who was considered one of the best American cookbook authors and teachers. She had always wanted to take one of his classes, but was afraid to fly and had never left the state of California. She finally made up her mind to say "yes" to opportunities, no matter what.

Marion's decision to take one of James Beard's classes in Seaside, Oregon really changed her life. She then went on to become his assistant, and it was James Beard who recommended that Marion be the one to revise the historic *Fannie Farmer Cookbook*.

I also admire what Marion Cunningham has strived to achieve. She's been dedicated to teaching millions of Americans the joys and satisfactions of home cooking, and the value of taking the time to sit down and share a home cooked meal with family and friends. Marion believes that "every meal should be a small celebration" and that it needn't be fancy. Home cooking doesn't have to be difficult; and the more you do it, the easier it becomes.

Kids, in particular, love home cooked meals: and not only for the food. They love the smells in the house, the activity, and the warm and special atmosphere that home cooked meals create. Home cooked meals are forms of sharing and caring for others, and they make family members feel loved.

Marion was born in California. Her grand-

Artichokes

The artichokes we eat in the U.S. are grown primarily along the coast of California, and were brought to California by the Italians. They range in color from green to purple.

Artichokes are actually the immature bud of a giant thistle plant. If allowed to bloom, it would be a lavender colored flower. The artichoke heart is the base of the bud. Artichokes can weigh up to one pound.

mother came from Italy; and though she moved to America, she never learned to speak English. She was, however, a great cook. One of Marion's favorite recipes that her grandmother made was garlic crumb-stuffed artichokes. The artichokes were boiled until tender and then garlic breadcrumbs were stuffed in between the artichoke's many leaves. Artichokes are fun to eat because each leaf is pulled from the base one by one, and there's a bite-sized portion on each leaf. In this dish, each bite included delicious, "garlicky" breadcrumbs.

One of Marion's favorite cakes that her mother made was a moist, oatmeal-flavored cake with a walnut, coconut topping. Many of the recipes in Marion's cookbooks can be considered comfort foods. Her cookbook, *The Breakfast Book*, is filled with recipes that adults loved as kids, and that kids today still enjoy. Two of those recipes are "knothole eggs" and popovers. "Knothole eggs" are made from pieces of toast that have a hole cut out in the center. Eggs are cracked into the holes and fried in butter with the toast around it.

I personally think that popovers are one of the all-time great food inventions. Popovers start with an "eggy" batter that's poured into muffin tins. As they cook, they inflate and puff up, leaving a hollow, soft center. There's nothing like a hot, fresh popover with melted butter. Marion's recipe goes one step further by adding a dollop of jam on the bottom that cooks into the batter.

GARLIC-CRUMB STUFFED ARTICHOKES

(makes 4 servings)

ARTICHOKES
4 artichokes

1. Fill a lage pot with water and bring to a boil.

2. Peel the fibers from the artichoke stems. Remove the tough bottom leaves, and then slice off about 1 inch from the top. With scissors, snip off the prickly tops of the remaining side leaves.

3. Place the artichokes in boiling water and boil gently until the bottom of the chokes are tender when pierced with a fork, about 15 to 20 minutes. Remove the artichokes from the water and turn them upside down on a large plate to drain.

CRUMBS
4 bread slices, white
2 large cloves garlic,
   finely chopped

¾ teaspoon salt
6 tablespoons olive oil

1. Tear each slice of bread into 5 or 6 pieces. Put the bread pieces into a blender and blend for a few seconds, until the pieces are crumbs.

2. Spread the crumbs on a baking sheet and dry them in a 250° degree oven until lightly golden,

about 15 minutes. Measure about 1 cup pf crumbs. If you have extra, you can save them for later use.

3. Toss together the crumbs, garlic, salt, and olive oil in a small bowl to mix well.

ASSEMBLY

1. Stuff the crumbs between the artichoke leaves. (You don't have to stuff between each leaf as the flavor will spread.)

2. Serve either warm or chilled.

THIS RECIPE BY
MARION CUNNINGHAM APPEARED
IN THE SAN FRANCISCO CHRONICLE

"KNOTHOLE" EGGS

(makes two servings)

This is a fun and easy breakfast recipe that kids especially enjoy.

2 slices sandwich bread	**2 eggs**
2 tablespoons butter	**Salt and pepper to taste**

1. Toast the bread lightly.

2. With a circular cutter or a wine glass about 2 inches in diameter, cut a hole out of the center of each slice.

3. Melt the butter over medium-low heat in a large skillet and put the bread slices side by side in the pan.

4. Crack an egg into each hole, letting the yolk fall into the center. Some of the white will run over the bread and down the side. Turn the heat to low and sprinkle with salt and pepper to taste.

5. Cover the pan and cook gently for 2 or, 3 minutes, until the whites are barely set.

6. Serve on warm plates.

RECIPE BY MARION CUNNINGHAM

OATMEAL CAKE
WITH WALNUT TOPPING

(makes 14 servings)

CAKE

1 ½ cups quick cooking (1-minute) oatmeal
½ cup (1 stick) butter, plus additional for greasing pan
1 ½ cups boiling water
¾ cup granulated sugar
1 cup light brown sugar, packed

2 eggs
2 teaspoons vanilla extract
½ teaspoon maple flavoring
1 ½ cups flour
1 teaspoon baking soda
1 teaspoon salt

1. Combine 1 cup oatmeal, butter, and boiling water in a large bowl.

2. Stir oatmeal mixture and add granulated sugar, brown sugar, eggs, vanilla, maple flavoring, flour, remaining ½ cup oatmeal, baking soda, and salt. Stir briskly until well blended.

3. Pour batter into 9 x 13-inch baking dish that has been greased with butter or shortning. Bake at 350° until a toothpick comes out clean when inserted in the center, about 20-30 minutes.

4. Remove cake and turn on broiler.

TOPPING

6 tablespoons butter, melted
½ cup chopped walnuts
½ cup light brown sugar, packed

½ teaspoon vanilla extract
¼ cup milk
1 cup coconut flakes

1. Stir together the melted butter, chopped walnuts, brown sugar, vanilla, milk, and coconut in a bowl.

2. Spread topping with a spatula over the top of the cake.

3. Put cake under broiler and broil until the topping bubbles all over, about 3 to 5 minutes.

4. Serve warm or cold.

THIS RECIPE BY
MARION CUNNINGHAM APPEARED
IN THE **SAN FRANCISCO CHRONICLE**

OATMEAL POPOVERS

(makes 10 medium-size popovers)

Marion says that the trick for making "high-rising" popovers is to start them in a cold oven. The use of oatmeal and marmalade makes these popovers unique. While Marion suggests using orange marmalade, you can substitute your favorite flavor. You can also make fewer, larger popovers by using a larger muffin tin.

2 eggs
1 cup milk
1 tablespoon butter, melted, plus additional to grease the pan
⅓ cup rolled oats, coarsely ground, in a food processor or blender
¾ cup all-purpose flour
½ teaspoon salt
½ cup orange marmalade (optional)

1. Butter 10 cavities from a medium-size muffin tin.

2. Put a rounded teaspoon of marmalade or jam in the bottom of each cup.

3. Combine the eggs, milk, butter, oatmeal, flour, and salt in a bowl and beat just until well blended.

4. Fill the prepared tins about half full and place them in a *cold* oven.

5. Set the oven temperature to 450° and bake for 15 minutes. Reduce the temperature to 350° and bake another 10 to 15 minutes, or until golden and round.

6. Remove from the pans and serve piping hot with butter.

RECIPE BY MARION CUNNINGHAM

Alice Waters

Northern California

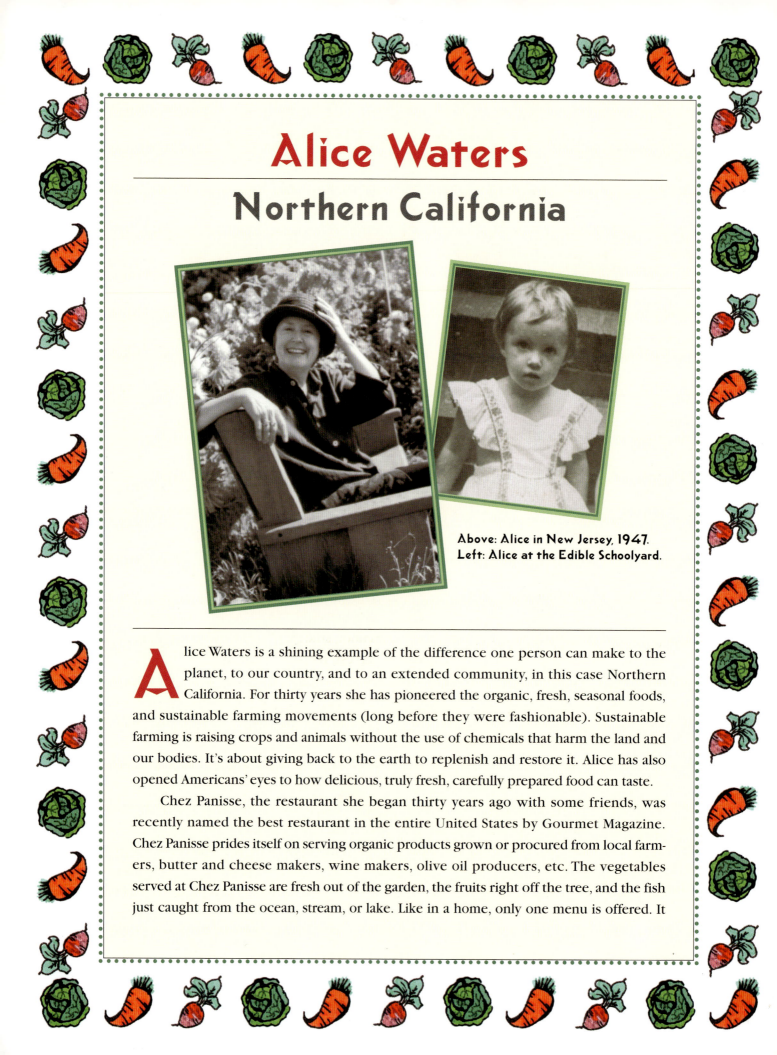

Above: Alice in New Jersey, 1947.
Left: Alice at the Edible Schoolyard.

Alice Waters is a shining example of the difference one person can make to the planet, to our country, and to an extended community, in this case Northern California. For thirty years she has pioneered the organic, fresh, seasonal foods, and sustainable farming movements (long before they were fashionable). Sustainable farming is raising crops and animals without the use of chemicals that harm the land and our bodies. It's about giving back to the earth to replenish and restore it. Alice has also opened Americans' eyes to how delicious, truly fresh, carefully prepared food can taste.

Chez Panisse, the restaurant she began thirty years ago with some friends, was recently named the best restaurant in the entire United States by Gourmet Magazine. Chez Panisse prides itself on serving organic products grown or procured from local farmers, butter and cheese makers, wine makers, olive oil producers, etc. The vegetables served at Chez Panisse are fresh out of the garden, the fruits right off the tree, and the fish just caught from the ocean, stream, or lake. Like in a home, only one menu is offered. It

changes daily based on the freshest ingredients available that morning.

A little over 20 years ago, Alice opened the Café at Chez Panisse, upstairs from the restaurant. The café has an open kitchen so guests can watch the chefs cook, a wood-burning oven, and a menu where people can order as few or as many courses as they like. In 1984 Café Fanny was opened nearby. Named after Alice's daughter, this tiny café serves breakfast and lunch. Approximately 500 people eat in Alice's restaurants every day.

Both Chez Panisse and the Chez Panisse Café collect their biodegradable waste, such as fruit and vegetable peels and cores, to compost. When the material decomposes, it makes a great, natural fertilizer that is given to a local, organic farmer to use.

When Alice is asked to be a guest speaker in other cities, she makes sure the food served is locally obtained, seasonal, and organic. As a result, the hotels and restaurants are forced to discover local suppliers they inevitably end up liking and using on a regular basis.

Because the food is so wonderful in her restaurants, and because of Alice's philosophy of serving only the highest quality, locally obtained organic products, a number of very positive things have happened. First, the restaurant has contented guests that return frequently. Second, local farmers, cheese makers, olive oil pressers, fishermen, wine producers, and flour millers, all of whom farm without chemicals in ways that respect and give back to the land, are recognized and have a place to sell their products. Third, the organic movement continues to grow, local small-scale farming has started to come back, farmers markets have "sprouted" up all around the country, and there are fewer chemicals in our food, our bodies, and our land. Still, however, much more progress needs to be made.

The quality of the food at Chez Panisse and the growth of these food suppliers has also helped America (long considered the "the fast food capital of the world") gain respect as a country that knows how to grow, prepare, and appreciate good food.

Of all her accomplishments, however, Alice is most gratified by the work of the Chez Panisse Foundation that she created in 1996. The Foundation supports a variety of youth and community projects that demonstrate how by working with the land to grow food organically and then by cooking and sharing it, people can become happy, productive, responsible, and more connected to each other. Two of the projects the Foundation supports are the Edible Schoolyard at Berkeley's Martin Luther King Jr. Middle School and the Garden Project at the San Francisco County Jail.

At the Garden Project, inmates grow fruits and vegetables and take them to the homeless. At the Edible Schoolyard and Kitchen Classroom at Berkeley's Martin Luther King Jr. Middle School, students learn to plant crops, garden, harvest, recycle, compost, prepare, serve, and eat good, fresh food. In this way, in addition to learning respect for the earth and each other, kids learn biology, chemistry, math, and life sciences such as gardening and cooking that will always stay with them. These classes are so popular, students consistently rate them their favorite subject. Alice hopes the Edible Schoolyard and Kitchen Classroom programs will be adopted by schools all over the country.

Alice grew up in New Jersey. When she was little, her parents had a Victory garden. Those were gardens that people all across America started in their backyards during World War II to

supply their families with whatever food they could grow. One Fourth of July when she was three or four years old, Alice's mother dressed her up as the "Queen of the Garden" in a homemade costume. It had an asparagus skirt, a lettuce leaf top, bracelets and a necklace of peppers and radishes, and a strawberry wreath for a crown.

Other memories include her mom canning rhubarb and applesauce for use during the winter. Alice's favorite vegetables were corn, tomatoes, frozen green beans, and sweet potatoes with marshmallows. Her favorite main dish was steak on the grill. For dessert she loved a parfait pie that had colorful layers of Jello. On her dad's birthday, which came during the summer when peaches were in season, her family had a tradition of making fresh peach ice cream to celebrate.

After attending the University of California at Berkeley, Alice spent a few years as a Montessori teacher. It was the year she spent in Paris, however, that changed her life. She loved the foods which were wonderful, new and different, and she sparked to the importance food seemed to play in French people's lives. She was impressed by the fact that the French ate foods only in season, because that was when it was least expensive and the best tasting. After experiencing the taste of just picked fruits and vegetables, just caught fish, and just baked bread and pastries, she realized what a tremendous difference the freshness made.

When Alice returned to Berkeley, she started Chez Panisse with some friends and a loan. In addition to applying her philosophy of using only fresh, local, seasonal ingredients, she wanted to create an atmosphere for the restaurant that would be like serving people at a dinner party in your own home. Today, because her restaurants are so special and welcoming, people come from all over to eat and celebrate there, and local customers return often.

What follows are some of the recipes Alice's knows that kids enjoy making and eating.

FRESH VEGETABLES
WITH VINAIGRETTE DIPPING SAUCE

(makes 4 servings)

Kids in the Edible Schoolyard program enjoy making this vinaigrette and dipping their freshly grown garden vegetables into the dressing. The vinaigrette is light and lets the flavor of the vegetables shine through.

VINAIGRETTE

1 shallot (optional)
Salt
2 tablespoons red wine vinegar

5 to 6 tablespoons extra virgin olive oil.

1. Peel the shallot and cut it into very thin slices. Put in a small bowl with a pinch of salt and the vinegar. Let the shallot soak in the vinegar for 15 to 20 minutes.

2. Add the olive oil and mix well. Taste to see if the balance of vinegar and olive oil is right— You might need to add more of one or the other.

FRESH VEGETABLES FOR DIPPING

This is completely your choice. Popular dipping vegetables include sliced carrots, celery, broccoli spears, red, yellow, or green pepper slices, asparagus spears, jicama slices, raw mushrooms, and cherry tomatoes. It's fun to arrange them colorfully on a plate or in a lined basket.

ADAPTED FROM ALICE WATERS

GRILLED CORN WITH GARLIC BUTTER

(makes 6 ears)

6 ears sweet corn
1 stick of unsalted butter at room
   temperature
1 large clove garlic

Handful of washed and dried
   Italian parsley
Pinch of cayenne powder
Salt

1. Build a medium fire in a charcoal grill.

2. Peel back the husk of each ear of corn. Try to make as few tears as possible and keep the husk attached to the ear at the bottom. Remove the corn silk from the cob. Pull the husk back into place to completely cover the kernels.

3. Pound the garlic into a paste with a mortar and pestle or squeeze it through a garlic press. Finely chop the parsley. With a wooden spoon, mix the garlic, parsley, and a pinch of cayenne together with the butter. Add salt to taste. Place butter mixture in a small serving bowl.

4. Once the coals are glowing and covered with a thin layer of ash, lay the corn on the grill. Turn the ears with tongs as the husks begin to blacken. They should cook for about 10 to 15 minutes.

5. Pile the corn in a basket and cover with a clean dish towel to keep them hot.

6. When ready to eat, peel back the husks, and smear the ears with the garlic butter.

ADAPTED FROM ALICE WATERS

PEACH CRISP

(makes 6 to 8 servings)

Y ou can make this recipe substituting other fruits as well, such as apples, nectarines, apricots, plums, pears, or berries.

CRISP TOPPING

1 cup flour

⅓ cup brown sugar

1 tablespoon granulated sugar

⅓ cup butter (about ¾ stick) at room
   temperature

4 pounds ripe, firm peaches

1 ½ tablespoons flour

1 tablespoon sugar

TO PREPARE TOPPING

1. Mix the flour and sugars in a bowl.

2. Cut butter into small pieces and add to the bowl. Mix in the butter by rubbing it in the flour mixture lightly and quickly between your fingertips. When the butter, flour, and sugar are evenly mixed and the mixture looks crumbly, it's ready.

TO ASSEMBLE THE CRISP

1. Preheat oven to 375°.

2. Cut the peaches in half, peel, and remove the pits. Cut into slices. You should have about 8 cups.

3. Mix the fruit with the flour and sugar. If using other fruits, taste to decide how much sugar to add.

4. Spread the peaches into a greased 2-quart or ceramic ovenproof dish, and sprinkle the topping evenly over the peaches.

5. Bake for about 40 minutes, until the topping is brown and the peaches are thick and bubbly.

6. Eat warm, after the crisp has cooled a bit, with some fresh cream poured around it in the dish.

ADAPTED FROM ALICE WATERS

1-2-3-4 CAKE

(makes two 8 or 9-inch layers or about 24 cupcakes)

Alice uses this recipe for birthday cakes. You can spread the layers with your favorite frosting. The cake also tastes great plain or topped with lemon curd. As you can see from the recipe below, the cake gets its name from the amounts of the ingredients used.

1 cup unsalted butter (2 sticks)
  at room temperature
2 cups sugar
3 cups cake flour
4 teaspoons baking powder

½ teaspoon salt
4 eggs
1 teaspoon vanilla extract
1 cup milk

1. Preheat oven to 350º.

2. Grease and flour two 8 or 9-inch cake pans. If making cupcakes, line 2 cupcake pans (12 cavities each) with cupcake liners.

3. Cut the butter into small pieces, and put in a large bowl. Measure the sugar and set aside.

4. Sift the cake flour, scoop it into a measuring cup, scrape a knife across the top of the cup to level it, and measure 3 cups. Put the flour in a separate bowl. Add the baking flour and salt and mix together well.

5. Separate the eggs. Put the whites in one bowl and the yolks in another.

6. Beat the butter with a wooden spoon or an electric mixer until light and fluffy. Add the sugar and beat again until very fluffy and light yellow. Add the yolks and beat them in briefly. Add the vanilla and mix it in well.

7. Add half the flour and lightly stir it in. Add the milk and use a spatula to gently mix it in. Incorporate the rest of the flour and then gently add the rest of the milk.

8. Beat the egg whites in a metal bowl with a wire whisk or electric mixer until they're very fluffy and hold a soft peak shape when you lift up the whisk.

9. Gently fold a small amount of the egg whites into the batter to lighten the batter. Then add the rest of the egg whites gently lifting up some of the batter from the bottom of the bowl and folding it over the whites. Fold several times, just until the egg whites are mixed in. The air bubbles in the whites give the cake its light, delicate texture.

10. Divide the batter between the layer cake pans, and put in the center of the oven to bake for about 25 minutes. If making cupcakes, fill the tins a little over half full and bake for about 20 minutes. When the cakes are lightly browned and a toothpick stuck in the center comes out clean, they're done. Remove from the oven and cool on a rack.

ADAPTED FROM ALICE WATERS

Thomas Keller

Northern California

Above: Thomas hard at work in the kitchen.
Left: Thomas relaxing in the dining room.

Thomas Keller, the chef-owner of the French Laundry Restaurant in the heart of Northern California's wine country, is widely considered one of the finest chefs in America. Having celebrated my twentieth anniversary at the French Laundry, I can attest that eating there is a heavenly experience. One of the reasons it's such an exciting restaurant is that you can choose from a five or nine course menu. Each features a variety of intensely flavored, beautifully presented mini courses "designed to satisfy your appetite and pique your curiosity". One of my favorite courses was the mini ice cream cone filled with salmon tartar (raw, chopped salmon), that Thomas says was inspired by a trip to a Baskin & Robbins ice cream shop.

Unlike some chefs who knew at a young age they wanted to pursue a career in cooking, Thomas Keller didn't make that decision until he was twenty years old. At that time he was considering different professions, and what he knew about the life of a chef appealed to him. It seemed challenging and athletic because you are always moving around when

you cook and you need lots of energy. There would be travel involved, both in terms of where you worked and where you learned to cook (both studying from other chefs and trying different local ingredients and dishes).

Thomas also liked the teamwork he observed in restaurant kitchens. Large, successful restaurants have a number of chefs who each prepare a different part of the meal. For example, there might be a pastry chef, a meat chef, and an appetizer chef. There are also assistants who prepare ingredients for the chefs to use. They peel and chop fruits and vegetables, clean fish, etc. Chefs also work closely with the servers to make sure customers are satisfied, and to hear customer feedback.

Even though Thomas didn't decide to become a chef until he was twenty, he was exposed to the world of cooking at a young age by his mother, Betty. Thomas's mother ran restaurants in different parts of the country. His dad worked for the military so they moved fairly often. His mom was and still is a big influence in his life. As he says in the *French Laundry Cookbook*, "Long before she put me to work, she taught me how to clean our home. Everything had to shine. That standard of cleanliness was its own gift, given the work I'd choose. I honestly don't know who I'd be if I'd been raised by, and had grown up watching someone other than her."

Thomas's philosophy about cooking permeates everything he does. He believes that making people happy is what cooking is all about. He also believes that the best food can only be made by using the freshest ingredients and proper cooking techniques. One of the many secrets to the success of his restaurant is that Thomas has researched and selected the best ingredients from all over America: from California to Pennsylvania to Maine.

Since Thomas admits to having no special food memories as a child other than perhaps chili dogs, he provided recipes for this book that he knows children like. When kids come to his restaurant, many order off the adult menu. If it's specially requested, however, he will prepare more traditional "kid food". By using the freshest ingredients and proper cooking techniques, these "kid foods" can be very delicious. Some of the recipes Thomas thought kids and adults would like include Yukon Gold Potato Blini, Eric's Staff Lasagna, Honey-Vanilla Ice Cream with Chocolate Sauce, and a very special Peach "Jello".

Inspiration

Before moving to California, Thomas stopped for dessert at Baskin & Robbins in New York City's Chinatown. He'd recently been challenged to create a dish for a benefit that would be a conversation piece. When he was handed his cone, a light went off and his signature salmon tartar in a tuile cone was conceived.

The French Laundry

The French Laundry was actually a French steam laundry at one point in its history. In keeping with the theme, each place setting has a beautifully folded napkin with a French Laundry clothespin on it that guests can take home as a souvenir. I still have mine.

Magical Melting Pot

YUKON GOLD POTATO BLINI

(makes about 3 dozen small blini)

The French Laundry's Yukon Gold potato blini (a type of pancake) use puréed potatoes, unlike many potato pancake recipes that call for shredded potatoes. These small blini are golden colored and have a wonderfully light texture. You can make them larger if you like.

1 pound Yukon Gold potatoes
2 tablespoon all-purpose flour
2 to 3 tablespoons crème fraîche, at room temperature (If hard to find you can make your own by combining ½ cup heavy cream at room temperature with 1 tablespoon buttermilk or ¼ cup sour cream. Leave at room temperature for 24 hours or until very thick. Stir once or twice during this time. This will give you a little more than you need. As a last resort, substitute 2 to 3 tablespoons heavy cream or sour cream.)
2 large eggs
1 large egg yolk
Kosher salt
Freshly ground white pepper

1. Place the potatoes in a saucepan with cold water to cover by at least 2 inches. Bring to a boil over high heat, reduce the heat, and simmer until the potatoes are thoroughly cooked and tender.

2. Peel the warm potatoes and purée them in a food processor or mash them extremely well so there are no lumps.

3. Immediately weigh out 9 ounces of the puréed potatoes and place them in a medium-size metal bowl.

4. Working quickly, whisk the flour into the warm potatoes, then whisk in 2 tablespoons of crème fraîche. Add 1 egg, whisking until the batter is smooth, add the second egg, and then add the yolk.

5. Hold the whisk with some of the batter over the bowl. The batter should fall in a thick stream but hold its shape when it hits the batter in the bowl. If it's too thick, add a little more crème fraîche. Season to taste with salt and white pepper.

6. Heat an electric griddle to 350°, or a large non-stick skillet over medium-low heat.

7. Spoon a rounded teaspoon of batter onto the griddle or skillet for each pancake. Cook until the bottoms are browned, 1 to 2 minutes. Then flip them to cook on the second side, about 1 minute. Transfer the blini to a baking sheet and keep warm in a very low oven (225°) while you make the rest.

8. Served plain with a little butter, or with your choice of topping such as sour cream or applesauce.

ADAPTED FROM THOMAS KELLER

ERIC'S STAFF LASAGNA

(makes about 9 servings)

The staff meal is eaten by the restaurant's employees in the late afternoon, before guests arrive. It's often a hearty meal because it must sustain the employees for the long night ahead. The staff cook makes food from scraps left over after the preparation of other foods. The challenge is to prepare tasty, satisfying meals for the restaurant's staff, all of whom know and appreciate good food.

SAUCE
½ cup olive oil
1 ½ cup minced yellow onions
2 tablespoons minced garlic
½ cup tomato paste
8 cups cut-up peeled tomatoes
 (about 12 to 14 medium tomatoes, cut into 1-inch pieces)
¼ cup chopped fresh oregano, or ¼ cup plus 2 tablespoons chopped fresh basil

TO PREPARE SAUCE

1. Heat the oil in a large, heavy pot. Add the onions and garlic and cook gently for 4 to 5 minutes, or until translucent. Add the tomato paste and cook, stirring frequently over low heat, for 10 minutes. Add the tomatoes and stir to combine. The sauce can be completed on the stove top or in the oven. The stove top method takes less time but requires more attention.

2. To complete on the stove, simmer the sauce gently for 1½-2 hours, stirring every 10 minutes to prevent scorching.

3. To complete in the oven, bring the tomatoes to a simmer on top of the stove, cover the pot with parchment paper, and place the pot in a preheated 325°oven for 3 to 4 hours.

4. Whichever method you choose, the sauce is done when it is thick, slightly chunky, and reduced to about 1 quart. Add the oregano or basil and let cool to room temperature (about 1 hour) before assembling lasagna.

FILLING
1 ½ pounds whole-milk
  ricotta cheese
3 large eggs

½ cup parsley
Kosher salt
Freshly ground black pepper

TO PREPARE THE FILLING

1. In a large bowl, whisk together the ricotta and eggs until completely blended. Add the parsley and salt and pepper to taste and mix until well combined.

2. Refrigerate until ready to use.

3. Cook the noodles in a large pot of boiling salted water according to the package directions.

4. Drain the noodles and allow them to cool slightly.

TO ASSEMBLE

1. Preheat oven to 350°.

2. Spread a thin layer (¾ to 1 cup) of sauce over the bottom of a 9 x 13-inch baking pan.

3. Place a layer of noodles (no more than one fourth) in the pan, slightly overlapping them.

4. Spread half the ricotta mixture evenly over the noodles and top with another layer of noodles.

5. Reserve 1 cup of the remaining sauce and spread the rest over the noodles, completely covering them.

6. Arrange another layer of noodles on top and cover with the remaining ricotta mixture.

7. Top with a final layer of noodles and spoon the reserved sauce over them.

8. Toss the grated mozzarella with salt and pepper to taste (to give the cheese more flavor), and sprinkle it over the top.

9. Bake for 45 minutes to 1 hour, or until the mozzarella is a spotted golden brown.

ADAPTED FROM THOMAS KELLER

PEACH "JELLO"

(makes 6 servings)

This "Jello" is surprisingly delightful, light, and refreshing. It's unlike any Jello you've ever tried. Make it during the summer months when fresh peaches are in season. As a result of making the "Jello", you get two added bonuses: delicious "left over" poached peaches, and you're halfway to making a truly wonderful peach sorbet.

10 yellow freestone peaches

POACHING LIQUID
13 ounces white wine, i.e. Mondavi Sauvignon Blanc
26 ounces water
13 ounces sugar
Juice of 1 lemon
½ cup grenadine syrup
3 envelopes powdered gelatin, ¼ ounce each (¾ ounce total)

TO POACH PEACHES

1. Bring white wine to a boil. Skim any particles that float to the surface. Add water and sugar. Bring to a boil again and continue to skim. Add the lemon juice and grenadine.

2. Make an "x" on the bottom of each peach. Poach them in the liquid until the skin starts to peel away from the "x" area. Remove from liquid and peel while still warm. Cut in half and remove the pits.

TO MAKE JELLO

1. While the liquid is still very hot, measure 34 ounces (4¼ cups) in a bowl.

2. Add the 3 envelopes powdered gelatin and stir well to make sure it dissolves completely. This is important because otherwise the gelatin at the bottom will be thicker than the gelatin on top when the "Jello" is set. Dice two of the poached peaches into ¼-inch size cubes and add them to the "Jello".

3. Pour it into a medium-size glass bowl, a 9 x 5-inch glass loaf pan, or an 8-cup capacity ring mold. The diced peaches will float to the top.

4. Refrigerate about 2 hours until set.

5. If using a mold, when ready to serve, place it in hot water for about 30 seconds, until the sides start to loosen. Place a serving plate over the mold and invert it.

ADAPTED FROM THOMAS KELLER

PEACH SORBET

(makes 6 servings)

17 ounces peach purée
6 ounces water (¾ cup)
5 ounces sugar (1 cup)
1 teaspoon almond liquor such as Marousquin or Amaretto (optional)

1. In a food processor or blender, purée enough of the peaches to make 17 ounces (a little more than 2 cups).

2. In a small saucepan add the sugar and the water and stir over very low heat until the sugar is dissolved. This is what's known as simple syrup.

3. Add the simple syrup to the peach purée and

cool the mixture completely. After the mixture is cool, add the liquor.

4. Spin the mixture in an ice cream machine, following the manufacturer's instructions.

5. Store in the freezer until ready to serve.

ADAPTED FROM THOMAS KELLER

Magical Melting Pot

HONEY-VANILLA ICE CREAM

(makes about 1 quart)

The French Laundry's rich, smooth, honey-vanilla ice cream gets it's unique, delicate flavor from the wildflower honey. The chocolate sauce is so easy to make and so good, you'll never buy a commercially manufactured version again.

2 cups milk
2 cups cream
½ cup sugar
10 large egg yolks
½ cup wildflower honey

1. In a saucepan, combine the milk, cream, and 2 tablespoons of the sugar and bring to a simmer.

2. Meanwhile, in a mixer or other metal bowl, whisk the egg yolks and the remaining 2 tablespoons sugar until thickened and lightened in color.

3. Gradually whisk in one third of the warm milk mixture to temper the egg yolks. This will prevent the eggs from "cooking" when the rest of the warm milk is added.

4. Return the mixture to the saucepan and stir over medium heat until the custard has thickened and coats the back of a wooden spoon.

5. Pour the custard into a bowl set in an ice-water bath and stir in the honey to combine. Let the mixture cool to room temperature.

6. When cool, strain the mixture into a container and refrigerate at least 5 hours, or overnight (for the creamiest texture).

7. Freeze the custard in an ice-cream machine following the manufacturer's directions. Remove to a covered container and freeze for several hours, or until hardened.

ADAPTED FROM THOMAS KELLER

CHOCOLATE SAUCE

**8 ounces bittersweet or semi-sweet
   chocolate, finely chopped
1 cup heavy cream
1 tablespoon light corn syrup**

1. Place the chocolate in a bowl.

2. Bring the cream and corn syrup to a boil.

3. Pour the hot liquid over the chocolate and allow it to sit for a few minutes to melt the chocolate. Stir until smooth. (The sauce can be refrigerated for several days.)

4. Serve over ice cream. Add whipped cream and chopped nuts and maraschino or candied morello cherries if desired.

ADAPTED FROM THOMAS KELLER

Loretta Barrett Oden

Oklahoma

Above: The little chef to be, at age 2.
Left: Chef Loretta Oden.

Loretta Oden is doing what she loves best: educating people throughout the country about North American, Central American, and South American Indian cooking. After Loretta divorced and her children were grown, she found an exciting new life for herself. In the process, she became the owner/creator of a successful Native American Indian restaurant in Santa Fe, New Mexico, and the leading expert in the country on Native American cooking. She started by traveling from Indian reservation to Indian reservation over a three-year period, throughout North, Central, and South America; and her research continues.

Loretta's highest priority in life is educating people of all ages about Indian foods, agriculture, and customs. She is also giving back to her own tribe, the Citizen Potawatomi Nation that has its reservation in Oklahoma, by developing programs to help the tribe rediscover its language, its health, its agricultural roots, and its identity.

Starting in the 1880's, many Indian tribes were forbidden to speak their native

languages; and, as a result, much of the language was lost to younger generations. With her brother, John "Rocky" Barrett, who is the leader of the Citizen Potawatomi Nation, Loretta is helping her people set aside plots of land to develop gardens. The elders and the children in the community garden together. In this way, the children learn the language and agricultural traditions of their ancestors, and the elders feel useful and respected.

In the 1830's under President Andrew Jackson, the U.S. government passed the Indian Removal Act. Indian tribes or nations east of the Mississippi River were forced to relocate to reservations in the central part of the United States. A diverse mix of Indian nations settled in Oklahoma, which today has the second largest Native American Indian population of any state in the country. Because so many different Indian nations were forced to live close to one another, they were exposed to each others' food, lore, and customs.

When Loretta was young, one of the ways she learned about other Native American groups was by going to the pow-wows and feast days that many different tribes attended. At pow-wows, dancers and drum groups from different Indian tribes would compete. Women cooked foods over open fires and fed all who attended. In late June there would be fry bread contests to see who could cook the best fry bread. The practice continues today.

Many of the Indians were poor as the result of having been taken from their lands and having to start life all over with very little. The U.S. government had what was called a commodities program to help these Indian families. Twice a week the government would give out free commodities, such as refined white flour, spam (canned

Three Sisters

The three most common foods in Native American cooking are beans, corn, and squash. They're known as "the Three Sisters" and have traditionally been planted together in the same mound. The vegetables were often eaten together, as in the Native American dish succotash.

As "the three sisters" grow, the beans climb by wrapping their vines around the corn stalk. The squash plant's large leaves and vines spread out around the base of the corn stalk, covering and shading the mound so it will better retain the moisture in the soil.

lunchmeat), cheese, lard, canned salmon, saltines, beans, and dried corn. The Indian women learned to cook with these ingredients. Ironically, some of the foods they made, such as Indian fry bread, became known as Indian foods; but they were really developed to use the available ingredients.

Loretta's mom came from a large family. She was one of nine brothers and sisters, so Loretta grew up with lots of aunts, uncles, and cousins. They were a happy, close knit group, always singing and laughing. Many of their activities revolved around food, and everyone had a job to do. Many families had gardens, which provided food throughout the year. They also gathered foods that grew on the prairies, such as chokecherries, wild blueberries, blackberries, possum grapes, wild onions, dandelion and poke greens, pecans, walnuts, and wild sand plums. Each year in the springtime, when the wild sand plum flowers bloomed, her family would go out to the wild sand plum thicket, bringing along

distinctively colored pieces of cloth. They would stake a claim to a thicket and reserve or identify it for their family with the cloth. When late summer came, and the sand plums ripened, they knew which were theirs by the color of the cloth. With the wild sand plums they'd make a crystal clear jelly, which was a great source of pride. Families would compete to see who made the clearest, most perfect jelly.

Black walnut and pecan trees grew near their reservation. The women in Loretta's family enjoyed sitting on their front porches, talking and shelling the nuts, and then making pralines, which are candy-like patties, brimming with nuts.

Family outings sometimes involved hunting and fishing. They'd pack up lunches, and the men would hunt rabbits and squirrels while the women would fish for catfish, perch, and bass, and the kids played in the fields.

Loretta's very first food memory was rolling Saltine crackers between waxed paper to make the crumbs to coat salmon croquettes. Another early memory was making chicken and dumplings. The dumplings were more like big, thick noodles. Her mom would make a big batch of dough, and the kids would roll it out onto a big sheet, covering a whole Formica table top. Loretta would start at one end, cutting the noodle dumplings one by one and dropping them into the big soup pot.

The story of Loretta's restaurant's success is a very nice one. After Loretta spent three years visiting Indian reservations all over the Americas researching Indian foods and agriculture, she decided to open a restaurant where she could experiment and apply much of what she'd learned. She considered potential locations all around the country and decided on Santa Fe, New Mexico, as the area that would be most interested in the type of cooking she wanted to introduce.

Loretta plowed all her savings into (as she describes it), a tiny, funky, adobe style restaurant near downtown Santa Fe. She named it the Corn Dance Café. She'd never worked in a restaurant before. At the start, there was one server, one dishwasher, and Loretta was the cook and host. Shortly after the restaurant opened, a local food critic named Pancho Epstein gave her little restaurant a glowing review. The following day when she opened her door, there were fifty people waiting outside to come in. The next thing Loretta knew, she was asked to appear on *Good Morning America* to prepare and talk about a Native American Thanksgiving feast.

Today Loretta is filming a wonderful TV series for PBS called *Seasoned with Spirit—A Native Cook's Journey*. A companion book of the same name will be published in fall 2004. The show is shot at locations all across the U.S., where Native American people are growing, harvesting, catching, or preparing foods such as wild rice in Minnesota, buffalo in South Dakota and Montana, and fresh salmon in Washington State. Loretta has also appeared on *Rebecca's Garden* and *House & Garden TV*. In addition, she writes for magazines such as *Prevention, Self*, and *Cooking Light*. Loretta just opened a new restaurant, Corn Dance Café at Fire Lake, in Shawnee, Oklahoma.

Below are the recipes for some of Loretta's favorite childhood dishes. While corn was only one of the many ingredients used by Native American Indians, these recipes demonstrate how versatile that ingredient is. The recipes utilize almost all the different forms of corn, from kernels cut from the cobs, to ground fresh corn, to popcorn, to cornmeal, to masa harina, a flour made from dried corn.

SKILLET CORN

(makes 6 servings)

9 medium ears of corn with kernels
cut from the cob (If fresh corn is
not in season, substitute 4 ½ cups
of frozen corn thawed and drained,
or canned corn that's been rinsed
and drained.)
½ onion, finely minced
1 teaspoon honey, warmed

1 jalapeño or serrano chile,
seeded and minced (optional)
1 large egg, lightly beaten
⅓ cup flour
½ teaspoon salt
¼ teaspoon black pepper
2 tablespoons canola oil
for the skillet

1. Pour the canola oil into a large cast iron or ovenproof skillet and tilt it all around to coat the bottom. Place in a 425° oven until very hot (about 15 to 20 minutes).

2. Combine all the ingredients and press them into the hot skillet to compact it. Then smooth the top.

3. Return the skillet to the oven and let it bake until a good crust is formed on the bottom (about 15 to 20 minutes). When you think it's

done, lift an edge of the corn to make sure the crust is nice and brown.

4. When ready, loosen the edges all around with a spatula and place a round serving plate (larger than the skillet) over the skillet. Invert it onto the plate, and while still hot, cut into wedges. (Use potholders, as the pan will be extremely hot.)

5. Serve immediately.

ADAPTED FROM LORETTA BARRETT ODEN

MAPLE POPCORN

(makes 6 servings)

This maple popcorn is so good, I can assure you it won't last long!

1 cup popcorn kernels
1 cup salted peanuts or
coarsely chopped pecans
(optional)
¾ cup unsalted butter

1 ½ cups pure maple syrup
½ cup light corn syrup
1 teaspoon salt
¼ teaspoon cream of tartar
⅓ teaspoon baking soda

1. Pop the popcorn in a large pot with 2 tablespoons of oil, or use a popcorn popper.

2. Distribute the popped corn equally between 2 oiled 9 x 13-inch pans. If adding nuts, divide them equally as well.

3. Preheat the oven to 200°.

4. In a large saucepan, melt the butter. Add the maple and corn syrups, salt, and cream of tartar, mixing well. Cook over medium-low heat, without stirring, until a candy thermometer registers 240° degrees, or until a spoonful of syrup forms a soft pliable ball when dropped in cold water. Remove from heat and stir in the baking soda.

5. Pour the syrup over the popcorn and stir to coat it thoroughly. Bake, stirring several times, for 1 hour.

6. Let cool until no longer too hot to handle. If you let it stay in the pan until completely cool, it will be harder to remove.

7. Store in a tightly covered container. If exposed to air for too long, the maple popcorn will pick up moisture and not be as crunchy.

ADAPTED FROM LORETTA BARRETT ODEN

CACHAPAS PANCAKES

(makes 4 servings)

6 ears of fresh corn with the kernels removed (about 3 ½ cups) (If fresh corn is not in season, use an equivalent amount of frozen corn (about 16 ounces) thawed and drained, or canned corn rinsed and drained.)
¼ cup sugar
4 tablespoons masa harina or instant corn masa mix (If not available substitute 4 tablespoons flour plus 2 tablespoons cornmeal.)
¾ teaspoon salt
3 egg whites
2 tablespoons oil (or more if needed) for the skillet or griddle
Sour cream, maple syrup, or honey for garnish

1. Combine corn, sugar, salt, and egg whites with 3 tablespoons masa mix (or flour and cornmeal mixture) in a blender or food processor. Purée until smooth, about 1-2 minutes. If too loose, add remaining 1 tablespoon masa mix or flour.

2. Add enough oil to coat the bottom of a skillet or griddle and heat on medium-low.

3. Pour ¼ cup batter into the hot skillet and cook until the sides of the pancake begin to turn golden brown, bubbles start to form, and the surface begins to look slightly dry. Gently turn the pancakes over and cook an additional 1-2 minutes. This batter is a little soft and the pancakes have a tendency to stick, so make sure there is enough oil coating the pan for each additional pancake.

ADAPTED FROM LORETTA BARRETT ODEN

SWEET INDIAN PUDDING

(makes 6 servings)

This is one of the ultimate comfort desserts. It always makes me think of Autumn and New England. Dried cranberries are a great addition.

4 cups milk
1 cup maple syrup
¼ cup unsalted butter
⅔ cup cornmeal

½ teaspoon ground ginger
¼ teaspoon ground allspice
1 ½ cups dried cranberries

1. Preheat oven to 300°. Butter a 2-quart casserole.

2. In a medium saucepan, combine 3 cups of milk and the maple syrup over medium heat. Heat until it simmers and then add the butter.

3. In a small bowl, combine the cornmeal, ginger, and allspice.

4. Using a wire whisk, stir the milk mixture as you slowly pour the cornmeal mixture into the milk. This will keep it from becoming lumpy.

Reduce heat to low and cook until thickened, stirring occasionally. Fold in the cranberries.

5. Spoon into prepared casserole and pour remaining milk over the top of the pudding. DO NOT STIR. Bake for 2½ hours until milk has been absorbed and the top is golden brown.

6. Serve plain, or with a dollop of honey-sweetened whipped cream.

ADAPTED FROM LORETTA BARRETT ODEN

Patrick O'Connell

Virginia

Above: Patrick at age 10.
Left: Patrick O'Connell today.

Patrick O'Connell is a man who likes to smile, and these days he has a lot to smile about. Patrick recently received the James Beard Award for Best Chef in America. Patrick and his partner Reinhardt Lynch own The Inn at Little Washington, a magnificent inn and restaurant located in the tiny town of Washington, Virginia, nestled between the foothills of the Blue Ridge Mountains and Virginia's Shenandoah Valley.

The town was named for George Washington, who surveyed and helped lay out the town in 1749, when he was just 17 years old. It has since been declared a National Historic District. The Inn is located about an hour and a half south of Washington, D.C.; and it's worth the drive just to see the decor, just to taste the food, and even to just see the food which is so beautifully and imaginatively presented.

The Inn at Little Washington is a dream that began about 25 years ago; and each year it gets better and better. What is now The Inn was once an abandoned gas station that was operating as a country store on the bottom floor, with a basketball court and dance hall above. Patrick and Reinhardt initially converted the downstairs into a restaurant; and, after a number of years of customers asking where they could spend the night, the upstairs was transformed into guest bedrooms.

To figure out exactly how they wanted to make their inn special, Patrick and Reinhardt traveled to the best inns they could find all around the world. Then they hired Joyce Evans who lived in London, to decorate the rooms. Joyce was an unusual and brilliant choice because her "real" job was designing stage sets for the London theatre. She has great taste in furniture, fabrics, and wallpaper; and she knows how to combine them in ways that are incredibly beautiful.

The Inn has recently added an enormous new kitchen with large picture windows, an oversized fireplace with tables on either side, and the type of padded bench chairs that Patrick remembered from his grandmother's kitchen years ago. It's the most magnificent and cheerful kitchen I've ever seen. A limited number of guests can actually dine at one of the two large tables by the fireplace and from there watch the chefs cook, if they make reservations far enough in advance. A farmhouse was recently added to The Inn, where guests can also stay. In the morning a chef comes to the farmhouse to prepare a special breakfast.

Two Dalmatians, Rose and DeSoto, are so much a part of The Inn that they often greet visitors when they arrive. When dinner guests want to take home leftovers, they get a "doggie bag" that has a Dalmatian spot pattern on it. The chefs in the kitchen all wear specially designed pants with a Dalmatian print, creating an atmosphere that can't help but make you smile.

A beautiful swan sculpture sits high above the center of the dining room. It's an ancient symbol of plenitude or bounty, grace, and elegance.

Dalmations

Dalmatian puppies are pure white when they're born. After about 3-4 weeks, their spots start to appear. Dalmatians have served as watchdogs, hunting dogs, and years ago as coach dogs that would run alongside carriages..

Besides being attractive to look at, its purpose is to remind the employees of the restaurant's goals and the dining experience they're trying to create. After dinner, each guest receives a small wicker basket with the swan decoration on top and miniature cookies and candied grapefruit rind inside. This has been a tradition at the restaurant for years.

Patrick first experienced restaurant life when he was 15. His first restaurant job was cooking frozen hamburgers at a carryout restaurant, and he loved the excitement and fast pace. Though he toyed with becoming an actor, he preferred running a restaurant because as he says, it gave him the opportunity "to be the producer, director, set designer, and lead player" and to combine "the world of complete illusion in the dining room with the reality of the kitchen".

Patrick grew up in a quiet Maryland suburb of Washington, D.C., near Andrews Air Force Base. His ancestors came from Norway, Ireland, and Wales. During summers, Patrick and his family would visit his grandmother in the Midwest. She had a big yellow house, and the kitchen with its cozy breakfast nook and padded bench chairs, was the center of activity. Outside her kitchen there was a rhubarb patch; and, past that, there were apple trees and grape arbors.

His grandmother loved to bake apple pies and to keep the cookie jar full with peanut butter cookies for her five grandchildren. She also made wonderful chocolate fudge.

Patrick's grandmother was extremely resourceful. She could whip up an elegant dinner for 12 based on a tiny piece of meat. Baked beans were a favorite side dish at picnics and family get-togethers. They baked for hours with bacon, sugar, and butter; and were delicious eaten either hot or at room temperature.

His mother's "signature" dish that she was known for and that she served at parties when Patrick was young, was called "Little Nancy Etticoat in Her White Petticoat" and was also known as "Candlelight Salad". It was inspired by a nursery rhyme. It consisted of a banana (meant to replicate a candle) coming straight out of a Dole pineapple ring, surrounded by lettuce. It had a dollop of mayonnaise running down the side to replicate the dripping candle wax, a strand of coconut to replicate the wick, and a maraschino cherry to simulate the flame. It was a very popular dish in its day. Needless to say, it was challenging to eat.

Patrick has included several of his own childhood favorite recipes as well as a few recipes that he's since developed that are delicious and fun to make. Included is a fantasy (sweet dessert) pizza that he prepared on *Good Morning America*. It's extremely clever, as it uses puff pastry for the pizza dough, rhubarb, cranberry, or strawberry purée in place of tomato sauce, shaved white chocolate in place of cheese, and prunes and pistachio nuts to replicate black and green olives. You'll also find a very special pineapple upside-down crêpe recipe that appeared in the *New York Times* and was inspired by his mother's pineapple upside-down cake.

THE INN
AT LITTLE
WASHINGTON

MY GRANDMOTHER'S BAKED BEANS

(makes 4 servings)

These beans are a little different and unusually good. Sugar gives them their unique caramelized flavor. They're easy to make, but you'll have to start them the day before you need them.

1 pound (16 ounces) dried Great Northern Beans
1 tablespoon salt
1 cup sugar
3 strips bacon, cut into ½-inch pieces
2 tablespoons butter

1. Place the beans in a 2-quart saucepan, cover with cool water, and soak over night.

2. Drain the beans, cover them with fresh salted water, and cook over medium heat until barely tender. Do not drain.

3. Preheat oven to 300°.

4. Add the sugar and bacon to the beans and cooking liquid. Pour into an ovenproof earthenware crock or bean pot. Top with the butter and bake, uncovered, for 3 hours. If the top layer of beans begins becomes too dry, cover the pot with aluminum foil.

ADAPTED FROM PATRICK O'CONNELL

"CANDLELIGHT SALAD"

(makes 1 serving)

This whimsical salad was the vogue when Patrick was growing up. It looks like a melting candle.

1 large iceberg lettuce leaf
1 Dole canned pineapple ring
½ banana cut at its mid-section
   so it can stand flat

1 teaspoon mayonnaise
A shred of dried coconut
A small piece of red pimento
   or a maraschino cherry

1. Arrange the lettuce leaf decoratively on an individual salad plate.

2. Place the pineapple ring in the center of the lettuce.

3. Place the banana half in the center of the pineapple ring which will anchor it. The banana should stand upright.

4. Carefully place the mayonnaise along the top of the banana, running down about 1½ inches so it resembles melting candle wax.

5. Place a long shred of coconut into the tip of the banana so it looks like a wick.

6. Place the piece of red pimento or the cherry just below the wick to simulate the candle's flame.

ADAPTED FROM PATRICK O'CONNELL

RHUBARB PIZZA

(makes 10 individual 5-inch round "pizzas")

This dessert is a great example of Patrick O'Connell's tremendous creativity and inventiveness, his artistic eye, and his sense of playfulness. The recipe can be cut in half.

FOR THE CRUST
1 ½-pound package puff pastry dough (2 sheets)
¼ cup yellow cornmeal

On a floured board, roll each sheet of dough into a square about 11 x 11 inches and about ⅛-inch thick. Lay a bowl about 5 inches in diameter upside down on the dough, and using the rim as

a pattern, cut out 4 circles per sheet with a paring knife. Combine the remaining scraps of dough and roll them out to ⅛-inch thickness.

You should be able to get at least two more 5-inch circles.

FOR THE RHUBARB PURÉE (TO SIMULATE TOMATO SAUCE)

3 cups of roughly chopped fresh rhubarb, or frozen (a 16-ounce package)
1 cup sugar

1. Wash the fresh rhubarb, trim off any leaves, and cut out any brown or bruised spots. Using a very sharp knife, roughly chop the stalks. If using frozen rhubarb, thaw and then chop it.

2. In a 4-quart saucepan, combine the sugar and rhubarb over medium heat. Bring just to a boil.

Simmer until the rhubarb is soft, and looks thick like applesauce. Mash any lumps with a spoon. The frozen rhubarb may be more watery, so cook it down until it makes a nice purée, stirring periodically.

FOR THE TOPPINGS

1 cup pistachios, lightly toasted (to simulate green olives)
12 large strawberries cut into thin,
    circular disks (to simulate tomatoes)
1 cup dried prunes, pitted and diced (to simulate black olives)
8-ounce block of white chocolate,
    for grating (to simulate cheese)
1 cup Galliano liquor (to simulate olive oil)

TO ASSEMBLE PIZZAS

1. Preheat oven to 350°.

2. Sprinkle cornmeal on 2 large cookie sheets to prevent the dough from sticking. Lay the rounds of dough so they don't touch.

3. Spread about 1 ½ tablespoons of the rhubarb purée evenly over each of the circles, leaving a ⅓-inch border of crust.

4. Bake for 15 minutes or until the pastry is crisp and golden brown.

5. Remove from the oven and place the strawberry slices, pistachios, and prunes on top to resemble pizza toppings.

TO SERVE

Place each of the pizzas on a dessert plate. Grate the white chocolate on top, and then sprinkle with Galliano. (This can be done at the table, just like getting Parmesan and olive oil sprinkled on top of a pizza.) Serve each with a scoop of ice cream.

ADAPTED FROM PATRICK O'CONNELL

PINEAPPLE UPSIDE-DOWN CRÊPES

(makes 5-6)

FOR THE CRÊPE BATTER

1 cup all-purpose flour
3 tablespoons unsalted butter, melted and cooled
2 tablespoons sugar
2 medium eggs
Pinch of salt
½ cup milk, or as needed

1. Combine the flour, melted butter, sugar, and salt in a food processor or blender. With the motor running, add the milk to make a fluid batter. Add more milk if necessary. The batter may be covered and refrigerated up to 24 hours in advance.

TO MAKE THE CRÊPES

1 large ripe pineapple, peeled, cored, and cut lengthwise into quarters
3 tablespoons butter, plus extra for greasing the pan
½ cup coarsely ground macadamia nuts
¼ cup sugar
⅜ cup of cream, or as needed
10 to 12 miniature scoops vanilla, buttermilk, or coconut ice cream

1. Line 2 baking sheets with parchment paper, and set aside.

2. Slice pineapple quarters lengthwise, ⅛-inch thick.

3. In a 7-inch non-stick pan over medium heat, lightly coat the pan with butter. Remove pan from heat.

4. Ladle in about 3 tablespoons batter and roll around pan until bottom is evenly coated. Sprinkle with 1 tablespoon macadamia nuts.

5. Return pan to medium heat. Just as the crêpe sets, but while it's still wet on top, remove pan from heat and arrange pineapple slices in an overlapping circular pattern, completely covering the surface.

6. Sprinkle pineapple with 2 teaspoons sugar and about ½ tablespoon cold butter, cut in bits. Use a rubber spatula to loosen edges of crêpe and underside. When bottom is golden brown, loosen crêpe by running a rubber spatula around edges and carefully flip crêpe over in pan. Continue cooking until sugar underneath begins to turn a light caramel color.

7. Add 1 tablespoon cream around sides of pan, and tilt it so the cream blends with the sugar and runs under edges of the crêpe.

8. Spray a flat metal surface like the bottom of a cake pan with nonstick cooking spray. Place sprayed side over crêpe, and invert skillet to remove crêpe. Slide onto prepared baking sheet. Repeat process, wiping pan clean between crêpes, to make 5 to 6. Crêpes may be covered and refrigerated up to 4 hours.

9. To serve, reheat crêpes in a 350° oven until hot, about 4 minutes. Transfer to individual serving plates. Garnish each with a miniature scoop of ice cream.

ADAPTED FROM PATRICK O'CONNELL

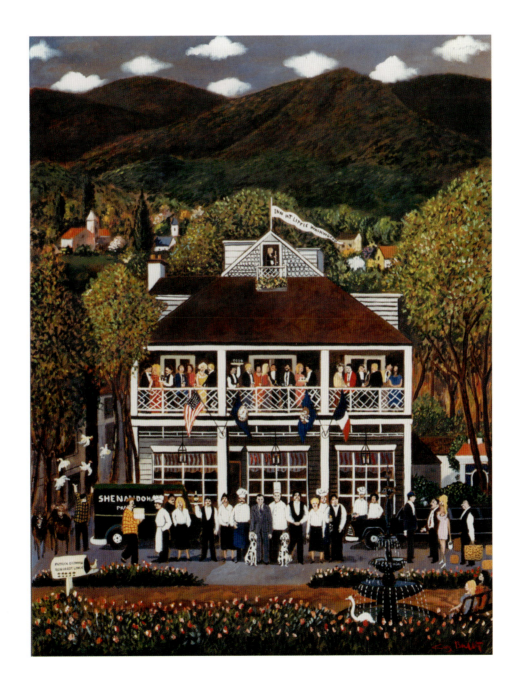

Michelle Greenwald

Southern California

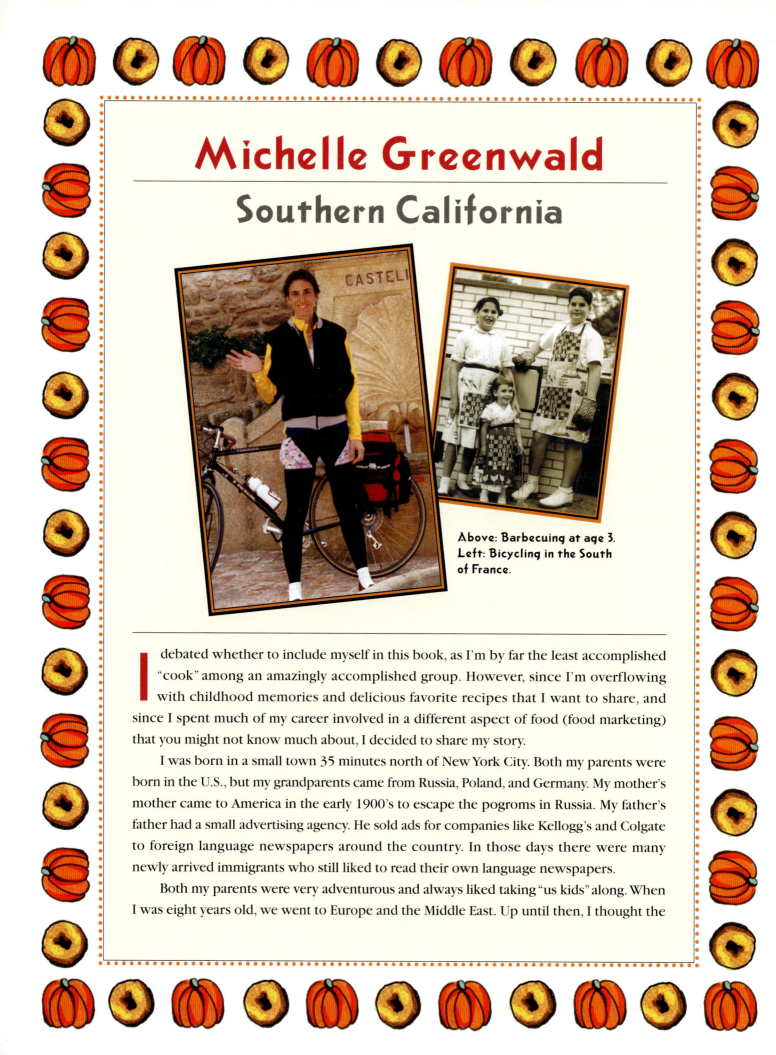

Above: Barbecuing at age 3.
Left: Bicycling in the South
of France.

I debated whether to include myself in this book, as I'm by far the least accomplished "cook" among an amazingly accomplished group. However, since I'm overflowing with childhood memories and delicious favorite recipes that I want to share, and since I spent much of my career involved in a different aspect of food (food marketing) that you might not know much about, I decided to share my story.

I was born in a small town 35 minutes north of New York City. Both my parents were born in the U.S., but my grandparents came from Russia, Poland, and Germany. My mother's mother came to America in the early 1900's to escape the pogroms in Russia. My father's father had a small advertising agency. He sold ads for companies like Kellogg's and Colgate to foreign language newspapers around the country. In those days there were many newly arrived immigrants who still liked to read their own language newspapers.

Both my parents were very adventurous and always liked taking "us kids" along. When I was eight years old, we went to Europe and the Middle East. Up until then, I thought the

whole world spoke English. I remember being very frustrated when I saw kids in other countries that I couldn't communicate with because I didn't speak their language. That might have been one of the reasons I majored in International Relations in college and studied Spanish, French, and Italian.

On Sundays my family would explore New York City, which has always been known as "a melting pot" because so many different types of people live there. We loved eating at the Benihana Restaurant and watching the Japanese chef cook at the big grill built into our table. He'd do food tricks, like throwing a shrimp tail in the air and catching it in his hat, or making a steaming volcano out of a stack of sliced onions. At other Japanese restaurants we sat on the floor and made sukiyaki in the middle of our low table, or we'd sit at the tempura bar and watch the chef dip shrimp and vegetables into a batter and fry them until they were golden brown.

We'd visit the "Lower East Side" of New York and buy pickled tomatoes and cucumbers out of great big barrels, or baked, flavored pot cheese from a tiny "dairy" store. We looked forward to visiting "Little Italy" during the San Genaro Festival when the streets were filled with colored lights, and stands overflowed with sausages and peppers and other Italian specialties. After we'd go to Ferrara's for their wonderful ricotta cheesecake and sfalladelle, a cheese filled pastry, wrapped it seemed a thousand times, in an overlapping ribbon of crisp, paper thin dough that crackled when you took a bite.

My parents liked progressive meals through Chinatown. They'd start at "Big Wong's" for their hearty Won Ton Soup, then move on to Hop Lee's Rice Shop for Crab with Ginger and Scallions, and Steak with Chinese Broccoli. For dessert

Pumpkins

Pumpkins are members of the gourd family. The precursor to pumpkin pie was made in colonial times by filling a hollowed out pumpkin with milk, spices, and maple syrup and then baking it.

Pumpkin seeds make a delicious, nutritious snack. After cutting the pumpkin, wash the seeds and spread them out on a greased cookie sheet. Dot with butter and sprinkle with salt. Bake in a 350° oven until golden brown. Stir once in between to make sure they brown all over.

we'd go to a Chinese bakery for giant almond cookies that crumbled when you ate them. Lastly, we'd stop at a Chinese grocery store to buy Chinese vegetables and on occasion, an air-dried, roasted duck to take home.

The seasons also brought new food adventures. We frequented farm stands in summer and early fall. My father was a well-known, fresh corn fanatic. When sweet corn was in season, he'd buy it at the farm and go right home to cook it, before the sugar turned to starch. He was known to eat 8-10 corn in one sitting. New York is the "Apple State" and in the fall, when apples were in season, we'd go for a hayride at an apple orchard, pick a few barrels of apples, and then go home and make fresh applesauce. The fresh apple cider that was pressed at the farm was incredible. It tasted like liquid apples. Along with the cider, we had fresh, warm donuts that we watched fry in oil and then rolled in cinnamon sugar. Around Halloween, we loved the just-made slices of coconut custard pie and pumpkins from the "Old

Log Cabin". To decorate the pumpkins my dad took us to an old fashioned, penny candy store to buy licorice lips and jelly slices for the eyes.

We had friends from Peru, Spain, Italy, and Denmark and looked forward to invitations to their houses. We enjoyed their company and really liked their food! I could go on and on.

In college I went on the Experiment in International Living to Spain and France and stayed with families that didn't speak any English. I did projects for credit on the local cooking. That included going to a French bakery in the middle of the night to watch the baker work his magic making crisp loaves of French bread and pastries, visiting a farm where cheese was made, taking part in a fall grape harvest to make wine, and taking French cooking classes. After graduating from college, I attended graduate school in business administration and majored in Marketing.

For 15 years I worked for large, multinational food companies marketing products like Post Cereals, NesQuik, Nestlé Candy Bars, Kraft Mayonnaise, Pepsi-Cola beverages, and even dog food. One of my claims to fame was the creation of the Laffy Taffy brand. I came up with the name, the idea to put jokes on the wrappers, and worked with others to develop the characters for each flavor. When I was assigned to NesQuik, I developed the NesQuik Syrup "bunny bottle" and worked with the people at Macy's to develop the gigantic NesQuik Bunny balloon that for years was in Macy's Thanksgiving Day Parade. At Pepsi-Cola I was responsible for introducing new beverage products into the U.S. market. Several years ago I was selected by Advertising Age Magazine as "One of the 100 Best and Brightest Women in the U.S. in Advertising and Marketing".

Today I'm a part-time graduate business school professor and I teach a variety of marketing courses. I love teaching because I learn so much in preparing for each class, and also from my students who teach me as much as I teach them.

Living in California has been wonderful because there's so much ethnic diversity here. We shop at Middle Eastern, Korean, and Japanese grocery stores and eat at Ethiopian, Thai, Peruvian, Mexican, and Chinese restaurants that are delicious and inexpensive. Luckily, my kids have allowed me to drag them all around on "food adventures".

I had wanted to write this book for years, and finally decided I could do it if I put my mind to it. Being able to interview and learn from all the amazing people in this book has been a dream come true.

Below are my favorite childhood recipes. My grandmother made the most delicious egg salad with fried onions. My grandfather had his own version, which he made with crumbled bacon. It was crunchy and had a wonderful flavor. A friend of our family, Sadie Mack, used to carve out oranges, fill them with sweet potatoes, and then bake them with marshmallows on top until they turned golden brown. In the winter I used to love a soup called sweet and sour, cabbage borscht with its delicious chunks of soft, flavorful, short rib meat.

Lastly, I enjoyed making and eating Rugelach cookies. The rich cream cheese and butter dough was rolled into a circle and cut into slices like a pizza. It was sprinkled with cinnamon sugar and chopped nuts, currants, mini chocolate chips, or spread with jam. Each slice was rolled into a crescent shape and baked until golden brown. The aroma that filled the house was wonderful.

Happy eating!

SWEET AND SOUR BEEF AND CABBAGE BORSCHT

(makes 8 servings)

Served with a fresh loaf of bread, this hearty soup makes a satisfying meal. I loved it as a kid, and it's been my own family's favorite.

3 pounds beef flanken or short ribs
1 pound beef marrow bones
2 ½-3 quarts water
1 ½ teaspoons salt
2 large onions, peeled and coarsely chopped
3 cloves garlic, minced
1 16-ounce can chopped tomatoes with their liquid

1 head green cabbage, shredded
3 tablespoons butter
3 tablespoons flour
Juice of 1 large lemon, or to taste
4 tablespoons brown sugar, or to taste

1. Place the beef flanken and marrow bones in a large soup pot and cover with the water. Bring to a boil and continue to boil about 10 minutes. A grayish foam will come to the surface. Skim it off, lower the heat, cover, and simmer about 45 minutes more.

2. Add the onion, garlic, the chopped tomatoes with their liquid, and the shredded cabbage. Simmer 30 minutes more.

3. Remove the beef from the soup and let it cool. Remove the bones and grizzle from the meat. Cut into small cubes and add meat back to the soup.

4. Make a roux by melting the butter in a small saucepan. Add the flour and cook, stirring for several minutes until it starts to darken in color. Over low heat, gradually add several tablespoons of the soup stock, stirring constantly, until you have about ½ cup total. The roux shouldn't be too stiff. Add to the soup pot and stir. It will melt into the soup and become uniformly incorporated.

5. Add the lemon juice and brown sugar. Taste to make sure you like the sweet and sour balance and the amount of salt.

6. Simmer about 30 minutes more.

7. The soup will keep up to two days. If you make it in advance, refrigerate and remove any fat that comes to the surface.

ORANGES STUFFED WITH SWEET POTATOES AND GOLDEN MARSHMALLOWS

(makes 6)

I really loved these as a kid. They were a Thanksgiving favorite.

3 large navel oranges
3 yam-type sweet potatoes, about ½ pound each
1 tablespoons butter, cut in small pieces

½ cup orange juice
4 tablespoons brown sugar, packed
½ teaspoon salt
2 cups mini-marshmallows

1. Preheat oven to 400°.

2. Wash the yams, removing any dirt from the surface. Dry them and wrap in aluminum foil.

3. Bake for 1 hour or until soft when pierced with a fork.

4. Meanwhile, with a serrated knife, slice each navel orange in half. Use a serrated, curved grapefruit knife to remove the orange fruit. Place these hollowed out shells in a baking dish.

5. When the yams are cool enough to handle, peel off the skin and mash them well in a bowl. Add butter pieces and mix until melted. Add the orange juice, brown sugar, and salt and mix well.

6. Lower the oven temperature to 350°.

7. Spoon the yam mixture into the orange shells, allowing the filling to rise above the edges. Bake approximately 10-15 minutes to heat through. Remove from oven.

8. Cover the tops of each yam-filled orange with about ⅓ cup of mini-marshmallows. Make sure to push the marshmallows in well so they don't fall off as they bake. Return to the oven.

9. Heat about 8 more minutes. When the marshmallows turn golden brown, they're ready. Watch them carefully, as you don't want the marshmallows to burn.

EGG SALAD TWO WAYS

(makes 4-6 servings)

I've made this egg salad for nearly every brunch I've ever had. People always rave about it.

8 large eggs
4 tablespoons mayonnaise
   (or more to taste)
½ teaspoon salt (or more to taste)

1. Place eggs in a saucepan and cover with cold water. Bring water to a boil over medium heat and boil uncovered for approximately 20 minutes.

2. Drain eggs and cover with cold water. When cool enough to handle, peel and rinse them.

3. Mash the eggs with a fork (not too fine) and place them in a medium mixing bowl.

FOR THE SAUTÉED ONION VERSION
½ cup finely chopped onion (If you love onions, use ¾ cup.)
1 ½ tablespoons canola oil

Heat the canola oil in a skillet and add the chopped onions. Sauté the onions until they turn golden brown. Add the onions, mayonnaise, and salt to the chopped eggs and mix thoroughly. Taste and adjust the level of salt. If you like a creamier texture, add a little more mayonnaise.

FOR THE CRUMBLED BACON VERSION
4 strips of freshly made,
   crisp bacon

1. Crumble the cooked bacon into ¼-inch size and combine them with the chopped egg, mayonnaise, and salt. Mix well. Taste and adjust the level of salt and mayonnaise.

2. Serve immediately (it will be slightly warm), or if you prefer to serve later, refrigerate until ready to serve. The egg salad tastes great on bagels, in sandwiches, or on a bed of lettuce with fresh tomato wedges on the side.

RUGGELACH

(makes 48)

This is a very traditional recipe. It uses equal parts of butter and cream cheese. You can vary the fillings using chopped walnuts, currants, mini chocolate chips, or jam.

TO MAKE THE DOUGH
8 ounces butter (2 sticks), at room temperature
8 ounces "brick" cream cheese (not the soft tub kind), at room temperature
½ teaspoon salt
2 cups all-purpose flour

1. Cream together the butter and cream cheese in an electric mixer until completely blended. Gradually add the salt and flour. When completely incorporated, stop the mixer, remove all the dough around the beaters, and form into four equal size balls.

2. Flatten the balls of dough into discs and wrap them in wax paper or plastic wrap. Refrigerate for 6 hours or overnight.

FILLINGS

If using currants, mini chocolate chips, or chopped walnuts, spread melted butter over the dough and sprinkle with cinnamon sugar before sprinkling on the toppings. If using jam, omit the butter and cinnamon sugar base.

⅓ cup sugar
2 teaspoons cinnamon
¼ cup melted butter
1 cup miniature semi-sweet chocolate chips (if all chocolate chip)

1 cup currants (if all currant)
1 cup finely chopped walnuts (if all walnut)
1 cup raspberry or apricot jam (if all jam)

EGG GLAZE (OPTIONAL)
1 egg beaten with 1 tablespoon water (optional)

TO ASSEMBLE COOKIES

1. Preheat oven to 375°. Grease two cookie sheets.

2. Flour a work surface and rolling pin. Roll each dough ball into a 12-inch circle.

3. Brush the circle with 1 tablespoon melted butter.

4. Mix the cinnamon and sugar together. Sprinkle 1½ tablespoons of the mixture over the dough, leaving a ¼-inch border.

5. Cut the circle into 12 pie-shaped wedges.

6. Sprinkle ¼ cup of the chopped nuts, currants, or chocolate chips over the circle. Starting with the wide end, roll each wedge toward the center.

7. If making the jam only version, omit the butter and cinnamon sugar. Spread ¼ cup of jam on each circle, leaving a ¼-inch border.

8. Place cookies on the sheets about 1-inch apart. Repeat with remaining dough and fillings.

9. If you would like them glazed, brush each cookie with the beaten egg and water mixture.

10. Bake for about 20 minutes, or until golden brown.

PUMPKIN PIE

(makes 6–8 servings)

Pumpkin pie was one of the first desserts I ever made. I used the ingredient ratios on the Libby's® can. After all these years, I still make it the same way because it always comes out great.

1 deep dish pie crust or 2 regular
   pie crusts, home made (p. 39),
   or frozen, pre-prepared
¾ cup sugar
½ teaspoon salt
1 teaspoon cinnamon
½ teaspoon ginger
¼ teaspoon cloves
2 large eggs beaten
1-15 ounce can "pure pumpkin"
1 can (12 ounces) evaporated milk

1. Preheat oven to 350°.

2. Prick pie crust all over with the tines of a fork. Bake for about 15-20 minutes, or until light golden brown. Remove from oven.

3. Raise oven temperature to 425°.

4. Combine sugar, salt, cinnamon, ginger, and cloves in a small bowl.

5. Beat eggs in a large bowl. With a whisk, add the canned pumpkin. Then add the sugar and spice mixture. Lastly, whisk in the evaporated milk.

6. Pour into one deep pie crust, or two regular pie crusts.

7. Bake at 425° for 15 minutes. Then lower the temperature to 350° and bake 40-50 minutes more for the deep dish version, or 20-30 minutes for the regular size pies, until the filling is firm.

8. I sometimes make one regular pie and pour the remaining filling into individual size custard cups. The baking time will be shorter for the custard cups.

Zarela Martínez

Mexico

Above: Zarela taking orders from her cousins.
Left: Zarela today in New York.

Zarela Martínez grew up on a cattle ranch in northern Mexico. Her father taught her that she could do anything a boy could do. As a girl she had a baby coyote, she learned to kill a rattlesnake with a 12-foot whip, she tamed bucking broncos, and she had her own horse, which she loved very much, to ride around the ranch.

Because Zarela's family grew and raised most of their own food, she learned a great deal about animals and farming when she was a child. Her family invited guests to the ranch often, and her mother would cook elaborate meals. When she cooked, Zarela would take out her journal and copy down the recipes.

Mexican food is a combination of foods native to the New World such as beans, chiles, peanuts, tomatoes, chocolate, vanilla, corn, and squash, as well as foods brought by the Spanish and French conquerors that included pork, olives, olive oil, rice, onions, and wheat. The Europeans learned to cook the New World ingredients using their own familiar methods, and the native Mexican people learned to incorporate "Old World", European

ingredients into many of their traditional dishes.

Corn has always been the most important food in Mexican culture. It has a great deal of religious significance. It's considered a gift from the gods because it sustains life, and it's been used to make not only food and cooking oil, but also products such as medicines and dyes. Corn could easily be grown next to beans, and the two foods together complement one another to form protein as complete as steak. The "bread" of early Mexicans consisted of flat pancakes made of ground corn, called tortillas. Today while corn tortillas are still extremely popular, flour tortillas are also common.

Another very important Mexican food is chile. There are many different types, flavors, sizes, and colors of chiles that range from mild to "fiery" hot. There's a Mexican expression that "without chile, Mexicans don't believe they're eating". Mexicans use chile in dishes or as a condiment, for breakfast, lunch, and dinner. While chile was first discovered in Central and South America, over the centuries its popularity has spread to Europe, Asia, and Africa.

Two of Zarela's favorite holidays as a kid were Feast Days, and Days of the Dead. Feast Days honor the saint for whom each person is named. It's even more important than a birthday. There would be a big party with music and lots of delicious food. Tamales were always a part of all celebrations. They have been since the time of the Aztecs, going back hundreds of years. Tamales are made from a mixture of corn dough and lard that's filled with pork, chicken, seafood or vegetables. The mixture is wrapped in cornhusks or banana leaves and then steamed.

The Days of the Dead are November 1st, for children, and November 2nd, for the adults (right after our Halloween). It's actually a very happy

Corn

Corn on the cob is sold from vendor carts all over Mexico. The corn is cooked on little hibachi-type grills, spread with chile powder, and sprinkled with lime.

Chilies

Chiles contain vitamins A and C and have been used as medicine over the years in Mexico. The Aztec Indians used chiles as an earache remedy, a cough medicine, an antiseptic, a toothpaste ingredient, a digestive aid, and a way to clear the nasal passages.

holiday because Mexicans feel they are communicating with those they have loved who have died. There is a traditional "Bread of the Dead" that's eaten. It's a sweet, cake-like bread that's made into different shapes such as humans, lizards, animals, or skulls and crossbones, and then decorated with colored sugar crystals.

Zarela attended boarding school in the United States through high school. At that point, her parents insisted she return to Mexico to finish her studies because they didn't want her to lose her culture. She enrolled for one year in what was called a finishing school in the large city of Guadalajara, to learn to be a capable housewife. Even though she wasn't happy about it at the time, she grew to like the school and it changed her life. In addition to making good friends and learning other skills, she learned to prepare foods from different parts of Mexico. Zarela loved exploring Guadalajara's expansive and lively market, El Mercado de San

Juan de Dios, with all its fresh ingredients and prepared dishes. After attending finishing school, she went on to the university where she studied mass communications.

After graduation, Zarela moved to El Paso, Texas, not far from Mexico. There she worked as a social worker helping others. When she wasn't working, she indulged her passion for cooking and began experimenting with recipes from a variety of cookbooks and cooking magazines. One day her sister, Aida, suggested that she try catering parties. Zarela loved cooking, but she felt she needed to study a lot more about Mexican cooking, which she set about doing. She decided she was ready to start cooking professionally around the time she learned she was pregnant with twins. Word of mouth spread that her food was delicious and her business grew.

Through a lucky break, Zarela became friends with Paul Prudhomme, a very famous Cajun chef from New Orleans. Through Paul, she was invited to cook a special meal in New York City for French Chefs who were visiting.

Her food was a big hit. One thing lead to another and Zarela moved to New York. Today she has a festive restaurant in New York City called Zarela that serves regional Mexican food. At dinner time, musicians serenade guests with lively Mexican music.

Zarela has written cookbooks about Mexican regional cooking and she has recipes on the Nick Jr. website. She also just finished a 13-part public television series about the cooking of the Veracruz region of Mexico. She considers herself a cultural anthropologist because in addition to providing recipes, her books and programs describe the customs and history of the local people and their foods.

Zarela's favorite childhood dishes include fresh tomato salsa that's a universally loved dip for tortilla chips, a wonderful casserole of corn, rice, poblano chiles and cheese, Polvorones de Nuez (sandy-textured nut cookies, that are traditionally wrapped in colorful tissue papers at Christmas time), and Mango Mousse (a delicious and very easy dessert).

TOMATO SALSA

(makes about 4 cups)

This is a great recipe to make in the summer and fall when fresh, local tomatoes are ripe and juicy.

2 to 4 fresh chiles, either jalapeño or serrano, tops removed, but not seeded
1 garlic clove, peeled
4 large, ripe, red tomatoes, peeled but not seeded (about 2½ pounds)
6 to 8 scallions with part of the green tops
¼ cup (loosely packed) fresh cilantro leaves
1 teaspoon Mexican oregano, crumbled
Juice of 1 large lime
Salt to taste

1. Chop the chiles very fine. Wear gloves so the heat from the chiles won't get on your hands and burn your eyes later. Place them in a bowl.

2. Coarsely chop the tomatoes. Finely chop the scallions, garlic, and cilantro. Add all the chopped vegetables to the bowl with the chiles and mix everything together well.

3. Add the oregano and then squeeze the lime juice into the salsa. Add salt, a little at a time, until it tastes right.

4. Serve at once in a medium-size serving bowl with a large bowl of tortilla chips on the side.

ADAPTED FROM ZARELA MARTÍNEZ

ARROZ CON CREMA Y POBLANOS
Creamy Rice Caserole with Poblano Chiles

(makes 6 servings)

This makes a great side dish or even a main meal. It's very popular in my house. The poblano chiles are not very hot.

1 ½ cups sour cream
⅓ cup chopped onion
1 small garlic clove, minced
2 tablespoons finely chopped fresh
    cilantro leaves
4 cups water
1 tablespoon butter
2 teaspoons salt, or to taste
2 cups converted rice
2 tablespoons vegetable oil

1 small onion, chopped
    (about ½ cup)
1 garlic clove, minced
2 poblano chiles, roasted, peeled,
    seeded, and diced (or use 2
    4.5 oz. cans)
2 cups fresh corn kernels, frozen
    corn, or canned corn, drained
2 cups shredded Monterrey Jack
    or Cheddar cheese
Salt to taste

1. Preheat oven to 350°.

2. Combine the sour cream, the ⅓ cup chopped onion, one clove of minced garlic, and chopped cilantro leaves in a small bowl and set aside.

3. Bring the water to a boil in a medium-size saucepan over high heat and add the butter and salt. When the butter has melted, add the rice and bring back to a boil. Reduce the heat to very low, cover the saucepan tightly, and cook for 20 minutes. Remove from heat and allow the rice to cool uncovered. (The water quantity is based on using converted rice. If you use a different type of rice, keep the rice amount at 2 cups, but follow the directions on the package for the amount of water to use.)

4. Heat the oil in a heavy skillet over medium-high heat until very hot but not quite smoking. Reduce the heat to medium and add the ½ cup chopped onion, and the other clove of minced

SOUTH AMERICA & THE CARIBBEAN

Guillermo Pernot

Argentina

José Fonseca

Brazil

Douglas Rodriguez

Cuba

Mechel Thompson

Jamaica

Jorge Chan

Peru

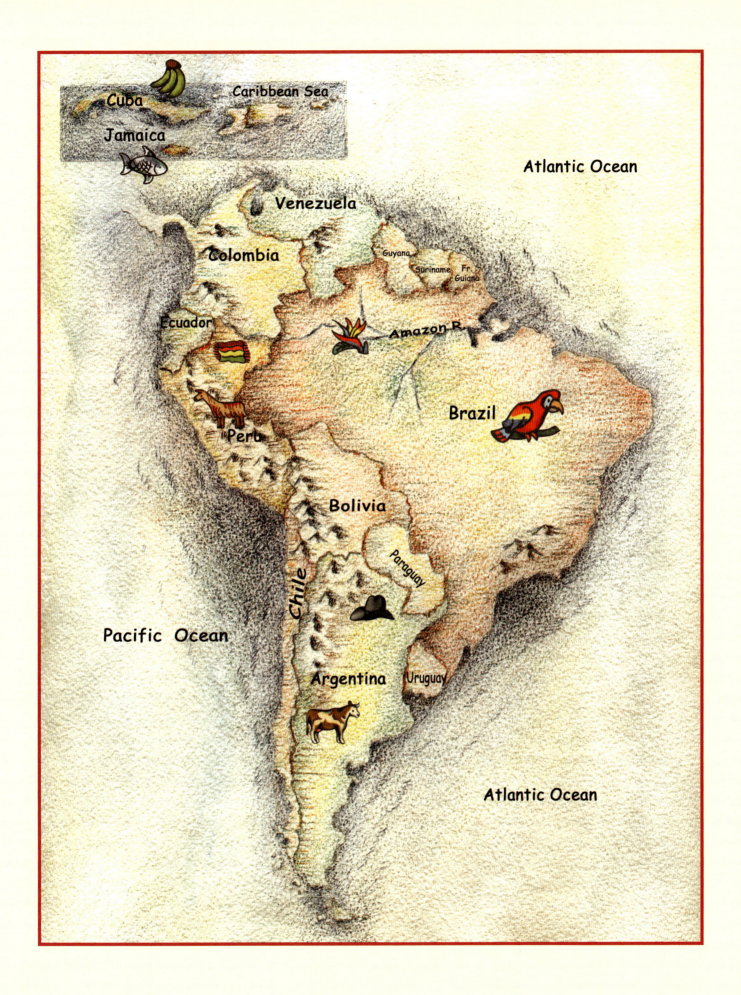

Cuba

Caribbean Sea

Jamaica

Atlantic Ocean

Venezuela

Colombia

Guyana

Suriname   Fr.
Guiana

Ecuador

Amazon R.

Brazil

Peru

Bolivia

Paraguay

Pacific Ocean

Chile

Argentina

Uruguay

Atlantic Ocean

Guillermo Pernot

Argentina

Above: Guillermo's 3rd grade
school picture.
Left: A picture of Guillermo in his
chef's coat.

G uillermo Pernot is the chef/owner of ¡Pasión!, an extremely popular restaurant in Philadelphia that serves Nuevo Latino cuisine. His cooking features new twists on traditional dishes from countries all over Latin American such as Brazil, Peru, Colombia, and Argentina. Guillermo named his restaurant ¡Pasión!, which means passion in Spanish, because he's passionate about good food. He enjoys creating delicious, exciting, and attractive foods that use ingredients and flavors, new to many of his customers.

Guillermo (William in Spanish), was born in Buenos Aires, the capital of Argentina. Argentina is itself a melting pot of many different cultures. It was colonized by the Spanish in the 1600's. During World War II, people came to Argentina from such diverse countries as Italy, Japan, Germany, and Yugoslavia. Guillermo's mother's family came to Argentina from Barcelona, Spain, and his father's family came from southern France.

Guillermo's love of food began at a very young age, and he remembers cooking for the first time when he was five years old. While his mother worked, his Spanish grandmother taught him how to cook. He began most mornings with a breakfast of café con leche, a sweet, milky coffee drink, and toasted bread with butter. Sunday mornings, however, a special breakfast was served with a special kind of French toast. The bread was soaked in red wine, rolled in sugar, dipped in beaten egg, and then sautéed in butter. Wine is widely consumed in Argentina. Children there are allowed to drink wine mixed with soda water. The younger the child, the more soda water is used.

Argentina is known all over the world for its exceptional beef and Argentineans eat a lot of it! They eat twice as much beef on average as Americans, and some Argentineans eat beef as often as three times a day: for breakfast, lunch, and dinner. Once a month, usually on Sundays, Guillermo's family would have a barbecue or grilled meat feast called a "parillada". It would last from 10:00 or 11:00 in the morning until 8:00 or 9:00 in the evening. All kinds of meats such as lamb, steak, and sausages called chorizos, would be cooked very slowly on a grill or parilla, over hot charcoals with no flames. It was a whole day of getting together with friends, talking, relaxing, playing card games, and singing songs while someone played the guitar.

In the days following the parillada, the leftovers would be made into other favorite dishes such as soups, lamb croquettes (a type of fritter), and empanadas (filled turnovers that are popular all over South America and the Caribbean). Empanadas have as many different types of fillings as sandwiches, and they can be filled with meats, vegetables, or sweets. They're eaten as snacks, appetizers, and picnic lunches; and children often carry them to school. The key to making empanadas is to stuff as much filling into the dough as possible and to seal them

Cattle

The Spaniards who settled Argentina in the 1500's brought cattle with them. The cows thrived in the climate and on the rich, green, grassy plains known as pampas.

tightly so the filling doesn't leak out during cooking. Guillermo uses a fork to press down and crimp the edges, like the seal on a double-crusted pie. He sometimes makes a decorative rope edge that his mother taught him. The empanadas can either be fried or baked. Both ways are delicious. Some of Guillermo's favorite empanadas include savory ones, like chicken with corn, or fish with pine nuts and raisins, and also sweet ones like quince and guava paste with cream cheese, or banana with chocolate.

Some other favorite childhood dishes include carbonada criolla, which is a complete meal baked in a pumpkin as the pot. It includes squash, peaches, short ribs, and corn, and is a summertime favorite when the peaches, corn, and pumpkins are in season. Guillermo also loved dulce de leche, a dessert of caramelized milk that was invented in Argentina and has become extremely popular all over Latin America and recently the United States. Dulce de leche can be made into ice cream as well. In fact, it's become Hagen Daz's second most popular flavor after vanilla. Dulce de leche can be spread on toast, drizzled over fruit, spread on cakes, rolled into balls and covered with chopped nuts, or even eaten right out of the jar. Guillermo has fond memories of raiding the refrigerator to spread a spoonful over a piece of

Gauchos

The "cowboys" who look after the cows are called gauchos. Their traditional garb consists of large black hats, high leather boots and colorful capes called ponchos.

Fontina type cheese. Another popular way of eating dulce de leche is as a filling between shortbread cookies called alfajores.

Guillermo came to the United States when he was nineteen to study psychology at Columbia University. When he graduated, he decided he was really more interested in food as a career than psychology, so he became a waiter in some of the finest restaurants in Philadelphia. During those years he learned a lot about food preparation and the skills it would take to run a fine restaurant. In the back of his mind he knew he wanted to open a restaurant one day, and so he taught himself how to cook. To create ¡Pasión!, Guillermo built on his early food memories which included the Spanish influence of his grandmother, his childhood in Argentina, and his travels all over Central and South America. Guillermo recently opened a second restaurant in Philadelphia called Trust. It features Mediterranean dishes. What follows are the recipes from some of Guillermo's favorite childhood dishes.

EMPANADAS

(Makes 24 Turnovers)

While it is customary to use lard in the dough and it will make a better and more authentic empanada crust, as an option you can omit the lard and substitute butter.

EMPANADA DOUGH (FOR BOTH SWEET AND SAVORY VARIETIES: MAKES 24)
4 cups all-purpose flour, plus more for kneading
2 teaspoons baking powder
1 teaspoon coarse salt
¾ cup lard
¾ cup (1 ½ sticks) unsalted butter
Cold water (about ¾ cup)

1. Place the flour, baking powder, and salt in a food processor fitted with the steel blade. Add lard and butter, cut in pieces, and pulse until it is the texture of coarse meal. With the processor running, slowly add enough water to form a firm dough. Transfer to a lightly floured work surface.

2. Knead the dough for about 5 minutes, until it comes together and becomes smooth. Shape into two flat disks and wrap each in plastic wrap. Chill in the refrigerator for one hour.

Chicken and Corn Empanadas

(makes 24)

¼ cup olive oil
1 ½ cups finely chopped white onion
1 teaspoon crushed red pepper flakes
1 teaspoon dried oregano, preferably Mexican
½ cup finely chopped red bell pepper
½ cup finely chopped green bell pepper
5 small ears corn, kernels removed
   (or about 1 ½ cups of frozen corn or canned corn, drained)
1 pound boneless, skinless chicken thigh meat, cut into ¼-inch pieces
2 tablespoons dry white wine
1 teaspoon salt
6 ounces Monterey Jack cheese, shredded
Empanada dough (see above)
1 large egg, lightly beaten with 1 tablespoon water

1. Preheat oven to 400°.

2. Heat olive oil in a large skillet over medium heat. Add onion, red pepper flakes, and oregano. Sauté, stirring occasionally until lightly browned, about 4 minutes. Add the chopped red and green peppers and corn. Cook until peppers soften.

3. To the same pan, add the chicken and wine, and then the salt. Cook until the chicken is just cooked through and almost all of the liquid has evaporated, about 3 minutes. Refrigerate the filling until chilled. If there is any liquid remaining, pour it off. Stir in the cheese. You can refrigerate again at this point, until you're ready to fill the empanadas.

4. Fill a small bowl with cold water. Roll out the dough to a thickness of ⅛ inch. Using a 5-inch diameter plate as a template, or the rim of a 5-inch bowl or plastic container, cut out approximately 24 circles in total.

5. Spoon about two tablespoons of chilled filling into the center of each circle, leaving a ½ inch border. Brush the border with cold water. Fold the dough over, stretching it slightly, to form a half-moon shape. The empanadas should be pretty full.

6. Beginning at one end, press the edges to seal well, while trying to remove any air pockets. Using a fork or your fingers, crimp the edges to form a decorative, tight edge, like for a pie crust. Repeat with the remaining filling.

7. Brush the empanadas with egg wash.

8. Refrigerate at least 30 minutes (but no longer than one day).

9. Line two baking sheets with parchment paper or tinfoil. Arrange empanadas on baking sheets. Bake until puffed and browned and the filling is bubbling inside, about 15 to 20 minutes. Serve immediately.

Fruit-Filled
Dessert Empanadas

(makes 24)

1 21-ounce can quince paste, cut into ½-inch cubes*
1 21-ounce can guava paste, cut into ½-inch cubes*
1 ½ pounds (24 ounces) cream cheese, cut into ½-inch cubes
Empanada dough (see above)
1 large egg, lightly beaten with 1 tablespoon water
Peanut oil, for frying
Confectioner's sugar
*You should be able to find the guava and quince paste in the Latin American
    section of your grocery store. If you can only find one type, then use approxi-
    mately 42 ounces of that fruit paste.

1. With a dull knife, cut the quince and guava paste into ½-inch cubes. Cut the cream cheese into ½-inch cubes and mix together with the guava and quince paste, trying to retain the cube shapes. Cover bowl with plastic wrap, and place it in the freezer for 15 minutes.

2. Fill a small bowl with cold water. Roll dough ⅛-inch thick. Using a 5-inch diameter plate as a template, or the rim of a 5-inch bowl or plastic container, cut out approximately 24 circles in total. Spoon about 2 tablespoons chilled filling into the center of each circle, leaving a ½-inch border. Brush border with cold water. Fold dough over, stretching it slightly, to form a half-moon shape. The empanadas should be pretty full.

3. Beginning at one end, press the edges together well to seal, while trying to remove any air pockets. Using a fork or your fingers, crimp edges to form a decorative, tight edge, like for a pie crust. Repeat with remaining circles and filling.

4. Brush the empanadas with egg wash.

5. Refrigerate at least 30 minutes (but no longer than 1 day).

6. In a large, deep saucepan, heat 4 inches of peanut oil to 375°. Fry empanadas in batches until puffed and browned and the filling is bubbling inside, about 3 minutes. Remove, and immediately sprinkle generously with confectioner's sugar. Serve hot.

7. As an alternative, you can bake these just as you bake the chicken and corn empanadas. You can also use semi-sweet chocolate chips and sliced bananas as a filling.

ADAPTED FROM GUILLERMO PERNOT

CARBONADA CRIOLLA
Beef Stew with Peaches and Corn Baked in a Pumpkin

This is a wonderful, fun, and festive dish to serve in autumn.

One 10-12-pound pumpkin or other
   large winter squash (It must be
   that large to hold all the filling)
2 tablespoons butter at room
   temperature
½ cup sugar
2 pounds short ribs, cut into
   2-inch pieces
2 tablespoons vegetable oil
2 cloves garlic, minced
½ cup onion, diced
1 tablespoons vinegar
1 cup canned chopped tomatoes
½ teaspoon oregano

½ teaspoon black pepper
1 ½ teaspoons salt
2-3 cups chicken stock, or enough
   to cover meat
¾ pound butternut squash, cut in
   ¾-inch chunks
1 ½ pounds (1 medium) sweet potato,
   cut in ¾-inch chunks
1 large ear of corn, sliced in ½-inch
   rounds
2 large ripe peaches, peeled
   and sliced, or one 16-oz.
   package frozen peaches,
   thawed

1. Preheat the oven to 375°.

2. Cut a hole in the top of the pumpkin and remove the seeds, just as you would to make a jack-o-lantern. (You can clean the seeds and bake with salt and butter until brown, to make a snack.)

3. Grease the inside of the pumpkin with the butter. Pour in the sugar and tilt the pumpkin all around so the sugar coats the inside. Turn pumpkin upside down to shake out the excess sugar.

4. Place the pumpkin in a large roasting pan or on a cookie sheet that has been greased lightly with oil, and bake it for about 45 minutes, or until it starts to soften but is still firm.

5. While the pumpkin is baking, start the stew. Heat the vegetable oil in a large pot and brown the meat on all sides. Remove the meat to a bowl or platter.

6. To the oil that remains in the pot, add the onions and garlic. Cook over medium heat, stirring constantly for approximately 5 minutes, until the vegetables are soft.

7. Add the chicken stock and bring it to a boil. Add back the meat. Add the tomatoes, vinegar, oregano, salt, and pepper. Cover the pan and let it simmer over low heat for about 15 minutes, or until the meat is soft.

8. Add the sweet potato chunks and cook about 20 minutes more.

9. Add the butternut squash chunks and corn and cook about 10 minutes.

10. Add the peaches and cook about 5 more minutes. Remove pot from the burner.

11. Spoon the stew into the cavity of the pumpkin. Put the pumpkin's lid back on and bake for approximately 20 minutes.

12. When ready to serve, carefully place the pumpkin on a large serving platter. It will look like a large tureen. Ladle the stew onto individual plates or into individual bowls, as there will be plenty of gravy or sauce.

ADAPTED FROM GUILLERMO PERNOT

ALFAJOR DE DULCE DE LECHE

Shortbread Cookie Sandwiches with Dulce de Leche Filling

(makes 40 cookies)

COOKIE DOUGH
4 cups all-purpose flour
6 tablespoons confectioner's sugar
1 ½ cups chilled unsalted butter
1 cup cold water

1. Preheat oven to 350°.

2. Sift together the flour and sugar.

3. Place dry mixture in a food processor fitted with a steel blade. Add the butter cut up in pieces, and process until it resembles a coarse meal. Add water until the dough comes together.

4. Knead well for at least 5 minutes, until the dough is very smooth and no butter particles are visible.

5. Divide the dough in two, and shape each into a large, flat disk. (This will make it easier to roll out later.) Wrap and chill in the refrigerator for at least 1 hour.

6. Roll out dough on a lightly floured surface, to a thickness of ⅛ inch.

7. Cut into 1¼-inch rounds or any other shape you like, and place on parchment paper, a Silpat®, or a greased cookie sheet.

8. Bake in a 350° oven until golden brown, about 10-12 minutes. Remove from the oven and let cool completely.

DULCE DE LECHE

This recipe is very easy, but it takes constant watching. You can store leftover dulce de leche in your refrigerator. Warm it slightly in a microwave to make it easier to spread, or to use it as an ice cream topping.

2 cans sweetened condensed milk (14 oz. each)

1. Empty the sweetened condensed milk into the top of a double boiler. Add water to the bottom compartment. Cook over medium heat for approximately 1 ¼ hours, stirring periodically to prevent scorching. The dulce de leche will be done when it turns a tan color and thickens to the consistency of a spreadable jam. It will get thicker as it cools.

COOKIE ASSEMBLY

1. Spoon a teaspoon of dulce de leche on top of one of the cookies and then place another cookie on top to make a sandwich.

2. Sprinkle with confectioner's sugar.

ADAPTED FROM GUILLERMO PERNOT

Spanish/English Translations

pan	bread	poncho	cape or jacket
vaca	cow	Domingo	Sunday
leche	milk	desayuno	breakfast
dulce	sweet	pollo	chicken
verde	green	abuela	grandmother

José Fonseca

Brazil

Above: José's school picture, age 10.
Left: José in the kitchen of Delicia Brazil.

Fun and good food are abundant at José Fonseca's cozy restaurant, Delicia Brazil, located in a brownstone building in Greenwich Village, New York. Each table has musical instruments such as tambourines and maracas. That's because some time during the meal Jose, who does much of the cooking, will come out of the kitchen and start singing Brazilian songs. He encourages his guest to join in. Each table also has crayons, not just for kids, but for adults to doodle with as well. Because he wants people to have a fun and relaxing time at his restaurant, guests are encouraged to stay as long as they like.

José's journey to America and to restaurant ownership is an interesting one. He grew up on a small farm in Minas Gerais State, two hours north of the large city Rio de Janeiro, with his mother and three sisters. They grew their own vegetables, raised their own farm animals, and got fresh milk from their cows and fresh eggs from their chickens. His mom and sisters were always cooking, and he liked to help whenever he could. When José was

17 years old, he won an American Field Service Scholarship to spend one year living with an American family in Elmira, a small town in upstate New York, where he also attended the local high school. He loved the United States.

José returned to Brazil to attend college and majored in journalism. After graduating, he went to work for a newspaper in the city of Juiz de Fora. Simultaneously he started his first culinary venture as the operator of a poultry shop that served chicken dishes. In the 1980's Brazil's government announced a price freeze to fight its runaway inflation. Restaurant and store costs were allowed to rise, but they were not allowed to pass on price increases to their customers. As a result, many went out of business, including José's luncheonette chain. Ever since he had lived in New York State during high school, José had thought about returning to America. In 1986, he decided it was a good time to move to the U.S. permanently, and he moved to New York City.

His first job was as a taxi cab driver. Following that experience he became a reporter for a Brazilian newspaper in New York. In his spare time he indulged his love for cooking by preparing wonderful Brazilian meals for friends. For several years, José's girlfriend encouraged him to open his own restaurant and finally he decided she was right. He now thinks it was one of the best decisions he's ever made.

José's restaurant, Delicia Brazil, features home-style cooking. Brazilian food has been influenced by the Portuguese who settled the country, the native Indians, and the West Africans who came in large numbers as slaves to work on the plantations. Fruits and vegetables that are common to Brazilian cooking include corn, sweet potatoes, peanuts, bananas, coconut, pineapples,

Amazon Rain Forest

The Amazon Rain Forest covers about 1/2 of Brazil. It has 1/3rd of the earth's oxygen and 1/5th of the earth's fresh water. It's a wonderful place for plants and animals of all kinds to live. 60% of the world's animal species live in the Rain Forest and 33% of the world's flowering species live there.

River Sea

Brazil is about half the size of all of South America, and its population is equal to the rest of South America combined. The Amazon River is known as Rio Mar (River Sea) because at some points it's so big, you can't see the opposite shore.

mangos, and a pale yellow root vegetable called manioc (also known as cassava or yucca) that is prepared in many different ways. Africans did much of the farming and cooking, and they had a great impact on the development of Brazilian cuisine. Because Brazil has an enormous coastline along the Atlantic Ocean, fish and shrimp are a large part of the diet.

Brazil is famous for the extremely festive holiday, Carnival. It's been described as "the biggest party on earth". Carnival takes place on the last days before the fast for Lent, prior to Easter. During Carnival, people all over the country dress up in bright, colorful costumes. There are grand parades with beautiful floats, lively music, and special "samba" dancing, a combination of European folk dancing and African dancing. The costumes often relate to historic

themes such as Brazilian Indian legends, or the discovery of Brazil by the Europeans. At many of the festive parties and balls people compete for the most imaginative costumes.

Some of José's favorite childhood dishes included fried yucca which is a bit like American French fries, baked cheese rolls that are shaped into small round balls, delicious shrimp cooked in a rich coconut milk sauce, and for dessert, a creamy, chocolate, truffle-like confection that's rolled in chocolate or colored sprinkles, called brigadeiros.

FRIED YUCCA

(makes 6 servings)

You can find frozen yucca in the Latin American section of the frozen food aisle of some grocery stores and fresh yucca in the produce section. Yucca is a root vegetable that's white inside, with a dark brown skin.

---

8 cups of water
1 teaspoon salt
24 ounces (1 ½ pounds) frozen yucca, or fresh yucca
Vegetable oil for frying

---

1. If using frozen yucca, add the salt to the 8 cups of water and bring to a boil. Boil approximately 8 minutes, until it turns cream color. Drain in a colander and let cool. Cut the yucca into wedges.

2. If using fresh yucca, peel the yucca and boil it until it turns cream color. Let it cool, and cut into French fry shaped pieces.

3. Heat about 3 inches of oil in a deep saucepan. Put one piece of yucca into the hot oil. If it floats to the top, the oil is ready.

4. Add the yucca to the oil a handful at a time, so as not to crowd them. When light golden brown, remove with a slotted spoon and drain on paper towels.

5. Salt to taste. Fried yucca can also be seasoned with garlic powder, black pepper, hot sauce, ketchup, or any dipping sauce.

6. As an alternative, you can make a bread crumb coating for the yucca by dipping the wedges in a beaten egg and then coating them in seasoned bread crumbs before frying.

ADAPTED FROM JOSÉ FONSECA

PAO DE QUEIJO
Cheese Rolls

(makes 12 rolls)

¾ pound (12 ounces) crumbled feta cheese
2 cups all-purpose flour or manioc flour (available in Latino Markets)
½ teaspoon salt
½ cup cooking oil
1 cup whole milk
2 eggs

1. Preheat oven to 400°

2. Mix feta cheese, flour, and salt together in a food processor. Add the cooking oil and process a few more seconds.

3. Warm milk for one minute in microwave and add to the processor mixture, along with the two eggs. Process until well blended. Place mixture in a bowl and refrigerate for ½ hour, or longer.

4. Roll the dough into round balls the size of golf balls and place on an ungreased cookie sheet.

5. Bake approximately 17 minutes, or until golden brown. The rolls are best warm, right out of the oven. If you have leftover rolls, you can briefly microwave them, or cut them in half, toast them, and spread them with butter.

ADAPTED FROM JOSÉ FONSECA

MOQUECA DE CAMARÃO
Shrimp in Coconut Milk Sauce

(Makes 6–8 servings)

2 ½ cups of chopped red pepper
  (in ¾-inch pieces)
5 cups of chopped onion
  (in ¾-inch pieces)
2 ½ cups of chopped tomatoes
  (in ½-inch pieces)
½ cup oil for cooking
  (olive, dende or vegetable)
4 cans of coconut milk (14 oz. each)
3 teaspoons of salt
1 ½ teaspoons black pepper
3 teaspoons of hot sauce such as
  Tabasco
1 tablespoon of finely chopped garlic
½ cup chopped fresh coriander
  (cilantro), for garnish

SHRIMP MARINADE INGREDIENTS
¾ teaspoon salt
¾ teaspoon garlic powder
¼ teaspoon ground black pepper
1 ½ pounds large shrimp,
  cleaned, pealed, and deveined

1. Measure the marinade ingredients and add them to the shrimp. Toss with a big spoon so the spices coat the shrimp. Refrigerate until needed.

2. Cut up and measure the red peppers, onions and tomatoes.

3. In a large soup pot, sauté the chopped red peppers, onions, and tomatoes in the oil until they all become soft.

4. Add the coconut milk, salt, black pepper, hot sauce, and chopped garlic. Cook over low heat for one hour, stirring occasionally.

5. Add the shrimp that have been marinating in the refrigerator. Stir well and cook for about 5 minutes, or until the shrimp are done.

6. Pour into a large serving bowl and sprinkle with chopped coriander. This dish goes great with plain rice.

ADAPTED FROM JOSÉ FONSECA

BRIGADEIROS
Rich Chocolate Truffle Balls with Sprinkles

(Makes 24)

3 tablespoons butter
2 cans (14 oz. each) sweetened condensed milk
6 tablespoons of Chocolate NesQuik™ powder (or more to taste)
Sprinkles (chocolate, colored, or some of each: you choose)
Vegetable oil or softened butter to grease your hands
Little muffin cup papers or foil

1. Melt the butter in a medium-sized saucepan over medium-low heat.

2. Add the two cans of sweetened condensed milk and the NesQuik™ powder and stir well. Continue stirring constantly for 10-15 minutes, until the mixture becomes very thick, like chocolate pudding. It should "slide" from side to side when the pan is tilted.

3. Pour the chocolate mixture into a shallow bowl and refrigerate until cool (about one hour).

4. Put the sprinkles in a shallow dish or pie plate and separate 24 little muffin cup papers, spreading them out on the table.

5. Grease your hands with the oil or butter. Take about one tablespoon of the cooled mixture and roll it into a ball shape. Then roll the ball in the sprinkles to coat it all around. Place each finished confection in a muffin cup. Repeat until all the confections are done. You will have to add more oil or butter to your hands to keep the candies from sticking.

6. As a variation, you can roll the chocolate balls in shredded coconut or finely chopped nuts.

ADAPTED FROM JOSÉ FONSECA

Portuguese/English Translations

queijo	cheese	pato	duck
tomate	tomato	galinha	chicken
pão	roll	chocolate	chocolate
camarão	shrimp	assado	baked
carne	beef	abobora	pumpkin

Douglas Rodriguez
Cuba

Above: Douglas's childhood school picture.
Left: Chef Douglas Rodriguez today.

Douglas Rodriguez is often called the father or inventor of "Nuevo Latina" cooking, a cooking style that creates fun, new variations on traditional goods from Latin America and and Caribbean countries such as Peru, Brazil, Cuba and Guatemala.

For as long as he can remember, Douglas wanted to be a chef. As a kid he preferred cooking utensils to toy cars. He credits Julia Child (who had the very first TV cooking show, where she taught French cooking) with inspiring him to be the chef he is today. He started watching Julia Child when he was 7 years old and remembers fighting with his brother & cousins about which TV show they would watch on Saturday mornings. Douglas wanted to watch Julia, while they preferred cartoon shows.

Douglas was raised in New York City, but both of his parents were born in Cuba. His mom worked for American Airlines and when he was 7, she took him to Spain, where he remembers ordering a Spanish tortilla omelet. He didn't like eating eggs without ketchup and there wasn't any available. The chef tried to improvise making him some by using tomato paste, sugar & water. Even though it wasn't very good, Douglas's mom made him eat it all because the chef had gone to the trouble of making it especially for him.

As in all Cuban households, in Douglas's home rice and beans were eaten with almost every meal. Either red, black or white beans were used. Plantains, light green colored bananas that are firmer and less sweet than regular bananas, were eaten as a side dish (usually fried) about three times a week. Caramel custards called flans were the most common desserts. A favorite after dinner treat was a rich, thick, delicious hot chocolate made with evaporated milk, vanilla, spices, and cornstarch. Special Spanish bitter-sweet chocolate was shaved and stirred into the hot milk mixture where it melted into a wonderful, creamy drink. It was a treat not only because it was so delicious, but because his family would sit around the table and talk and laugh and enjoy each other's company while they savored it.

When Douglas was 9 he bought his first cookbook (a Bicardi Rum cookbook) for $.25 at a New York City style garage sale (on a blanket on the street). Soon after, he bought himself a set of pots and pans. When he was 11, he cooked his first dinner for his parents. They always encouraged his love of cooking. The first time he made French onion soup, his mom bought him special crocks or soup bowls for it at Macy's. As Douglas got older, he began buying more & more cookbooks, and he started to memorize them. He loved the Time/Life Cookbooks that showed the foods, markets, holidays and landscapes of different countries around the world. It was one of the best cookbook series ever made.

Today Douglas still collects cookbooks. He figures he has about 3000 and that he buys about 120 each year. He loves cookbooks because

Chocolate

Chocolate comes from cocoa trees. The tree has large pods with cocoa beans inside. The cocoa beans are fermented, dried in the sun and then roasted to bring out the flavor. The beans are ground and turned into a liquid that contains cocoa butter. Milk and sugar are added to make milk chocolate bars.

they give him ideas, stimulate his creativity and help him to write cookbooks of his own that are exciting, interesting and different.

When Douglas was 14, his family moved to Miami and he got his first restaurant job as an apprentice at the Four Ambassadors Hotel. After high school, he became a breakfast cook at the Fountainbleu Hilton Hotel on Miami Beach. He then attended Johnson & Wales University in Providence, Rhode Island, one of the top cooking schools in the United States.

Douglas loves what he does so much, it doesn't feel like work. He never stops challenging himself to do things that are new and better, and he's constantly traveling and exploring to learn more. It's his dream that the cooking from Latin America will one day be well-known and well-liked all over the United States. Because of his hard work, talent and enthusiasm, his dream is fast becoming a reality.

Below are several of Douglas's favorite childhood dishes: his mother Gloria's black bean soup, which is the best he's ever tasted, plantain bread (like banana bread) made from very ripe plantains, croquetas or ham croquettes that are crispy on the outside and soft

and creamy inside, pumpkin flan that's a variation on a classic Cuban dessert, and his family's favorite, rich and creamy hot chocolate.

SOPA DE FRIJOLES NEGROS DE GLORIA
Gloria's Black Bean Soup

(makes 8 to 10 servings)

I recently made this for a large family, and everyone at the table, including all the kids asked for seconds. It's unusually delicious.

1 pound dried black beans
3 quarts water
2 bay leaves
1 cup extra virgin olive oil
2 large red bell peppers, seeded and chopped
2 shallots, chopped
2 medium onions, chopped
8 cloves garlic, minced

1 tablespoon ground cumin
2 tablespoons dried oregano
2 tablespoons chopped fresh oregano leaves
1 ½ tablespoons sugar
2 tablespoons salt
1 red onion, diced, for garnish
8 ounces sour cream, for garnish (optional)

1. Place beans in a non-reactive pan. Cover with 3 quarts of water and the bay leaves, and bring to a boil. Reduce the heat and simmer the beans for 2 ½ to 3 hours, stirring frequently and adding more water if necessary to keep them well covered.

2. Heat the oil in a large saucepan. Sauté the bell peppers, shallots and onions over medium heat until the onions are translucent, about 15 minutes. Add the garlic, cumin, dried and fresh oregano, and sauté for an additional 2 minutes. Remove from the heat and let cool slightly.

3. Transfer the sautéed vegetables to a blender and purée until smooth.

4. When the beans are almost tender, add the puréed mixture, sugar and salt to the beans and cook about 20 to 30 minutes more.

5. Dice the red onions to be used as a garnish.

6. Serve sprinkled with diced red onions and a dollop of sour cream.

ADAPTED FROM DOUGLAS RODRIGUEZ

CROQUETAS DE JAMÓN
Ham Croquettes

(makes 4–6 servings)

CROQUETAS
4 tablespoons butter
2 tablespoons diced onion
1 cup milk
¾ cup all-purpose flour
½ teaspoon salt
⅛ teaspoon pepper
½ teaspoon ground nutmeg
1 tablespoon dry sherry
1 pound smoked boneless ham, ground

BREADING
1 cup all-purpose flour
2 eggs
1 cup cracker meal or
   matzo meal
Canola oil, for deep-frying

1. Grind the ham very fine in a food processor and set aside.

2. Heat the butter in a heavy-bottomed saucepan and sauté the onion over high heat until translucent, about 3 to 4 minutes. Set aside.

3. Add the milk and flour to a food processor or blender and blend until combined. Pour into the sautéed onions. Add the salt, pepper and nutmeg. Simmer over low heat, stirring constantly, until the mixture reaches the consistency of very thick pancake batter. If it's too loose, the croquettes will not hold their shape.

4. Remove the pan from the heat. Add the sherry and ground ham, and mix well. Pour into a shallow pan and let cool for about 2 hours.

5. Measure the flour and put it in a shallow soup bowl. Measure the cracker meal and put it in another shallow bowl. In a third bowl, put the lightly beaten eggs.

6. Take about 2 tablespoons of the ham mixture and roll it into a log shape about 2 inches long. (It might be a little sticky). Roll the croquette in the flour to coat it all over. Then roll it in the beaten egg. Lastly, roll it in the cracker meal to coat completely. Place on a plate and repeat until you have used up all the ham mixture. Refrigerate the ham croquettes for at least one hour.

7. Heat the canola oil in a deep fryer to about 375°. Add the croquettes gently to the oil and fry them until golden brown, about 3 minutes. Drain on paper towels and keep warm in the oven until ready to serve.

ADAPTED FROM DOUGLAS RODRIGUEZ

Magical Melting Pot

PAN DE PLÁTANOS
Plantain Bread

(makes 2 large loaves)

4 ½ cups all-purpose flour
1 tablespoon baking soda
½ teaspoon salt
1 ½ cups butter, at room temperature
3 cups sugar
6 eggs
½ cup sour cream
2 teaspoons pure vanilla extract
2 cups mashed ripe plantains (peels should be black)

1. Preheat oven to 350°.

2. Measure the flour, baking soda and salt. Mix them in a bowl and set aside.

3. Mash and measure the ripe plantains and set them aside.

4. Grease and flour two large (9"x5") loaf pans.

5. In another bowl, cream the butter and sugar with an electric mixer at low speed until light and fluffy. With the mixer running, add the eggs, one at a time, scraping down the sides of the bowl so everything gets incorporated. Add the sour cream and vanilla, and mix well.

6. Alternate adding the mashed plantains and flour mixture to the creamed butter and egg mixture. When it's well blended, pour the mixture into the prepared pans.

7. Bake for 40-50 minutes, until a toothpick comes out clean when inserted.

ADAPTED FROM DOUGLAS RODRIGUEZ

FLAN DE CALABAZA
Pumpkin Flan

(makes 8-10 servings)

1 cup sugar, for caramel
8 ounces canned pumpkin
1 can (14 ounces) sweetened
  condensed milk

1 can (12 ounces)
  evaporated milk
8 eggs
3 tablespoons sugar

1. Preheat oven to 375°.

2. To make the caramel, place the cup of sugar in a heavy-bottomed saucepan and cook, stirring, constantly, over medium heat until it turns a light amber color, about 15-20 minutes. Pour the caramel into a 2-quart baking dish, two 8"x4" loaf pans, or 8 individual 8-ounce ramekins. Immediately tilt the caramel so it completely covers the bottoms and a little way up the sides. Set aside.

3. In a large bowl, beat the eggs well with a large wire whisk. Next, whisk in the sugar and then the canned pumpkin. Gradually add the condensed milk, the evaporated milk and the 3 tablespoons of sugar.

4. Pour the mixture into the loaf pans or ramekins.

5. Place the pans or ramekins in a larger baking dish that's filled half way up the sides with water. Bake at 375° for 15 minutes. Reduce the heat to 350° and bake for about 30 minutes more, or until a knife inserted comes out clean. Remove from the oven and let cool completely.

6. To serve, run a knife around the inside edges of the pans or ramekins and invert onto a serving platter or individual plates. The pumpkin custard will have a delicious caramel sauce.

ADAPTED FROM DOUGLAS RODRIGUEZ

CHOCOLATE CALIENTE DE CUBA
Cuban Hot Cocolate

(makes 8 to 10 servings)

Because this is so rich, it's as much a dessert as a beverage. As a result the suggested serving size is relatively small.

1 ¼ cups sweetened condensed milk
4 ½ cups evaporated milk
20 whole allspice berries
4 whole cloves
1 vanilla bean, or 1 teaspoon vanilla extract
10 ounces El Rey Bucare or other bittersweet or semi-sweet chocolate, chopped
5 tablespoons cornstarch dissolved in 5 tablespoons cold water

1. In a medium saucepan, combine the sweetened condensed milk, evaporated milk, allspice and cloves.

2. If using a vanilla bean, split it lengthwise, scrape the soft pulp inside into the pan, and add the outer pod.

3. Set the pan on medium heat and bring to a simmer, stirring constantly. Reduce the heat to low and cook 20 minutes more. Remove from heat and strain the mixture into a clean pot.

4. Add the chopped chocolate and whisk until it melts. Add the cornstarch and water mixture in a steady stream, whisking constantly. Whisk for 4 to 6 more minutes, until the mixture is thickened and smooth. Serve hot in cups. Eat with a spoon.

ADAPTED FROM DOUGLAS RODRIGUEZ

Mechel Thompson

Jamaica

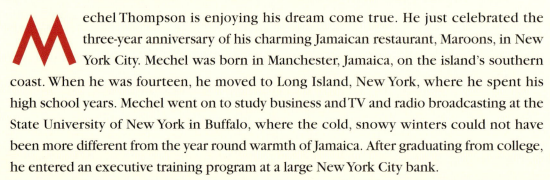

Above: Mechel at 3 years old in Manchester Jamaica.
Left: Mechel Thompson Restauranteur.

Mechel Thompson is enjoying his dream come true. He just celebrated the three-year anniversary of his charming Jamaican restaurant, Maroons, in New York City. Mechel was born in Manchester, Jamaica, on the island's southern coast. When he was fourteen, he moved to Long Island, New York, where he spent his high school years. Mechel went on to study business and TV and radio broadcasting at the State University of New York in Buffalo, where the cold, snowy winters could not have been more different from the year round warmth of Jamaica. After graduating from college, he entered an executive training program at a large New York City bank.

For a long time Mechel had dreamed of opening his own Jamaican restaurant. Ever since childhood, he'd loved being around good food, and the excitement and challenge of restaurant life appealed to him. He decided that by working in different New York City restaurants, he could learn many of the skills he'd need to be successful. He worked in the bank by day; and at night, for a number of years, he took a variety of restaurant jobs.

Mechel named his restaurant Maroons after a proud and well-known, darker skinned group of Jamaicans who were the descendents of African slaves. The Maroons were very strong and independent. They fought against the Spanish colonists and gained their independence in 1655, even though most Jamaican slaves were not freed until 1838. The Maroons, who lived in wild mountain country, in later years fought against the British colonists. Jamaica was a British colony until 1962, when it became an independent nation. The name Maroons comes from the Spanish word "cimarron" or wild.

Mechel grew up in the farm country of rural Jamaica and was cared for by his grandmother when he was young. She loved to cook, and he would often watch for hours as she prepared dishes over her coal stove. When Mechel was eight or nine, he began to cook by himself, under his grandmother's guidance. The first dish he ever made was sweet potato pudding, a delicious, sweet pudding made with grated sweet potatoes, eggs, coconut, brown sugar, and rum.

Because Jamaica was surrounded by ocean, fish was plentiful and was eaten often. Mechel's fondest childhood memory was waiting on the steps of his grandmother's house for Mr. Johnson, "the fisherman", to bring them that day's catch. Mr. Johnson would go to a place called Alligator Pond to buy fresh fish that had just been caught. He had a donkey with two hampers or lidded baskets that hung on either side, where the fresh fish was kept. After loading up his donkey, Mr. Johnson would ride it into Michel's neighborhood and sell the fresh fish door to door.

Another memory was of Mechel's aunt making fresh Blue Mountain Coffee from the coffee trees that grew in her backyard. This coffee, grown in Jamaica's Blue Mountains, is the most

Cod

In many European and Latin cultures throughout history, cod, a very common type of fish, was preserved by salting and drying. Before it could be used, it was soaked to make it soft again and to remove most of the salt.

expensive coffee in the world. It's considered by many to be the finest you can buy because of its rich, smooth, unbitter flavor. Coffee is made from coffee beans, which are the large seeds of small red fruit called coffee cherries. When the cherries were ripe, his aunt would remove the cherry flesh and then lay the coffee beans out to dry in the sun. When she was ready to make the coffee, she'd roast the beans and grind them by hand with a mortar and pestle made of wood. The coffee could not have been fresher.

Saturday mornings, Mechel's grandmother made fried dumplings, which he looked forward to all week. Ackee (a local fruit) and salt fish was also popular for breakfast. It's Jamaica's national dish.

The most special meal of the week was lunch after church on Sundays. It often consisted of rice and peas (the peas are actually Jamaican gungo peas, large red peas like kidney beans), brown stew chicken, fried fish or fried chicken, codfish fritters, and candied yams. Curried goat was a favorite at Christmas time and other special occasions such as large village parties and weddings. Immigrants from India who came to work on the large sugar plantations brought curries to Jamaica.

Another of Mechel's favorite foods was jerk

chicken or pork. It was developed by the Maroons and has become well-known and very popular. The meat is seasoned with a variety of seasonings and it's grilled over allspice or pimento tree wood. Jerk is sold at roadside stands all over Jamaica.

What follows are the recipes for some of Mechel's favorite childhood dishes, some of which are served in his restaurant today.

CODFISH FRITTERS

(makes 24-26 fritters)

You'll need to prepare this recipe 2 days before you plan to eat it.

½ pound dried salt cod
1 cup all-purpose flour
1 cup yellow cornmeal
1 teaspoon baking powder
½ teaspoon salt
¼ teaspoon freshly ground black pepper
¼ cup plus 2 tablespoons vegetable oil
2 tablespoons onion, minced
2 whole scallions, finely chopped

1 clove garlic, minced
¼ sweet green or red pepper, finely chopped
¼ scotch bonnet pepper (any color), seeded and minced. (If unavailable, use habanera or jalapeño peppers. Wear gloves and don't touch your eyes after.)
1 small tomato, finely chopped
½ teaspoon dried thyme
1 cup of water (or more)

1. Soak the dried salt cod for two days in enough water to cover it. Change the water each day.

2. Steam the salt cod in a covered pan in one inch of boiling water for about five minutes, until cooked through. Drain and let it cool.

3. Heat two tablespoons of the oil in a medium-size skillet and cook the onion, scallions, garlic, sweet pepper, scotch bonnet pepper and tomato for about two minutes. Let cool.

4. Flake the cooled salt cod with a fork and add it to the cooled vegetable mixture above.

5. Combine the flour, cornmeal, baking powder, salt, and black pepper in a large bowl. Add the salt cod and vegetable mixture to the flour and cornmeal mixture and mix it all together well.

Add the water. The mixture should be like a thick pancake batter. If it's too thick, add more water.

6. Heat the remaining ¼ cup of oil in a large frying pan until it's very hot. Drop tablespoons full of the batter into the oil. Cook until golden brown on the bottom and then flip the fritter over and cook until golden brown on the other side. It will look like a small, fat pancake. If you want the fritters to be round, you'll have to fry them in several inches of hot oil, in a high-sided saucepan. Drain on paper towels.

7. Serve with mango chutney. The fritters can be cooked in advance and reheated in the oven for about ten minutes.

ADAPTED FROM MECHEL THOMPSON

MANGO CHUTNEY

(makes about 5 cups)

5 mangoes, peeled, pits removed,
   and chopped (about 5 cups), or
   unsweetened mangoes that have
   been thawed
4 tablespoons fresh ginger, grated or
   chopped in very small pieces
1 medium size onion, chopped in
   small pieces

1 clove garlic, minced
½ cup raisins
½ cup sugar
1 ½ teaspoons salt
½ cup white vinegar
⅓ cup water

1. Combine all the ingredients above in a large saucepan.

2. Bring the mixture to a boil and then lower the heat and simmer for about one hour and twenty minutes until thick, stirring occasionally. Let the chutney cool.

3. Ladle the chutney into glass jars and store it in the refrigerator.

4. For a quick chutney version, warm a store-bought chutney in a saucepan over low heat. Dilute it with about ⅓ cup of orange juice until warm and blended together.

ADAPTED FROM MECHEL THOMPSON

RICE AND PEAS

(makes 6 servings)

1 cup (8 ounces) small dried red kidney beans
2 cans (15 ounces each) coconut milk
2-4 cups of water (It will depend. See step 3 of recipe.)
½ teaspoon black pepper
2 whole scallions
2 sprigs of fresh thyme or 1 teaspoon of dried
2 cups uncooked long-grain white rice
2 teaspoons salt

1. In a large strainer or colander, wash the beans thoroughly. Put them in a large saucepan with the coconut milk, 2 cups of water, black pepper, scallions, and thyme.

2. Bring the beans to a boil and simmer on low heat, partially covered for about 1 ½ hours, until they start to soften. Stir periodically to make sure they don't stick to the bottom of the pan.

3. Drain the beans over a deep bowl, keeping the liquid and removing the scallions and thyme sprigs. Measure the liquid and add enough water to make 4 cups in total.

4. Return the beans to the pot with the liquid and bring to a boil. Add the rice and salt and stir. Cover the saucepan and cook over low heat for about 20 minutes, or until the liquid is absorbed.

5. Before serving, fluff the rice and peas with a fork.

ADAPTED FROM MECHEL THOMPSON

CHICKEN FRICASEE

(makes 8 servings)

2 three-pound chickens, cut into eighths
3 limes, rinsed and quartered
1 teaspoon salt
½ teaspoon freshly ground black pepper
4 small yellow onions, thinly sliced
3 medium tomatoes, finely chopped
3 cloves garlic, minced
2 sprigs fresh thyme or 1 teaspoon dried
1 whole scotch bonnet pepper
   (If not available, use habanera or jalapeño.)
¼ cup vegetable oil
3 tablespoons ketchup
2 cups chicken broth

1. Rinse the chicken in cold water and pat dry with paper towels.

2. Put the chicken pieces in a large bowl and squeeze the lime juice over them. Sprinkle the chicken with the salt and pepper. Mix with a big metal spoon to make sure all the pieces are coated.

3. Prepare the vegetables and add them to the chicken. Mix well. Set aside to marinate for at least 15 minutes. You can marinate up to two hours if you leave the bowl in the refrigerator.

4. In a large frying pan, heat two tablespoons of the oil until hot. Fry half the pieces until brown all over (about 5 minutes per side). Remove the pieces to a large plate. Repeat with the rest of the chicken. Pour out remaining oil from the pan.

5. Add the reserved marinating mixture (lime rinds removed) to the frying pan and cook, stirring for several minutes. Add one cup of the chicken broth, then the ketchup and stir till com-

bined. Add the remaining cup of chicken broth and add back the chicken pieces. Lower the heat to medium-low, cover and cook the chicken about 45 minutes or until tender. Remove the Scotch Bonnet pepper.

6. Place chicken pieces with the sauce in a large serving bowl. This is great served with the rice and peas which will absorb the delicious sauce.

ADAPTED FROM MECHEL THOMPSON

SWEET POTATO PUDDING

(makes 8 servings)

3 pounds of sweet potatoes, grated
½ cup raisins
½ cup sugar
3 cups coconut milk
½ teaspoon vanilla

½ teaspoon cinnamon
½ teaspoon ground ginger
¼ teaspoon ground nutmeg
½ cup shredded unsweetened
    coconut

1. Preheat oven to 350°.

2. Peel the sweet potatoes and grate them, using the large holes of the grater.

3. Put the grated sweet potatoes in a large bowl. Add the remaining ingredients and mix together well.

4. Grease a 9 x 13-inch baking dish and pour in the sweet potato mixture.

5. Bake for one hour. Best served warm.

ADAPTED FROM MECHEL THOMPSON

Ackee

Ackee is a red fruit with a tough outer skin. It's poisonous when unripe. When the fruit is ripe and no longer poisonous, the pod will open by itself. Ackee has a creamy, yellow flesh that looks like scrambled eggs when cooked.

Jorge Chan

Peru

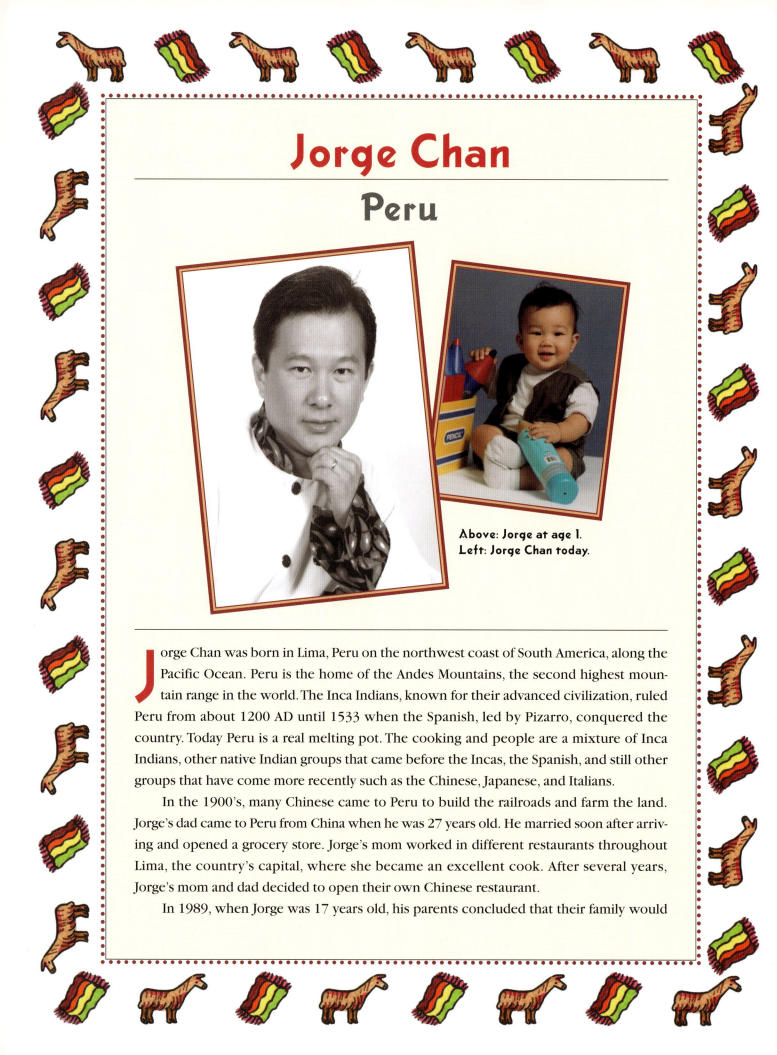

Above: Jorge at age 1.
Left: Jorge Chan today.

Jorge Chan was born in Lima, Peru on the northwest coast of South America, along the Pacific Ocean. Peru is the home of the Andes Mountains, the second highest mountain range in the world. The Inca Indians, known for their advanced civilization, ruled Peru from about 1200 AD until 1533 when the Spanish, led by Pizarro, conquered the country. Today Peru is a real melting pot. The cooking and people are a mixture of Inca Indians, other native Indian groups that came before the Incas, the Spanish, and still other groups that have come more recently such as the Chinese, Japanese, and Italians.

In the 1900's, many Chinese came to Peru to build the railroads and farm the land. Jorge's dad came to Peru from China when he was 27 years old. He married soon after arriving and opened a grocery store. Jorge's mom worked in different restaurants throughout Lima, the country's capital, where she became an excellent cook. After several years, Jorge's mom and dad decided to open their own Chinese restaurant.

In 1989, when Jorge was 17 years old, his parents concluded that their family would be better off living in the United States. They sent Jorge and his brother first, and followed themselves one year later. Jorge was familiar with the restaurant business from his parent's restaurant in Peru, so when he came to America he found jobs first at Pizza Hut and then at American Honda, Inc. He saved his money and earned good credit, so that one day he could open his own restaurant. When he'd saved enough, he opened his first restaurant called "El Rocoto" in Gardena, California. El rocoto is a type of red chile pepper used in Peruvian cooking. His restaurant specializes in seafood, which is plentiful in Peru, because much of the country lies along the Pacific Ocean. All the recipes used today in Jorge's restaurant were developed by his mom.

El Rocoto serves generous portions of wonderful food at very affordable prices, so it's always crowded, even after expanding into the space next door. On Saturday nights Peruvian musicians, dressed in traditional costumes, play a beautiful flutelike instrument called the sampona.

When Jorge was a child, his favorite way to begin a meal was with sopa al minuto (minute soup), a cream of chicken soup with thin spaghetti noodles. It's called minute soup because just before it's served, evaporated milk is added to the chicken broth. It's creamy and flavorful, and loaded with chunks of chicken and noodles.

Today Jorge and his wife, Jessica, have three small children, Jorge Jr., Christian, and Janelle. Their kids' favorite meal is tallarin verde or green spaghetti, a reflection of the Italian influence on Peru. The sauce for the pasta is made from spinach, fresh basil leaves and cream cheese, so it's green, rich, healthy, and delicious.

Two very popular ways to end the meal are the desserts, arroz con leche (rice with milk), a creamy, cinnamon flavored rice pudding, and leche asada, a simple baked custard. They're the ultimate comfort foods.

Other foods that are very popular in Peru include yellow potatoes, which are prepared in many different ways. They're even included in stir-fry dishes (of Chinese origin) called saltados that have French fries right in the stir-fry. Another extremely popular food is anticuchos: strips of marinated beef hearts that are grilled on little sticks and sold by street vendors. Anticuchos are also served at parties, and can be made of beef, chicken, or seafood. Kids sometimes compete to see who can eat the most. Peru is also famous for its ceviche: seafood that's marinated or soaked in lemon or lime juice and spices. The acid in the juice actually cooks the seafood without the need for any heat.

Blankets and Ponchos

Ancient Nasca and Paracas Indians were known for the beautiful fabrics they wove into detailed patterns, using nearly 200 different colors. They made colorful belts, scarves, blankets and ponchos which Peruvians are still known for today.

Llamas

Llamas (relatives of camels) have inhabited Peru for thousands of years. The Inca Indians had no horses and used llamas instead. Llama wool was made into rugs and ropes. Llamas are blessed at festivals, and tassels are attached to their ears, like earrings.

Like in Spain, the main meal of the day is eaten at noon. Stores, offices, and schools close from 12:00 – 3:00 so people can go home to eat with their families and rest.

What follows are the recipes for Jorge's favorite childhood dishes.

SALTADO DE POLLO
Stir-Fried Chicken with French Fries

(makes 4-6 servings)

This dish is different because the French fries are mixed in with the chicken and sauce. Once the French fries are cooked, it's very quick to prepare. You can make your own French fries, or used frozen ones that have been fully cooked. You can also use pieces of leftover boiled or baked potatoes.

- 1 pound sliced, peeled, raw potatoes, cut in wedges for French fries, or sliced, cooked potatoes
- Vegetable oil for frying potatoes
- 1 pound boneless chicken, cut in one-inch pieces
- 2 medium onions, cut in half, and each half cut in thirds
- 1 teaspoon chopped garlic
- 1 tablespoon minced, fresh cilantro (coriander)

- 2 tablespoons red wine vinegar
- 2 medium tomatoes, chopped in large pieces
- 1 tablespoon chopped parsley
- 1 tablespoon soy sauce
- 1 tablespoon chopped scallion
- 1 ½ teaspoons salt
- ½ teaspoon pepper

1. If using French fries, fry the potatoes in oil and drain on paper towels

2. In a large sauté pan or wok, heat 4 tablespoons of oil and stir fry the onions and chicken pieces over medium-high heat until brown. Add the tomatoes, potatoes, and garlic and stir-fry for 2 minutes.

3. Sprinkle with soy sauce and red vinegar and sauté 2 more minutes. Add the cilantro, parsley, chopped scallions, salt and pepper and cook 3 minutes more.

4. Serve with ketchup.

ADAPTED FROM JORGE CHAN

SOPA AL MINUTO
Cream of Chicken Soup with Spaghetti

(makes 4-6 servings)

This soup is delicious, comforting, and fun to eat. It can make a great lunch or a light dinner.

3 tablespoons of vegetable oil
½ medium onion, chopped
1 teaspoon of garlic, minced
2 tablespoons of chopped tomatoes
1 teaspoon salt
¼ teaspoon black pepper
1 teaspoon oregano

8 ounces (1 cup) cooked chicken, shredded
5 cups of chicken broth
6 ounces of thin spaghetti, broken in half and then half again
1 cup evaporated milk

1. Fry the chopped onion, garlic, tomato, and shredded chicken until golden.

2. Add the four cups of broth, bring to a boil, add the spaghetti and cook for about 7-10 minutes, or until the pasta is fully cooked. Add the salt, pepper, and oregano.

3. Just before serving, add the evaporated milk.

4. Serve in individual bowls with spoons and forks to twirl the spaghetti.

ADAPTED FROM JORGE CHAN

TALLARIN VERDE
Green Spaghetti

(makes 6 servings)

The leafy greens in this creamy sauce make this pasta very nutritious.

1 pound package (16 ounces) of thin spaghetti
¼ cup walnuts
¼ pound (4 ounces) cream cheese, cut into cubes
1 cup fresh basil leaves
3 cups fresh spinach leaves
½ cup evaporated milk

2 cloves garlic, chopped
1 tablespoon chopped red onion
1 teaspoon salt
2 tablespoons olive oil
Grated Parmesan cheese
2 cups grilled chicken or beef steak, cut in strips (optional)

1. Bring two quarts of salted water to a boil and boil the spaghetti until done to your liking. Drain the spaghetti.

2. While the pasta is cooking, add the remaining ingredients (except the Parmesan) to a food processor or blender, and blend until smooth.

3. Warm the sauce over low heat in a saucepan for a few minutes, or in a microwave.

4. Toss the sauce with the pasta (and optional sliced meat) in a large serving bowl. Sprinkle Parmesan cheese on each serving.

ADAPTED FROM JORGE CHAN

LECHE ASADA
Baked Custard

(makes 8 servings)

6 cups of whole milk
¾ cup sugar
6 eggs
2 teaspoons of vanilla extract

1. Preheat oven to 375°.

2. Bring the milk to a boil. Remove from heat and add the sugar and vanilla.

3. Beat the eggs well in a medium-size bowl.

4. Add the hot milk to the eggs, a little at a time, whisking constantly so the eggs don't cook or curdle.

5. Pour the mixture into a 2-quart baking dish. Place that dish in a larger baking dish and add water so it comes halfway up the sides. Alterna-tively, you can fill 12 individual 6-ounce custard cups and place them in two large baking pans filled halfway up the sides with water.

6. Bake approximately 1 hour (45 minutes for the individual cups), or until a knife inserted in the custard comes out clean.

ADAPTED FROM JORGE CHAN

ARROZ CON LECHE
Rice Pudding

(makes 6–8 servings)

This is another comforting dessert that's incredibly delicious and easy to make, though it requires frequent stirring.

5 cups of water
1 large cinnamon stick
½ teaspoon salt
1 cup of rice
1 can (12 ounces) of sweetened condensed milk
1 can (12 ounces) evaporated milk
½ cup raisins
Ground cinnamon

1. Heat the water in a medium saucepan with the cinnamon stick and salt. When it starts to boil, add the rice. Cover the pot and cook over medium heat for about 15 minutes.

2. Add the sweetened condensed milk, evaporated milk, and raisins and cook about 10 minutes more, stirring frequently. When the pudding starts to get thick and the rice becomes soft, it's done. It will thicken further as it cools.

3. Pour the pudding into a bowl and refrigerate for several hours.

4. Sprinkle individual servings with cinnamon.

ADAPTED FROM JORGE CHAN

Spanish/English Translations

arroz	rice	cuchara	spoon
papas fritas	French fries	tenedor	fork
canela	cinnamon	cuchillo	knife
huevo	egg	pollo	chicken
minuto	minute	azúcar	sugar

ASIA AND ASIA MINOR

Ming Tsai

China

Dmitri Dimitrov

Russia

Shoba Narayan

India

Su-Mei Yu

Thailand

Nobu Matsuhisa

Japan

Najmieh Batmanglij

Iran

Samuel Oh

Korea

Hava Volman

Israel

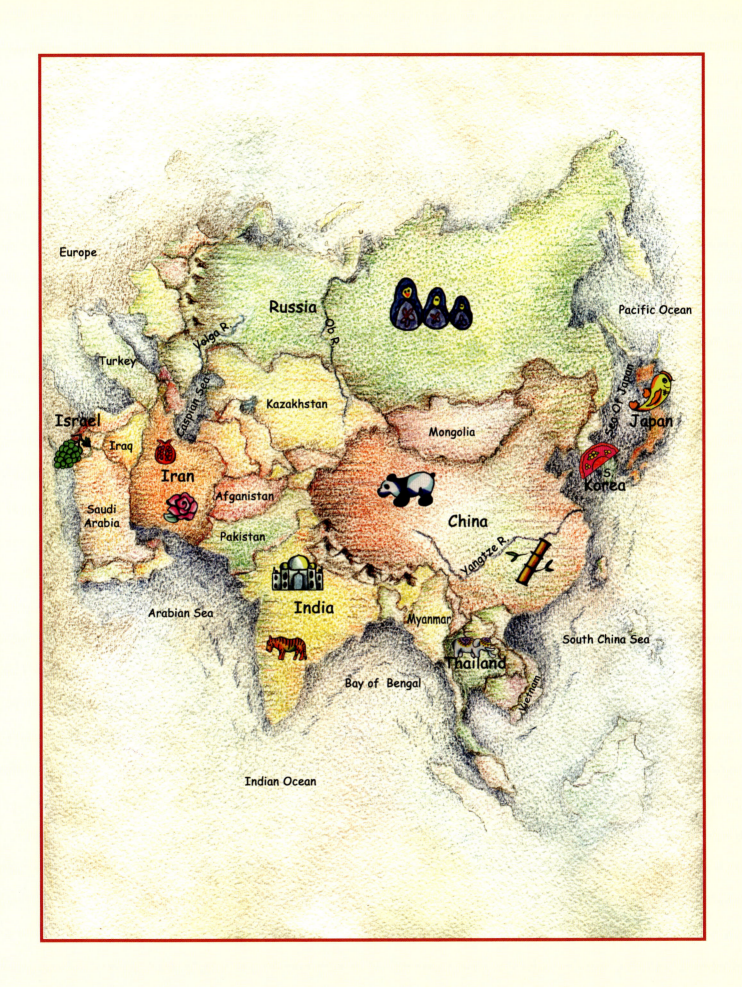

Ming Tsai

China

Left: Ming at his restaurant, Blue Ginger.

Ming Tsai was born in Newport Beach, California. Both his parents were born in Beijing, China. Ming's father, Stephen, came to the United States to study engineering at Yale University, just as his father, Ming's grandfather, had done. Stephen Tsai met Ming's mom, Iris, at Yale, where her parents taught Mandarin Chinese. Stephen and Iris named their son Ming, which means brilliance in Chinese. It's symbolized by the sun and the moon together because between the two, there's always brightness and light.

Ming spent most of his childhood in Dayton, Ohio. He always knew he wanted to be a chef. When he was thirteen, his mother opened a restaurant called Mandarin Kitchen in the food court of a shopping center in Dayton. There he experienced a variety of restaurant jobs including janitor, dishwasher, manager, cook, and cashier. During summers he also sold egg rolls from a cart outside the mall. Ming enjoyed working in the restaurant because he liked creating and selling a product, and he saw people leaving the restaurant happy.

As a kid, Ming loved to eat. He wasn't exactly thin, and so he tried to cook foods that were relatively low calorie. He'd make frosted Duncan Hines cakes for his brother and plain cakes for himself. One day when he was ten, some unexpected guests came to visit. Though his parents weren't in, he wanted to be hospitable, so he decided to make fried rice. He'd never made it before, but thought he remembered how his mom made it. It came out a bit too greasy, but it was tasty; and Ming was pretty proud of himself.

Throughout his childhood, Ming's parents took him on trips to Asia and Europe, and he loved seeing new places and trying new foods.

Growing up, Ming was taught the Chinese respect for family and food. Every Friday night he went to his grandparents' home for a traditional Chinese dinner. As part of Chinese tradition, no part of the food was wasted. After a whole fish dish was served and eaten, nothing was left but the bones. When his father and uncles went out to eat with their families at a restaurant, they'd fight for the check as a point of honor.

Meals often started with pot stickers, which are pork filled dumplings that can be steamed, boiled, or pan-fried. They were invented during the Ming Dynasty when a cook for the Emperor accidentally left the dumplings in the pot too long and all the water evaporated. They stuck to the bottom and got a little crispy. The Emperor liked them so much, they became a permanent dish and were named "pot stickers". Ming's mom's recipe is still his favorite.

Another favorite was Chinese fire pot. It's a communal meal during which the whole family sits around the table and slowly cooks and eats together. It starts with a pot of chicken broth placed in the middle of the table over a burner. Plates of sliced raw meats, fish, and vegetables

Bamboo

Bamboo is a member of the grass family, and it's one of the most diverse plant species there is. Bamboo ranges from a thin, low, ground cover, to stalks that are one foot wide and 100 feet high. Most bamboo varieties have solid "nodes" or rings connecting each segment, and long hollow sections in between.

are brought to the table; and using chopsticks, each person dips their own into the broth to cook it. The cooked meats and vegetables are then dipped into a variety of sauces such as sesame paste and peanut butter. It's an adventure to cook your own, and the dish is especially fun to eat and warming on cold winter nights.

Red-roast pork, made with rock sugar, soy sauce, and Asian spices was another favorite. The pork was braised slowly on the stove for hours and it filled the house with its wonderful aroma. The family would wait with great anticipation for dinner. It was served over white rice, which absorbed the rich, flavorful sauce. Duck and chicken were also prepared in a similar manner.

Since the Chinese don't use butter, cream, or ovens for baking, their desserts are different and lighter than most Americans are used to. Almond Jell-o with Mandarin oranges was a soothing and refreshing way to end the meal.

Ming studied engineering at Yale University, but decided before graduating that he really wanted to be a chef. He attended the Cordon Bleu Cooking School in Paris and then worked at a bakery and restaurant in Paris to refine what he'd learned in cooking school. After that experience, Ming went to Japan to study under a sushi

Pandas

There are believed to be only about 1000 giant panda bears alive today in the world. Most live in China. Pandas are related to raccoons and bears. They live in bamboo forests high in the mountains, and bamboo is their primary source of food. While they weigh less than half a pound at birth, when full grown, they can weigh up to 300 pounds.

master. Next he wisely decided he needed to learn the business aspects of running a restaurant and he enrolled in the renowned Cornell School of Hotel Management in Ithaca, New York. After graduation, Ming went on to work at restaurants in Chicago, San Francisco, and Santa Fe, New Mexico, learning as much as he could wherever he went from other talented and experienced chefs.

Today Ming is the star of two very popular TV shows. On his show East Meets West with Ming Tsai, he teaches the style of cooking that he's pioneered. It combines Asian ingredients and cooking techniques with French techniques and "Western" ingredients from Europe and America. On Ming's Quest, he travels to different parts of the United States to capture and then cook indigenous ingredients such as alligators in Florida, lobsters in Massachusetts, ostriches in Texas, salmon in Alaska, and shark in the Caribbean.

Ming and his wife, Polly, have an extremely popular restaurant in Wellesley, Massachusetts called Blue Ginger. They designed the restaurant using the principles of feng-shui, the Chinese art of arranging your environment to achieve harmony with your surroundings, positive energy, and success in life. Ming's first cookbook, *Blue Ginger*, is already in its fifth edition and in the Fall of 2003, his second book, *Simply Ming*, will hit the shelves.

There's a tremendous amount that's impressive about Ming. However, what impressed me most is his dedication to children's charities. Immediately following my interview with Ming, he invited a boy who was terminally ill to cook with him. Through the charity, "The Make a Wish Foundation", the boy wished he could come to Blue Ginger to cook with Ming; and his wish was granted.

What follows are some of Ming's favorite childhood recipes.

PORK & GINGER POT STICKERS WITH SPICY SOY DIPPING SAUCE

(makes 20–24 pot stickers)

Below is a recipe for pot sticker wrappers. As an alternative if you're pressed for time, you can buy already made 3-inch, round gyoza wrappers found in the refrigerated section of most grocery stores. You can also buy egg roll skins that are 7-inch squares. Cut out four circles from each egg roll wrapper with a sharp-edged, 3-inch, circular cookie cutter. A third option is to buy wonton wrappers and cut 3-inch circles with a cookie cutter.

DOUGH & WRAPPERS
2 cups water
4 cups all-purpose flour
½ teaspoon salt

1. Mix flour and salt in a mixing bowl.

2. Bring water to a boil. Add the boiling water ¼-cup at a time, mixing with chopsticks until a ball is formed and the dough is no longer too hot to handle. All the water may not be needed.

3. Knead the dough on a floured work surface until it becomes smooth and elastic (15-20 minutes). Form dough into a ball, return it to the bowl, and cover with a damp cloth. Allow dough to rest for 1 hour.

4. To form the wrappers, dust the table or counter top with flour. Divide the dough in half. Shape each half into a thin log shape, about one inch in diameter, and 5 to 6 inches in length.

5. Cut each log into ½-inch pieces. One by one, stand each piece on end, flatten it with the palm of your hand, and roll it into a circle about 3 inches wide and 1/16th of an inch thick. Repeat with remaining dough.

FILLING
4 cups finely chopped napa cabbage
1 tablespoon salt
½ pound ground pork
  (not too lean)
2 tablespoons finely chopped
  fresh ginger

1 ½ tablespoons finely
  chopped garlic
2 tablespoons soy sauce
3 tablespoons toasted sesame oil
1 egg, lightly beaten

1. Finely chop the cabbage, sprinkle 1 ½ teaspoons of salt over it and toss. Set aside for 30 minutes. Spread out a clean dish towel or a double layer of cheese cloth and dump the cabbage on it. Gather up the ends and twist to squeeze as much water as possible from the cabbage.

2. In a second large bowl, combine the cabbage with the pork, ginger, garlic, soy sauce, sesame oil, and egg, and mix well.

ASSEMBLY

1. To fill the pot stickers, place about ½ tablespoon of the filling in the center of each wrapper. Avoid getting filling on the edges of the wrapper so it can seal tightly. With your finger, brush a little water around the edge of the circle. Fold each wrapper in half to form a half-moon shape.

2. Seal the top center of each dumpling by pressing dough between the fingers and, starting at the center, make 3 pleats or "pinches", working toward the bottom right. Go back to the middle and make three pleats going from the center to the bottom left. Now press the entire dumpling down gently to make a flat bottom.

3. Heat a large, nonstick frying pan over high heat. Add the two tablespoons of oil and swirl to coat the pan. When the oil shimmers, add the pot stickers, flattened bottoms down, in rows of five. Cook in batches without disturbing until brown, about 6 minutes.

4. Add about ½ cup of water and immediately cover to avoid splattering. Lift the cover and make sure about ⅛ inch of water remains in the pan; if not, add a bit more. Steam until the pot stickers are puffy yet firm and the water has evaporated, 8 to 10 minutes. If the pot stickers seem done but water remains in the pan, drain it and return the pan to the stove top. Continue to cook over high heat to allow the pot stickers to recrisp on the bottom, 2 to 3 minutes.

5. Transfer the pot stickers to a platter and serve with the dipping sauce.

SPICY SOY DIPPING SAUCE

(makes about 1 cup)

⅓ cup soy sauce
⅓ cup rice wine vinegar
⅓ cup scallions, green parts only, sliced ⅛-inch thick
1 tablespoon toasted sesame oil

1 tablespoon sambal oelek, optional if you want it spicy (this is a hot chile pepper paste that can be found in Asian markets)

Combine the soy sauce, vinegar, scallions, sesame oil, and sambal oelek in a medium-size bowl. Stir to blend, and serve or refrigerate for up to two weeks.

TRADITIONAL MANDARIN FRIED RICE

(makes 4 servings)

4 tablespoons canola oil

3 eggs, beaten lightly

2 tablespoons finely chopped garlic

2 tablespoons finely chopped, fresh ginger

1 la chang sausage cut into a ⅛-inch dice, or 4 strips cooked bacon, crumbled (La chang is a dry, hard, sweet Chinese sausage, available in Asian markets. It must be steamed before using.)

1 bunch scallions, white and green parts chopped and reserved separately

5 cups cooked cold rice

2 tablespoons soy sauce

½ teaspoon white pepper

Salt, if needed

1. Heat a wok or large nonstick frying pan over high heat. Add 2 tablespoons of the oil and swirl to coat the pan. When the oil shimmers, add the beaten eggs, which will puff up. Allow eggs to set, about 5 seconds, and slide them onto a dish; do not overcook. With the edge of the spatula, break the eggs into small pieces. Set aside.

2. Add the remaining 2 tablespoons of oil to the wok and swirl to coat the pan. When the oil shimmers, add the garlic and ginger and stir-fry until soft, about 2 minutes.

3. Add the sausage or bacon pieces, the white parts of the scallions, and the rice and toss thoroughly until heated through.

4. Add the soy sauce, pepper, and reserved eggs and toss. Correct the seasonings, adding the salt if necessary.

5. Transfer to a platter, and garnish with the scallion greens. Serve immediately.

RED-ROAST PORK

(makes 4 servings)

I t's fun to make the liquid the red-roast pork will cook in. It has so many wonderful ingredients!

1 bottle dry red wine

2 cups Shaoxing wine, or 1 cup dry sherry

1 cup dark soy sauce

3 cups regular soy sauce

4 cups water

6 pounds pork butt with fat caps (ask your butcher)

2 boxes rock sugar, or 2 cups dark brown sugar

1 5-inch piece fresh ginger, cut into ¼-inch slices

1 whole head garlic, unpeeled and halved horizontally

**2 bunches scallions, white parts sliced into 3-inch lengths,
   green parts sliced ⅛-inch thick**

2 star anise (a spice shaped like 1-inch stars)

**4 Thai bird chiles (Both star anise and Thai bird chiles, a fiery, small chile,
   are available at Asian markets. If unavailable, use serrano chiles.)**

2 cinnamon sticks

8 baby bok choy, halved and cored

1. Combine the wines, soy sauces and water in a large, deep pot.

2. Bring liquid to a boil over high heat and add the pork. If the liquid doesn't cover the pork, add more water. Bring to a boil again, then reduce the heat and simmer, skimming the liquid until no more scum forms on top, about 30 minutes.

3. Add the rock sugar, ginger, garlic, white scallion pieces, star anise, chiles, and cinnamon sticks. Stir to dissolve the sugar and taste for sweetness. It should be pleasantly sweet; if not sweet enough, add more sugar. Place a second pot or stainless steel bowl, half-filled with water into the first, to keep the pork submerged. Simmer until the pork is very tender, 2 ½ to 3 hours. Do not overcook. During the last 10 minutes of cooking, add the bok choy.

4. Using a large-mesh spoon, carefully remove the pork and bok choy to a platter and cover with foil to keep warm. Strain and skim the stock, return it to the pot, and reduce it over high heat until lightly syrupy, about 20 minutes.

5. When ready to serve, slice the pork and place on a serving platter. Surround with the bok choy. Spoon sauce over the pork, garnish it with sliced green scallions, and serve.

ALMOND FLOAT
Almond Jell-O

(makes 6 servings)

2 packages (¼ ounce each) Knox unflavored gelatin
2 cups boiling water
1 cup cold water
1 cup sweetened condensed milk
1 tablespoon almond extract
Fruit cocktail or mandarin oranges in syrup

1. Completely dissolve the gelatin in 2 cups of boiling water.

2. Add 1 cup of cold water and one cup of sweetened condensed milk. Then add 1 tablespoon of almond extract. Stir well. Refrigerate until it becomes solid (several hours).

3. Remove from refrigerator and cut into small cubes. Put in a bowl and mix with fruit cocktail or mandarin oranges in syrup.

4. Serve in individual bowls.

Mandarin Chinese/English Translations

chá	tea	pai-fan	cooked rice
ch'aau faan	fried rice	ya	duck
hsia	shrimp	yú	fish
chu-jou	pork	yim	salt
mein	noodles	Chung-Kwok	China

Shoba Narayan

India

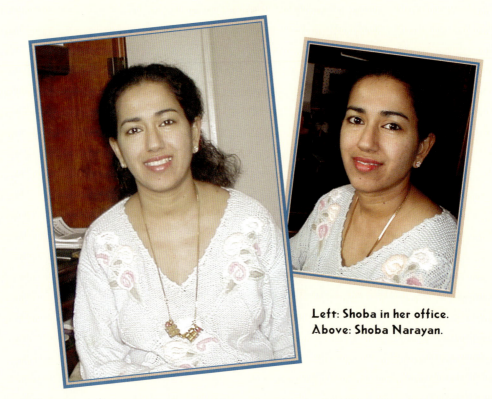

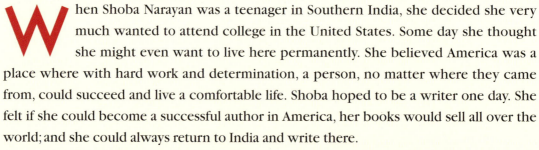

Left: Shoba in her office.
Above: Shoba Narayan.

When Shoba Narayan was a teenager in Southern India, she decided she very much wanted to attend college in the United States. Some day she thought she might even want to live here permanently. She believed America was a place where with hard work and determination, a person, no matter where they came from, could succeed and live a comfortable life. Shoba hoped to be a writer one day. She felt if she could become a successful author in America, her books would sell all over the world; and she could always return to India and write there.

Today, sixteen years after coming to America, and after attending college at Mount Holyoke and graduate school in journalism at Columbia University, she has achieved her dream: she's a successful writer and has decided to make the United States her home. Shoba has won the MFK Fisher Award, the most prestigious award in food journalism, named after perhaps the greatest food writer of all time. She's written articles about food for *Gourmet*, *Saveur*, and *Food and Wine* magazines, as well as for the *New York Times*

newspaper. While she loves writing about her childhood memories of food in India, she also writes for magazines, newspapers, and radio about non-food subjects.

Shoba grew up in a very large household in India that was headed by her very spirited and energetic grandmother, Nalla-ma. Nalla-ma was an exceptional cook, and she had plenty of people to cook for. There were fourteen cousins, four pairs of aunts and uncles, plus servants, and visiting relatives. The family's religion was Hindu, the largest religion in India. Hindu's are vegetarians, as they believe that all animals are holy and should not be killed for food or clothing. Meat, fish, and even eggs are avoided. The vegetarian cooking in India is considered the best and most varied in the world.

Shoba's family was not happy about her desire to attend college in America. They feared for her safety, knew they'd miss her tremendously, and felt she should get married before making such a big decision to move so far away. Nevertheless, they allowed her to apply to Mount Holyoke College in South Hadley, Massachusetts. When she was accepted, she begged her family to let her go. The elders in the family decided to give her a test that they expected her to fail. If she passed the test, she could go to college in America. The test was that she had to cook a vegetarian feast with a perfect balance of spices and flavors. Good Indian meals are supposed to include six primary flavors or rasas which are sweet, sour, salty, bitter, pungent or tart, and astringent or acidic.

After carefully selecting the dishes and making sure she had all the right ingredients, Shoba worked all day preparing the feast. She made crisp lentil wafers, tomato-lentil soup, lemon rice with peanuts, fresh cheese with

Tigers

There are believed to be only about 5,000–7,000 tigers in the world today, and over half reside in India. For centuries they've been revered for their strength, power, and fertility. Various parts of their bodies are believed to have medicinal properties, and as a result, over the years they've been decimated by hunters. Today hunting tigers is a crime.

spinach, curried string beans, a vegetable and yogurt salad, and rice pudding with pistachios, raisins and saffron for color. Her entire extended family came to the important feast dressed in their best outfits and wondering what to expect. To their surprise the food was wonderful and Shoba earned their permission to come to the United States for college.

Shoba had learned to cook by watching her grandmother and listening to the wisdom and lore her mother passed on. Many foods in India were thought to have medicinal or healing properties: for instance, fenugreek tea is thought to make your hair shiny, coriander seeds to make you feel cooler in the summer heat, mustard and sesame seeds to warm you in the winter, cardamom to aid digestion, and lentils to build muscles. The tomato-lentil soup that Shoba prepared for the feast was considered the "chicken soup" or "comfort soup" of vegetarian Indian cooking. All new brides were expected to know how to make it.

One day a year all the children were allowed to help in the kitchen. That was before the day-long celebration of the anniversary of her grand-

Taj Mahal

The Taj Mahal, located in Agra in north central India was built of white marble by the emperor Shah Jananan around 1640 to house the tomb of his wife. The marble color changes with the light and time of day. It's the most famous structure in all of India.

father's death. On that day, the whole family paid their respects to their ancestors. All the cousins helped to prepare a twenty-four course feast to feed the entire family, as well as twelve Brahman (Hindu) priests, two cows, and the neighborhood crows. The crows were believed to carry the souls of the ancestors.

Sadly Shoba's grandmother died seven years ago. Today when Shoba cooks the dishes her grandmother made, it brings back memories of Nalla-ma and her childhood. Carrot halwa is one of those dishes. Halwa are sweets. This particular dessert is a delicious, rich pudding made of grated carrots, half-and-half cream or milk, sugar, butter, cardamom, raisins, and nuts. If the mixture is cooked a little longer and spread in a baking pan and allowed to cool, it can be cut into squares and eaten like brownies.

What follows are the recipes for lemon rice with peanuts, carrot halwa, a sweet, golden colored milk pudding with vermicelli noodles, golden raisins, and pistachio nuts, and the samosas Shoba still makes today. Somosas have been described as the "pizza of India: everybody likes them and eats them". They're three-dimensional triangles shaped like pyramids, that are filled with mashed potatoes, peas and spices, then covered with a flaky dough and fried. Samosas are often served with a reddish-pink, sweet tamarind sauce, a bright green, mint and coriander sauce, or with mango chutney. They're as fun to make as they are to eat.

SAMOSAS
Spiced Potato-Stuffed Pastries

(makes 18)

This dough has a wonderful taste and texture, and it's very easy to work with.

PASTRY DOUGH
2 ¼ cups self-rising flour
¾ teaspoon salt
6 tablespoons (¾ stick) butter, cut in small pieces
9 tablespoons water

1. Mix the salt and flour together in a medium bowl or a food processor.

2. With a pastry blender, fork, or food processor blade, incorporate the butter until crumbs have formed.

3. Add the water a few tablespoons at a time, until you can form a ball.

4. Knead the dough for about 5 minutes. Let it rest for about 15 minutes more. You can prepare the dough in advance and refrigerate it.

FILLING

1 ½ pounds potatoes

1 cup fresh or frozen mixed peas, corn, and carrots

2 tablespoons vegetable oil

1 medium onion, chopped

½ habanero chile, minced

1 ½ teaspoons finely chopped fresh ginger

1 teaspoon finely chopped garlic

½ teaspoon garam masala spice blend

½ teaspoon turmeric

1 teaspoon red chili powder

1 ½ teaspoons salt

2 tablespoons chopped fresh coriander leaves

Juice of ½ lemon

Vegetable oil for frying

1. Boil the potatoes until tender. Let cool. Peel and mash them. Set aside.

2. If using fresh carrots, chop and simmer in water to cover in a small pot. Add the corn and peas to barely cook. Set aside to cool.

3. Heat the oil in a pan and fry the onion until golden. Add the garlic, ginger, and chili and cook for two minutes. Add the garam masala, turmeric, chili powder, and salt and cook two minutes more.

4. In a bowl combine the mashed potatoes, the onion and spice mixture, carrots, peas, corn, lemon juice, and chopped coriander. Mix well.

ASSEMBLY

1. Divide the dough into 9 equal size balls. On a floured surface, roll each ball into a 5-inch circle. Cut each circle in half.

2. Brush the straightedge side with a little water, fold it in half, and align the two straight sides so they overlap to form a cone shape. Squeeze the edges together to make a tight seal. Place approximately 1 generous tablespoon of filling inside each cone, leaving the top edge clean. Moisten the inside top rim of the cone and press the edges together to make another tight seal. Place the samosas on a tray until ready to fry. Repeat with remaining dough and filling.

3. Heat approximately 3 inches of vegetable in a deep saucepan.

4. Fry several samosas at a time, being careful not to crowd them. When one side turns golden brown, flip it over to brown on the other side. Drain on paper towels.

5. Serve with Chutney on page 113.

ADAPTED FROM SHOBA NARAYAN

LEMON RICE WITH PEANUTS

(makes 6 servings)

2 cups basmati rice
3 cups water
1 teaspoon salt
1 tablespoon vegetable oil
2 teaspoons black mustard seeds
    (or white if black are unavail-
    able)
1 tablespoon minced,

    peeled fresh ginger
½ cup finely chopped, salted
    roasted peanuts
½ teaspoon turmeric
3 tablespoons fresh lemon juice
1 tablespoon thin strips of fresh
    lemon zest or peel

1. Wash rice several times in water, until the water no longer turns white from the starch. Bring rice and water with salt to a boil in a large saucepan. Cook, covered, over very low heat until water is absorbed and rice is tender. Remove from heat and let stand, covered, for 10 minutes. Fluff rice with a fork and place in a medium-size serving bowl.

2. Heat oil in a deep, 12-inch frying pan over moderately high heat until hot, but not smoking.

Cook mustard seeds, stirring, until seeds begin to pop. Add ginger and ½ cup peanuts and cook, stirring, for 2 minutes. Add turmeric and stir one minute more.

3. Add spice mixture to cooked rice and mix thoroughly.

4. Stir in lemon juice and sprinkle with lemon zest.

ADAPTED FROM SHOBA NARAYAN

CARROT HALWA
Carrot Pudding

(makes 6 servings)

4 tablespoons butter
5 medium carrots, peeled,
    trimmed, and grated
1 ½ cups half-and-half or
    whole milk
1 cup sugar
10 shelled raw cashews,

    coarsely chopped
2 tablespoons raisins
½ teaspoon ground cardamom
¼ cup blanched, sliced almonds

1. Melt butter in a medium, nonstick frying pan over medium-low heat, skimming the foam off the top. Cook until the milk solids fall to the bottom of the pan and begin to brown, about 15 minutes. Pour the clear melted butter on top into a small dish and set aside. Discard the milk solids.

2. Heat two tablespoons of the clear melted butter in the same skillet over high heat. Add the grated carrots and fry, stirring constantly until they begin to brown, about 5 minutes.

3. Add half-and-half (or milk) and sugar, reduce heat to medium, and cook, stirring occasionally, until thick, about 35-45 minutes.

4. Heat the remaining clarified butter in a small frying pan over medium heat. Add the cashews, raisins, and ground cardamom to the carrot mixture, stirring well to combine.

5. Serve warm in small dishes, sprinkled with sliced almonds.

6. If you prefer the halwa as brownie-like squares, cook longer on stove, stirring often, until pudding is fairly stiff. Spread in a greased 9-inch square pan and allow to cool.

ADAPTED FROM SHOBA NARAYAN

VERMICELLI PAYASAM
Milk Pudding with Thin Noodles, Pistachios, Raisins, and Saffron

(makes 6 servings)

2 quarts whole milk
1 cup very fine egg noodles (the thinnest you can find)
1 cup sugar
6 green cardamom pods, lightly crushed
½ teaspoon crumbled saffron threads
2 tablespoons ghee (clarified butter, see step 2 in carrot halwa recipe)
½ cup shelled pistachios
½ cup golden raisins

1. Combine milk, sugar, cardamom, and saffron and put into a large, heavy pot.

2. Simmer approximately 40 minutes, stirring often. Add the egg noodles and cook until soft but not mushy, about 12-15 minutes more, stirring so the pudding doesn't stick to the bottom of the pan. Remove from stove. When cool, remove cardamom pods.

3. Heat ghee in a heavy skillet over medium heat until melted. Add the pistachios and raisins, stirring until the nuts are lightly browned, about 2 minutes. Stir half into the rice pudding. When cooked, place the pudding in a serving bowl and sprinkle the rest of the raisin and nut mixture on top.

ADAPTED FROM SHOBA NARAYAN

Nobu Matsuhisa

Japan

Above: Nobu with his grandmother, aunt, and cousins.
Left: Chef Nobu Matsuhisa.

After meeting Nobuyuki Matsuhisa (Nobu for short), it's easy to understand why he's so successful. Nobu, who was named one of the top 10 chefs in the world, is a very special person. He works hard, has a passion for what he does, and he gets tremendous pleasure when his customers are made happy by his food. Nobu is dedicated to creating delicious, innovative Japanese dishes, using only the highest quality ingredients.

From the time he was 10 years old, Nobu knew he wanted to become a sushi chef. That year his older brother (12 years his senior) took him to eat a special meal at a sushi restaurant in Japan. At this impressionable age, he was thrilled by the energy of the restaurant, the tastes and smells he experienced, and he loved watching the skill and artistry of the sushi chefs.

Nobu never wavered in his career choice and when he was eighteen he began a 7-year apprenticeship (with only 2 days off each month). The first 3 years were spent learning about different types of fish, how to buy the freshest and best quality, and how to remove the skin and bones properly. The next four years were spent learning how to cut, shape, season, and artfully arrange sushi and sashimi. Sushi consists of fish, usually raw, and always with rice, while sashimi is made from raw fish alone. It takes as long to train to be a sushi chef in Japan as it does to become a doctor, and it's an extremely well-respected profession.

After Nobu became a sushi chef, he worked at restaurants in Peru and Argentina where he learned to cook with ingredients not commonly used in Japan, such as chile, lime, and cilantro. His unique cooking style today incorporates some South American seasonings into Japanese dishes. When Nobu felt he was ready to open his own restaurant, he decided that Anchorage, Alaska was where he wanted it to be. Unfortunately, shortly after the restaurant opened, there was a fire and he lost everything, as he had no insurance. Needless to say this was a difficult period for him, but with the love and support of his family, he got through it. Undeterred, he decided to try opening his own restaurant again (which he named Matsuhisa), this time in Beverly Hills, California.

When he opened Matsuhisa in 1987, for the first few months, the restaurant made just enough money to cover its costs. Soon after, however, he had the good fortune to be visited by a food critic from the *Los Angeles Times* newspaper who gave his restaurant rave reviews and customers started coming in droves. Matsuhisa created a stir with its exciting, new variations on Japanese cooking, and because the ingredients Nobu used were so impeccably fresh and of such high quality. Within a relatively short time Nobu and his restaurant became well-known throughout the country.

Today Nobu has 13 extremely popular restaurants on 3 continents. He's a happy man, with a loving family, happy customers, and happy employees. He succeeded because he had a

Koi Fish

Koi fish are members of the carp family. They've been bred in Japan for centuries for ornamental purposes and they primarily adorn outdoor garden ponds. Their bright orange and white colors stand out from the dark pond bottoms. Unlike indoor fish which are viewed from the side, Koi are primarily viewed looking down.

dream, a dedication to quality, a creative talent, and he never gave up.

Some of Nobu's favorite childhood dishes were sticky rice with red azuki beans, yakisoba, sukiyaki, and rice balls. There were four children in Nobu's family. On each child's birthday, his mother would make a special meal with whole red snapper and sticky rice with red azuki beans. The red azuki beans which are like little red kidney beans, turn the rice a reddish, pink color. Red is the color for celebrations in Japan, and this red rice dish is known as festival rice.

Noodles are consumed more often in Japan than any other dish. Soba are the buckwheat noodles that are favored in Tokyo and Northern Japan. Traditionally these noodles have been given as gifts to new neighbors, and they're the last food eaten at the end of the year. Yakisoba is sold at stalls around Japanese temples and shrines on festival days. The dish is quick, easy and inexpensive to make. Egg noodles are stir fried in a wok with vegetables, meat, chicken or fish, and a delicious brown sauce. It's eaten fast and very hot, in a slurping, somewhat noisy manner.

Sukiyaki is a cross between a soup and a stew. It's made with meat and vegetables cooked

Magical Melting Pot

in a special, low-sided pot on the table right in front of you. It's fun to make because everyone adds their own meat and vegetables to the broth and watches it cook. It's dished over rice into individual serving bowls. Sukiyaki got its name from a spade or "suki" that farmers used years ago to grill chicken or meat. Later, a heavy cast iron pot called a sukiyaki was created, and vegetables and broth were added to the meat. Sukiyaki is nutritious, filling, and comforting.

Rice balls have been eaten since olden times for religious festivals. They're a very common, portable dessert and they're fun to make. Sticky rice is rolled by hand into balls that are then covered with a layer of sweetened red bean paste or black sesame seeds. Alternatively, the bean paste can be placed in the center, and the sticky rice wrapped around it. What follows are the recipes for Nobu's favorite childhood dishes.

BEEF SUKIYAKI

(makes 4 servings)

If you have an electric skillet, you can place it in the center of the table and make this dish in front of everyone. If not, you'll have to cook it over the stove and bring it to the table in the pan it was prepared in.

3 tablespoons vegetable oil
1 pound (16 oz.) thinly sliced beef
1 Tofu package (14 oz.), drained
  and cut into ½-inch cubes
1 package Shirataki noodles,
  drained of their liquid
8 oz. Chinese cabbage,
  cut in ½-inch slices
9 fresh Shitake mushrooms, cut
  in half (or dried Shitakes,

soaked in boiling water for at
  least 20 minutes, then drained)
1 bunch green onions (about 6),
  cut in 1 ½-inch pieces

SUKIYAKI BROTH
½ cup soy sauce
½ cup Mirin (rice wine)
3 tablespoons sugar
1 cup water

1. Combine the ingredients for the sukiyaki broth and set aside.

2. Heat half the oil in a large frying pan and stir-fry half the meat. When the meat is no longer pink, add half the remaining ingredients. Stir fry for about two minutes.

3. Pour half of the Sukiyaki broth into the skillet and cook the meat and vegetables in the simmering broth until the vegetables are cooked.

4. Serve with individual bowls of steamed rice.

5. Place the skillet on a hot plate in the center of the table. Guests use chopsticks to help themselves out of the skillet.

6. After you've eaten the first batch, prepare the rest with the remaining ingredients.

ADAPTED FROM NOBU MATSUHISA

YAKISOBA
(Stir-fried Noodles with Vegetables and Meat)

(makes 4 servings)

2 tablespoons vegetable oil
7 ounces chicken or pork, thinly sliced
1 small carrot, peeled and thinly sliced
4 cabbage leaves, sliced and cut in 1-inch pieces
¼ onion, sliced and cut in half
1 10-ounce package yakisoba noodles (they come already cooked, usually
    with a seasoning packet, in the refrigerated section of grocery stores)
Tonkatsu sauce (if the yakisoba noodles come with a seasoning packet, use
    it as the sauce; otherwise use this bottled sauce found in Asian markets)
Salt and pepper

1. Heat 2 tablespoons of vegetable oil in a wok. When the oil is hot, add all the vegetables and stir-fry for 4-5 minutes. Place in a serving dish.

2. Heat remaining tablespoon of oil and stir-fry pork or chicken until cooked through. Add to the vegetables.

3. If using the seasoning packet, remove the yakisoba from the cellophane packets, add ½ cup of water and the seasoning packets. Stir until the seasonings are dissolved and the noodles absorb the sauce and become soft.

4. Add back the vegetables and meat and toss with the seasoned noodles.

5. If using Tonkatu sauce, add the vegetables back to the noodles in the wok. Season with Tonkatsu sauce to taste (about ½ cup), salt and pepper. Toss to coat completely.

ADAPTED FROM NOBU MATSUHISA

SEKIHAN
Sticky Rice with Red Beans

(makes 8 servings)

If japanese azuki beans are not available, use small red kidney beans instead.

1 cup dry red azuki beans
   (available in Asian markets)
   or small kidney beans
3 cups sticky rice
   (mochigome, available in
Asian markets)
1 cup regular Japanese rice
2 teaspoons salt
2 tablespoons black sesame seeds (or
   white if black are unavailable)

1. Soak beans in water to cover for about 6 hours.

2. After draining the beans, fill a saucepan with six cups of water, add the beans, cover, bring to a boil, and simmer for about 15 minutes.

3. Drain the beans, reserving the red liquid.

4. Mix together the 3 cups sticky rice and 1 cup regular Japanese rice. Rinse the rice to remove the starch and soak in enough water to cover, for about 1 hour. Drain rice.

5. Add the beans and rice to a rice cooker, along with the 2 teaspoons of salt. Combine the reserved red bean liquid with enough water to measure 5½ cups of liquid. Start the rice cooker.

6. When rice is done, sprinkle with sesame seeds and salt to taste.

ADAPTED FROM NOBU MATSUHISA

OHAGI
Sticky Rice Balls with Red Bean Paste

(makes about 36 balls)

2 cups sticky rice (mochigome,
   available in Asian markets)
2 cups water
¼ teaspoon salt
1 can (18 ounces) of sweet red bean
   paste (available in Asian markets)
   or make your own (see recipe)

1. Rinse rice. Soak in 2 cups of water in the rice cooker pot for about one hour. Add salt, turn on rice cooker, and cook until done. Let cool.

2. When cool, beat rice with a whisk or mash with a wooden spoon until it becomes sticky.

RED BEAN PASTE

This recipe makes more red bean paste than you'll need for the sticky rice balls. With the extra you can make Japanese parfaits by simply layering vanilla ice cream with red bean paste and crushed corn flakes in parfait glasses.

1 12-ounce package dried red azuki beans or kidney beans
1 ½ cups sugar
1 ½ teaspoons salt

1. Wash the beans.

2. Cover them with water and boil until soft, about 1 hour.

3. Blend in a food processor with just enough water to form a purée.

4. Return the puréed beans to a heavy saucepan, add the sugar and salt, and cook, stirring frequnetly, until the beans develop a jam-like consistency. It should be fairly stiff. Let cool.

ASSEMBLY

Try some of each version and alternate them in a pattern on a serving plate.

VERSION 1 (RED BEAN COATING)

1. Moisten your hands with water (as the rice is sticky). Roll enough rice to form a ball the size of a golf ball.

2. Cover the rice ball with a thin layer of the bean paste.

3. Repeat for each ball.

VERSION 2 (RICE COATING)

1. Moisten your hands with water.

2. Flatten about one heaping tablespoon of sticky rice in the palm of your hand.

3. Place about 1½ teaspoons red bean paste in the center. Wrap your hand and the rice around the bean paste to make a ball.

4. Repeat for each ball.

ADAPTED FROM NOBU MATSUHISA

Japanese/English Translations

beef	gyunku	noodles	men
rice	gohan	onion	tamanegi
fish	sakana	dish	osara
skillet	onabe	red beans	azuki
soup	dashijiru	festival	matsuri

Samuel Oh

Korea

Above: Samuel Oh and his brother Dainel.
Left: Samuel Oh.

Samuel Oh is justifiably proud of what he and his family have accomplished. He's the owner of the popular restaurant Ham Hung in Los Angeles' Koreatown, by far the largest Korean community in the world outside of Korea. Over the past few years the number of Korean restaurants in America has doubled from 3000 to 6000. In Los Angeles' Korea town alone, there are approximately 500 Korean restaurants. Because there are so many restaurants and interesting shops in this area, it's a fun and exciting place to visit.

Samuel came to the United States with his parents from Korea when he was nine. When Samuel was fourteen, his parents bought a hamburger shop about twenty minutes from what is now L.A.'s Koreatown. A few years later his family decided to build their own Korean restaurant nearby. They named it Ham Hung for the North Korean city his ancestors came from. The restaurant quickly became popular and families have been going there for years. One of the things that has pleased Samuel most, is getting to know the families and watching their kids grow up and start their own families.

Because Korea was occupied at different times in its history by Japan (its neighbor to the east) and China (its neighbor to the west), Korean food has some similarities to both Chinese and Japanese cooking. Korean food is highly seasoned, and it includes a variety of tastes: spicy, salty, hot, sweet, and bitter. There is a great deal of tradition and history associated with Korean food and the way holidays are celebrated. Korea still follows a lunar calendar based on the rotation of the moon. This was important to the planting of crops throughout the year. Korean Thanksgiving Day, which is celebrated in September, is a holiday that thanks ancestors for the current harvest and asks for a bountiful harvest in the coming year.

Dduk Guk or rice cake soup is eaten throughout the country on New Year's Day. Slices of rice cake (oval-shaped, chewy, and noodle-like) are boiled in a rich beef broth. A beaten egg is often added to the hot broth to create a thicker base with little egg pieces, similar to Chinese egg drop soup. Dduk Guk is then sprinkled with the sautéed ground beef and seaweed flakes. The rice cakes became popular long ago because, like pasta, they could be dried and carried from place to place when families traveled; and they could be stored and eaten throughout the year, long after the rice was harvested.

In Korea, one's ancestors continue to be important, remembered, and respected long after they've died. A special ceremony called ancestor vowing honors the last two generations who have died, on both their birthdays and on Korea's Memorial Day. Two dishes that are customary for birthday parties and ancestor vowing are "job chae" and "kalbi jjim".

Job chae is an extremely delicious, cold noodle dish made with glass noodles. These

Fan Dance

Dance and music are very important parts of Korean culture. Two traditional and colorful dances are the Drum Dance and the Fan Dance. The border shows the beautiful decorations of the drum tops (also the symbol that appears on the Korean flag), as well as the decorative fans used in these dances. The Drum Dance requires considerable skill as the dancers wear the large, flat drums around their necks throughout the dance.

noodles are made from sweet-potato starch and are called glass noodles because they're clear. The noodles are tossed with sautéed vegetables and beef in a light, sesame flavored sauce. Noodles have come to symbolize long life because noodles themselves are long. Job chae was considered special in the olden days, because the glass noodles had to be bought rather than made at home, as more ordinary noodles usually were.

Kalbi jjim is the other traditional dish served at ancestor vowing festivities. Short ribs of beef are boiled in a delicious brown sauce for several hours until the meat becomes very tender and soft. This was so that the elders, who often lacked teeth, could eat the meat without having to chew too much. Many other ingredients such as carrots, potatoes, corn, turnips, fresh chestnuts, raw pistachio nuts, raisins, dates and pint nuts were added. The number and type of ingredients used depended on the wealth of the family. Finally each portion was topped with fried egg slices.

Bul goghi is another very popular birthday

and celebration dish. It's fun to make because everyone at the table cooks their own. While thinly sliced, seasoned beef is used most often, the dish which has been made in Korea for over 3000 years, has used any meat available during hunting season, including deer, turtle, snake, wild turkey, or chicken. What makes bul goghi so much fun to eat is that it's cooked over a small grill built into the center of the table. Before the 1900's it was cooked over a round, charcoal room heater. When the Japanese occupied Korea from 1909-1945, they showed the Koreans how to use their little habachi grills, which were small enough to fit on a table. In many Korean restaurants such as Ham Hung, the grills are built into the tables.

The national dish of Korea is kimchi, cold, wilted slices of Chinese cabbage that has been pickled or fermented and has a thin, hot, red pepper sauce. In the fall, families buy the cabbage by the cartload and for several days the women prepare the kimchi to be used all winter. In the olden days the kimchi was stored in giant pots that were buried in the earth. A little bit was taken out each day and eaten at every meal.

While desserts are not very common in Korea, a light way to end the meal is with white, black, or brown sesame seed and ginger candy called káe yeot kang jong. It was one of the first candies ever created. It's very easy to make and it makes a delicious, nutritious snack. Puffed rice or Rice Krispies®, chopped peanuts, sunflower seeds, or pumpkin seeds can be used instead of, or in addition to sesame seeds. While sweet rice syrup was used in the past, today corn syrup can be substituted to hold the seeds and other ingredients together and enable the mixture to harden into candy-like bars.

What follows are Samuel Oh's recipes for the Korean dishes he loved as a kid.

BUL GOGHI
Korean Barbecue Beef

(makes 3 servings)

1 pound (16 ounces) thinly sliced
  beef rib eye steak
2 tablespoons sesame oil
1 teaspoon minced garlic
2 tablespoons sugar
¼ teaspoon salt
1 tablespoons rice wine

3 tablespoons soy sauce
3 onion slices, cut in half
½ bunch green onions, cut in
  1 ½-inch pieces
½ carrot, sliced
3 large mushrooms, sliced

1. Combine all the ingredients in a large bowl and mix well. No marinating time is needed.

2. Cook the beef over a small hibachi.

3. As an alternative, you can spread the ingredients over a large broiling pan. Broil until beef is brown on one side. With tongs, turn beef slices over to brown on the other side.

4. Serve with rice.

ADAPTED FROM SAMUEL OH & HIS MOM

DDUK GUK
New Year Soup with Rice Cakes and Beef Broth

(makes 4 servings)

Sliced oval rice cakes can be found in some Asian markets. They are about ½-inch x ¾-inch, and are thicker and chewier than most noodles. A good substitute is the Italian, oval-shaped pasta called orecchiette.

- -

1 tablespoon cooking oil
6 ounces ground beef
1 teaspoon minced garlic
¼ teaspoon salt
⅛ teaspoon black pepper
2 quarts beef broth
8 ounces sliced rice cakes or any pasta that's not spaghetti
1 teaspoon sesame oil
1 egg, lightly beaten
1 bunch green onions, cut into 3-inch pieces
4 teaspoons dried seaweed flakes

- -

1. Heat oil. Sauté beef with garlic, salt, and pepper. Pour off any fat and set aside.

2. Bring beef broth to a boil in a large pot. Add the rice cakes or pasta. It will take the rice cakes about 20 minutes to cook and the pasta about 12 minutes.

3. While broth is still boiling, just before serving, add the beaten egg, sesame oil, and the green onion and stir.

4. Serve in individual soup bowls, topped with the ground beef. Sprinkle 1 teaspoon of seaweed flakes over each serving.

ADAPTED FROM SAMUEL OH & HIS MOM

JOB CHAE
Cellophane Noodles with Vegetables

(makes 6–8 servings)

8 ounces glass noodles (made of sweet-potato starch, available in Asian markets and
  some grocery stores)

1 teaspoon salt

1 gallon water

3 tablespoons vegetable oil

8 ounces beef or chicken breast, cut in thin strips (optional)

1 teaspoon minced garlic (optional)

1 carrot, peeled and cut in julienne strips

8 ounces raw cabbage, thinly sliced, or spinach that has been briefly blanched
  in boiling water

4 ounces sliced mushrooms

½ medium onion, sliced

4 teaspoons black fungus or tree ear mushrooms (available in Asian markets),
  cut in thin strips

3 tablespoons soy sauce

3 tablespoons sesame oil

1 tablespoon sugar

3 teaspoons sesame seeds

1. In a large pot add glass noodles, salt, and water and bring to a boil for about 5 minutes. Drain, and set aside. The noodles should be clear and translucent, but not "mushy".

2. Heat 1 tablespoon of oil in a wok until hot. Add the beef or chicken and stir-fry until cooked through. Set aside on a plate.

3. Heat remaining 2 tablespoons of oil in the wok until hot. Add the garlic, carrot, cabbage, and both mushrooms. Stir-fry until vegetables are crisp/tender.

4. Add the drained noodles, cooked beef or chicken, soy sauce, sesame seeds, and sugar to the vegetables in the wok. Toss to heat through and coat entirely.

ADAPTED FROM SAMUEL OH & HIS MOM

KÁE YEOT KANG JONG

Sesame Candy

(makes 25)

½ cup white, black, or brown sesame seeds, washed and drained
½ cup sugar
½ cup corn syrup
1 cup Rice Krispies®
2 tablespoons pine nuts
2 tablespoons raisins chopped
1 tablespoon sesame oil
1 tablespoon minced ginger

1. Line an 8-inch x 8-inch baking pan with aluminum foil and brush with sesame oil.

2. Toast sesame seeds over low heat in a dry frying pan for about 5 minutes.

3. Mix sugar and corn syrup together in a saucepan, bring to a boil, and simmer for about 5 minutes, until the syrup coats the back of a spoon and forms soft sugar "threads" when dropped into a small bowl of ice cold water.

4. Mix together the sesame seeds, puffed rice, pine nuts, ginger, and raisins in a bowl.

5. Pour caramelized mixture over the dry ingredients, stir together, and pour into the greased baking pan.

6. Pat the mixture evenly in the pan.

7. Before the candy cools, make 5 cuts in each direction to form 25 small squares.

ADAPTED FROM SAMUEL OH & HIS MOM

Korean/English Translations

kuk soo (myeon) .... noodle
sang kang .... ginger
bul .... fire
goghi .... meat
dduk .... rice cake

káe .... sesame
so .... beef
guk .... soup
bob .... cooked rice
bee beem .... mixed

Dimitri Dimitrov

Russia

Above: Dimitri as a young man.
Left: Dimitri at Diaghiev.

Dimitri Dimitrov is considered to be one of the finest maître d's in the United States. What also makes Dimitri so special, is how much he enjoys his job, and how much he cares about creating a great experience for his guests. He has been the maître d' at the restaurant Diaghilev in Los Angeles, the finest Russian restaurant in the United States, since it opened almost 15 years ago. He makes it his business to know his customers and their likes and dislikes well. Many are celebrities with Russian ancestors, who find the food and atmosphere at Diaghilev both elegant and comforting. Dimitri helps guests with their menu selection and choice of wine by providing honest advice. If there's any problem with the food, wine or service, he's there to rectify the situation.

Dimitri oversees other aspects of the restaurant as well, including the flower arrangements on the tables, and the coordination of the waiting staff so the food comes to the table hot and at the same time for everyone in the party. He also works with the chef to develop changes to the menu which can vary by season and the availability of fresh ingredients.

Diaghilev was named for the famous director of the Ballet Russe in Moscow in the late 1800's and early 1900's. At that time it was considered the finest Ballet Company in the world. Diaghilev was a perfectionist, famous for his creativity and discipline, and his ability to choreograph beautiful ballets and then train his dancers to perform them flawlessly. His ballerinas, Najinsky, Anna Pavlova, and George Balanchine rose to world fame, and to this day are ballet legends. The restaurant was named after Diaghilev because he was a man of art, great taste, and culture, who set very high standards for himself and for his ballet company. The owner of this new restaurant wanted to create a restaurant of great taste, and the name Diaghilev seemed appropriate.

Dimitri, who was actually born in Yugoslavia, learned his profession by training at the finest hotels in London, England, and Canada. Over the years he's been proud to have served several world leaders including Indira Ghandi and Queen Elizabeth.

While the food at Diaghilev is Russian, it includes a great deal of French influence. In the days of the Russian Czars of the 17th, 18th, and 19th Centuries, French chefs were brought to Russia to cook for royalty because they were considered the best chefs in the world. Russian food can be heavy, and the French chefs were able to "lighten up" traditional dishes. Because of the long winters and cold climate, fresh fruits and vegetables were not available during much of the year. As a result, root vegetables such as cabbages, potatoes, carrots, and beets, as well as dried fruits that could be kept all winter, are prevalent in Russian cooking.

Some of the dishes that Russian children love include Chicken Kiev, stuffed cabbage rolls, small, savory turnovers called pirozhki,

Matrushka Dolls

Matrushka (also spelled Matry-oshka) dolls are Russian stacking or nesting dolls. While the average set contains between 3 and 12 progressively sized dolls, rare sets can contain as many as 50 or more. Most start as large as 7-8 inches and get progressively smaller, while others start as small as 1 1/2-2 inches and go down to a tiny, 1/2-inch size. The width of the dolls is traditionally half the height.

Hand painted Matrushka dolls were first created in the late 1800's outside Moscow. Some are works of art that are on display in Russian museums. Today Matrushka dolls are sold by street vendors and shops in cities throughout Russia. Modern versions include sports figures, Russian leaders, and even Santa Claus.

and a special dessert served at Easter time called Pashka. Kiev is the largest city in the Ukraine, the area of Russia that borders on the Eastern European countries Poland, Czechoslovakia, and Rumania. Chicken Kiev is an extremely popular dish that's fun to eat and delicious. A piece of butter mixed with herbs is placed in the middle of a flattened chicken breast. The breast is rolled up and tied to seal in the herb butter. Then it's dipped in egg and breadcrumbs and fried until crisp on the outside. When you cut into Chicken Kiev, the herb butter squirts out, making a light, tasty sauce.

Cabbage is one of the most common vegetables in Russia. It can be a family activity to make stuffed cabbage by rolling the steamed, pliable leaves into bundles filled with a mixture of ground meat and rice. The bundles are cooked

in a delicious sweet and sour tomato based sauce. Pirozhki are savory, bite-size turnovers, filled with mashed potatoes, meat or cheese, and encased in a flaky, golden crust. Lastly, a childhood favorite of Dimitri's is pashka, the traditional, molded Easter dessert made with large curd pot cheese (a drier form of cottage cheese), butter, vanilla, sugar, eggs, candied fruits, and almonds.

POTATO & ONION PIROZHKI
Little Savory Pastries or Pies

(makes 2 dozen)

1 package frozen puff pastry
1 ½ pounds Yukon Gold potatoes
1 large onion, chopped
3 tablespoons vegetable oil

1 teaspoon salt.
1 egg, lightly beaten
   with 1 tablespoon water

1. Preheat oven to 400°. Lightly grease two cookie sheets with butter.

2. Boil the potatoes until cooked through. Cool, peel, and mash the potatoes.

3. Heat the oil in a frying pan and sauté the onions until they turn golden brown.

4. Add the onions and salt to the mashed potatoes and mix well.

5. Roll each sheet of puff pastry into a 9-inch x 12-inch square (or slightly larger), approximately ⅛-inch thick. Cut in 3-inch circles with a sharp cookie cutter. If you don't have one, a clean, empty tuna can works surprisingly well.

6. Place about ½ tablespoon in the center of each circle, keeping the edges clean. Moisten the edge with water and press together to form a tight seal. You can crimp the edges with a fork if you like.

7. Brush each pirozhki with the beaten egg.

8. Bake for approximately 25 minutes or until golden brown.

ADAPTED FROM DIMITRI DIMITROV

Russian/English Translations

cartofel	potato	spasiba	thank you
look	onion	Zima	Winter
kapusta	cabbage	sladkii	sweet
Pasha	Easter	ser	cheese
praznik	holiday	balayt	ballet

STUFFED CABBAGE

(makes 6 servings)

The traditional Russian stuffed cabbage recipe has been embellished by the creativity of the Diaghilev cooking staff.

1 ½ lbs. ground beef
¾ cup corn (fresh off the cob, canned or frozen)
¾ cup cooked wild or white rice, cooled
½ teaspoon salt
¼ cup chopped onions
¼ cup chopped pickles
2 eggs

5 ounces cream
4 ounces sun dried tomatoes
1 teaspoon salt
¼ teaspoon white pepper
1 Savoy cabbage
1 quart tomato sauce
Juice of 1 lemon
3 tablespoons of brown sugar

1. Steam the cabbage in 3 inches of boiling water in a covered pot.

2. Drain the cabbage and let it cool. When cool, remove the center core.

3. Cook rice according to package directions which will vary depending on the type of rice you choose, or use leftover plain rice.

4. Chop the onions and pickles.

5. Beat the eggs and mix them together with the onions, pickles, corn, rice, ground beef, salt, and pepper.

6. Remove an outer leaf of the cabbage. Put a heaping tablespoon of the filling at the bottom of the leaf (the thicker part). Roll the leaf up, folding in the outside edges as you go.

7. Put each stuffed cabbage leaf in the bottom of a wide-based pot. When all the leaves are finished, pour the tomato sauce over the cabbage. Squeeze lemon juice on top. Sprinkle with brown sugar.

8. Cover the cabbage and cook over medium heat for about 45 minutes. Check occasionally to make sure the cabbage doesn't stick to the bottom of the pot, and baste the sauce over the top so the sugar and lemon get incorporated into the sauce. If it's cooking too fast, lower the heat.

ADAPTED FROM DIMITRI DIMITROV

CHICKEN KIEV
Herb Stuffed Chicken Rolls

(makes 6 servings)

1 ½ lbs. flattened chicken breasts (6 pieces: have the butcher flatten them)
6 tablespoons butter (¾ of a stick), at room temperature
1 tablespoon minced garlic
1 tablespoon chopped chives, tarragon, or dill (or a combination)
3 tablespoons minced parsley
1 tablespoon lemon juice
¾ teaspoon salt
2 eggs beaten
2 tablespoons water
2 cups bread crumbs
1 teaspoon salt
1 cup flour
4 tablespoons butter

1. Cream the butter and add the garlic, parsley, herbs, lemon juice, and salt. Spread the mixture onto a piece of aluminum foil and roll it into a log shape about 9 inches long. Refrigerate seasoned butter log for about 1 hour, until it hardens.

2. Beat the two eggs with the two tablespoons of water in a shallow dish.

3. Place the breadcrumbs and salt in a zip-lock bag and shake it all around. Place approximately one cup of the bread crumb mixture in another shallow dish.

4. Place one cup of flour on a plate.

5. Lay wax paper over the counter or tabletop. Place a flattened chicken breast on the wax paper. Remove the seasoned butter and cut it into six, 1½-inch pieces. Put one piece in the middle of each chicken breast. Roll it up tight, making sure the butter doesn't stick out. Use a toothpick to keep it closed.

6. Roll the chicken in flour.

7. Dip the chicken in the beaten egg to coat it all around.

8. Then roll in the breadcrumbs.

9. Repeat steps 5-8 until all six chicken rolls are made.

10. Melt 2 tablespoons of butter in a large frying pan. Add three of the chicken rolls. Fry on all sides until golden brown, making sure the chicken is fully cooked inside. Repeat with remaining butter and chicken.

ADAPTED FROM DIMITRI DIMITROV

PASHKA
Easter Sweet Cheese Dessert

(makes 4 servings)

This has become one of my favorite desserts. I like it so much, I've even eaten it for breakfast. The use of a flower pot and weights in this recipe makes you feel scientific and somewhat adventurous!

1 new, clean, clay, medium-size
   flower pot
2 pounds large curd cottage cheese
   or pot cheese
⅔ cup heavy cream or half-and-half
2 large egg yolks
¾ cup sugar

½ cup raisins
½ cup chopped dried apricots
¼ cup chopped almonds
1 ½ teaspoons vanilla extract
4 tablespoons (2 oz. or ½ stick)
   unsalted butter

1. Line a colander with a double layer of cheese-cloth. If using cottage cheese, place it in the lined colander and set it over a bowl. Cover the cheese with a plate and put a heavy weight on top so the excess moisture will seep out. Drain for 2-3 hours in the refrigerator. Then press cottage cheese through a sieve.

2. Add the cottage cheese to a medium-size saucepan along with the remaining ingredients. Slowly bring to a boil and keep it at a low simmer for about 5 minutes, stirring constantly. Remove from the heat and let stand until thickened and completely cold.

3. Line the flower pot with a clean dish towel or cheesecloth that has been doubled over. Leave extra cloth hanging over both sides.

4. Pour the cooled mixture into the lined flower pot and fold the cheesecloth over the top.

5. Place the pot on a dish, to catch the moisture as it drains. Cover the cheese with a plate small enough to fit inside the flower pot. Place heavy weights on it to force out the liquid. Leave it to drain in the refrigerator for 8-24 hours. The longer you leave it, the firmer it will become.

6. When ready to serve, put a larger plate over the flower pot and invert it. Remove the cheese-cloth. You can decorate the Pashka with fresh fruits, candied fruits, or nuts, though it's delicious as is, without any additional embellishment.

ADAPTED FROM DIMITRI DIMITROV

Su-Mei Yu
Thailand

Above: Su-Mei Yu at
3 years old.
Left: Su-Mei Yu.

Su-Mei Yu has led an adventurous and courageous life; and she continues to challenge herself all the time. Su-Mei was born in Bangkok, Thailand, where her parents had moved from China before she was born. Her father had been a cloth salesman from northern China, and he traveled to Thailand often. He liked it so much that he decided to raise his family there. Following an arranged marriage in China, he moved with his new wife to Bangkok, the largest city and capital of Thailand.

Education was extremely important to Su-Mei's parents. Even though they didn't have much money, they wanted their daughter to attend the very best school for girls in Thailand: the school started by the King of Siam, King Mounkut, in the late 1800's. King Mounkut was the king on which the Rogers and Hammerstein musical *The King and I* and the movie *Anna and the King* were based. The book was *Anna and the King of Siam*.

The king, who was also a Buddhist monk and a scholar, encouraged his people to learn about other cultures and he was accepting of other religions. Because he wanted his

family and country to know about the world outside of Thailand, he asked women missionaries from the West to start a school in the back of his palace for his many children. King Mounkut was well-respected by his people because he gave them freedom and didn't try to suppress them. As a result, Thailand remained an independent and strong nation. His novel accomplishments included learning English from an American doctor, bringing the first printing presses to Thailand (or Siam as it was called then), and printing weekly announcements (a forerunner to the newspaper) for his kingdom. He was also an amateur astronomer.

The school the king later started became a boarding school for children of the very rich. Even though Su-Mei Yu was neither rich nor Thai by birth, her mother was able to enroll her because of the family's involvement in the Presbyterian Church in Bangkok. The school was difficult for Su-Mei Yu initially because she was one of the only Chinese-born students. Su-Mei, who had grown up eating Chinese food at home, learned about Thai food from her friends at school. One of her fondest memories was of the period 3 days before Christmas vacation when the school kitchen was closed. Families brought pots filled with all types of delicious Thai dishes to their daughters and turned the school courtyard into a potluck, picnic campsite.

When Su-Mei was 12 years old, she begged her family to send her to the United States. She had always felt like an outsider at her boarding school because of her differences; and she felt that if she came to America and learned to speak English and Western ways, she would be better accepted. Through a missionary in Los Angeles, Su-Mei was accepted by a church sponsored boarding school for girls in Kentucky. She

Elephants

Pale gray or white elephants have been a respected symbol throughout Thailand's history. They were considered celestial or almost god-like and related to kings. These proud and intelligent animals came to the aid of the Thai people by helping them fight during wars and by transporting them through the jungles. On special occasions they were colorfully decorated and paraded through the streets. .

was sent a handkerchief from Kentucky with goldenrod, blue grass, and horses; and that was enough to convince her to go.

Su-Mei stayed in Kentucky through her junior year of college. Her mission school had a sister school in Orange County, California, and she won a scholarship there for her senior at Chapman University. To earn extra money, Su-Mei worked at Chapman. There she heard about a summer job at Disneyland that was perfect for her. Because she spoke both Chinese and Thai, she gave tours of Disneyland to visitors from China and Thailand.

Su-Mei started cooking in college even though she'd never cooked before. She'd only watched others. She longed for foods from Thailand; so using the limited Thai ingredients that were available in grocery stores in the U. S. in those days, and with only an electric skillet, she cooked on the bathroom counter in her dormitory room.

Su-Mei went on to become a social worker, a career she pursued for twenty-five years. Then she made a radical career change; she decided to

open her own tiny Thai restaurant in San Diego. Today she owns two very successful Thai restaurants named "Saffron Thai Grilled Chicken" and "Saffron Noodles and Saté" that are right next to each other; and she's written two Thai cookbooks *Cracking the Coconut* and *Asian Grilling*.

Saffron Thai Grilled Chicken is a little shop where you order and eat at picnic tables outside. The special grilled chicken recipe was a favorite of Su-Mei's when she was a child. Her family would buy the tasty chicken from wooden huts in Bangkok, near the boxing arena, where it had been marinated in spices and grilled over hot charcoal. Her restaurant's version is served with a choice of five different sauces.

Su-Mei opened her second restaurant, Saffron Noodles and Saté, a few years ago. It's a little sit-down restaurant that serves the food she remembers from a noodle stand in an alley near her home in Bangkok. That noodle stand consisted of a wooden cart equipped with everything needed to make noodles, as well as a few wooden tables and stools. As a treat, Su-Mei's father would let her brother go down to the stand to place the order. A few minutes later, the owner's young son would come to their house with a tray holding bowls filled with the delicious, steaming hot noodles.

Safron Noodles and Saté also serves saté (grilled, skewered meats & shrimp), like the ones Su-Mei fondly remembers "the saté man" bringing to her house. In Bangkok, food vendors sold their products door-to-door, offering everything you could imagine. You never had to leave your house. In the case of the saté man, he would go door-to-door with his portable charcoal brazier or hibachi type grill, a basket of pork that had been marinated and skewered, and cucumber relish and peanut sauce. Bamboo sticks were used to skewer the meat, which he would grill right on their doorstep. It couldn't have been fresher or more delicious!

In describing the cooking of Thailand, Su-Mei explains that rice is central to all Thai cooking. Thai cooking is packed with different flavors and textures, each distinct, yet each helping to elevate and enhance all the other flavors. The flavors are a mixture and balance of hot, sweet, and salty. Typical ingredients in Thai cooking include slippery noodles, peanuts, fried garlic and shallots (a small, delicate onion), crunchy vegetables, shrimp, coconut milk, and fish sauce, (a salty, pale brown liquid made from fermented small fish or shrimp). Aroma is also very important. It's the first thing that hits you before you eat. A mortar and pestle, most often made of granite, is one of the most important pieces of equipment used in Thai cooking. When Su-Mei left Thailand for the United States, the one treasure she took was her mother's mortar and pestle. It's used to bruise, blend, and combine spices.

Women in Thailand are expected to be great cooks, but Su-Mei's mother was exceptional. Although their family lived in a cramped antiques warehouse stacked up with furniture next to her father's antique shop, her mother's reputation as a fine cook was known far and wide. People from the Chinese Embassy in Bangkok relished invitations to eat under her roof. They didn't care if they sat on boxes. She'd make fresh dumplings and steamed buns; and every weekend she prepared Chinese noodles, which she rolled by hand on something that looked like an ironing board. She'd buy live fish, crabs, and shrimp at the market and keep them in a big tank of water at home. When she was ready to cook the meal, she'd take them out and add them to the pot. Her dishes could not have been fresher!

When Su-Mei's family went to the temple shrine to honor Budhha, they'd bring sticky rice wrapped in banana leaves as an offering. In preparation for banquet time during the Chinese New Year, her mother planned the food for months. The special red bean paste she used in her steamed buns was made with date sugar and took weeks to make. A special type of pork fat was also used. It was hung in cotton bags to dry out and develop a unique flavor and texture. Food was an extremely important part of holiday celebrations and life in Thailand. What follows are the recipes for Su-Mei Yu's favorite childhood foods.

CHICKEN SATÉ
Chicken Skewers with Peanut Sauce

(makes 15 to 18 skewers)

1 teaspoons sea salt
1 teaspoon freshly ground white pepper
1 teaspoon coriander seeds, roasted and ground, or ½ teaspoon ground coriander
1 tablespoon minced garlic
1 teaspoon turmeric powder
½ teaspoon ground cayenne pepper

½ cup coconut milk (available canned in grocery stores)
1 pound skinless, boneless chicken breasts
15 to 18 6-inch bamboo skewers, soaked in water for 30 minutes, then dried
Vegetable oil spray

1. Slice the chicken breasts, paper thin, across the grain.

2. Combine all the ingredients except for the chicken in a large zippered plastic bag and seal. Shake the bag around to mix the ingredients.

3. Add the chicken. Seal and shake the bag to coat the chicken.

4. Refrigerate at least 30 minutes or overnight

5. Start the grill.

6. While waiting for the grill to get hot, remove chicken from the refrigerator. Thread chicken with the bamboo skewers, leaving ½-inch exposed at each end. Repeat with the remaining chicken. Save the remaining marinade in a bowl.

7. Spray the chicken generously with vegetable oil and place on the grill. Turn frequently to ensure even cooking and prevent burning. Baste frequently with the marinade and cook until the chicken is lightly browned on the outside, and the inside turns white and firm, about 9 to 10 minutes.

8. Remove from the grill and serve hot with peanut sauce.

ADAPTED FROM SU-MEI YU

PEANUT SAUCE

(makes 1 cup)

This sauce is great on chicken and steamed vegetables. If you thin it with water and refrigerate it, it makes a wonderful salad dressing.

1 tablespoon vegetable oil
2 tablespoons minced shallots
½ cup smooth peanut butter
½ teaspoon ground cayenne pepper
2 tablespoons sugar

1 tablespoon fish sauce (Nam Pla)
½ cup coconut milk (available canned in grocery stores)
2 tablespoons lime juice

1. In a medium size sauce pan, heat the oil over high heat for a minute before adding the shallots. Stir until shallots turn translucent, about 1 to 2 minutes.

2. Add the remaining ingredients, except for the lime juice. Reduce heat to medium-high. Continue to stir until the peanut butter is dissolved and the sauce begins to boil. Let cook for another 1 to 2 minutes.

3. Remove from heat and let cool before adding the lime juice. Taste for a balance of saltiness, sweet, and sour. Serve or refrigerate. It will keep for a couple of days. If it's been refrigerated, heat over a low heat and add a little water if it seems too thick.

ADAPTED FROM SU-MEI YU

YUMM WOON SEN

Glass Noodle Salad

(makes 6-8 servings)

DRESSING (MAKES 1 CUP)
1 ½ teaspoons sea salt
1 tablespoon minced garlic
1 tablespoon minced Jalapeno chiles

¾ cup sugar
3 tablespoons fish sauce (Nam Pla)
3 tablespoons distilled white vinegar
6 tablespoons lime juice

SALAD

6 ounces glass noodles (also called
   bean thread or mung bean thread)
2 cups cooked chicken, torn into
   bite-size pieces
2 cups cooked medium-size shrimp
1 cup diced celery
⅔ cup thinly sliced white onion

1 cup cherry tomatoes, halved
⅔ cup shredded cabbage
⅔ cup coarsely chopped cilantro leaves
⅔ cup mint leaves,
   bruised and hand-torn
⅔ cup coarsely chopped
   roasted peanuts

1. Mix the dressing ingredients in a small bowl.

2. Soak the glass noodles in luke-warm water until supple, about 15 minutes. Drain through a strainer in the sink.

3. Bring 2 cups water to a boil in a medium-size saucepan. Add the glass noodles and boil for 25 seconds. Empty into a strainer over the sink and rinse with cool water until the noodles are completely cool. Squeeze out all excess water before chopping into bite-size lengths. Transfer to a serving bowl.

4. Add all the ingredients except for the cilantro, mint and peanuts. Pour on the dressing and toss to combine.

5. Sprinkle the top with the cilantro, mint, and chopped peanuts and serve.

ADAPTED FROM SU-MEI YU

BANANA JOINED THE NUNNERY
Bananas in Sweet Coconut Milk

(makes 6 servings)

1 can (13.5 ounces) coconut milk
¾ cup sugar
¾ teaspoon sea salt
3 firm, ripe bananas peeled, sliced across into 1 ½ inch pieces
   (approximately 2 ½ cups)

1. In a medium-size saucepan, combine all the ingredients except for the banana over medium heat. Stir to dissolve the sugar and salt.

2. When the sauce begins to boil, about 5 minutes, add the bananas. Lower the heat to medium-low and let cook until the bananas soften, about 5 minutes: no longer or the bananas will become mushy.

3. Serve hot or at room temperature. The sauce will thicken if allowed to cool.

ADAPTED FROM SU-MEI YU

Najmieh Batmanglij

Iran

Above: Najmieh in
the 3rd grade.
Left: Najmieh at
the Farmer's Market.

Najmieh Batmanglij was raised in Teheran, Iran. She's the third-youngest in a family of eleven children. When Najmieh was growing up, her mother discouraged her from cooking because she was afraid it would distract her from studying. She wanted her daughter to have the type of university education that she never had.

Najmieh came to the United States to study when she was eighteen. Prior to that, the farthest she'd been away from home was an occasional sleepover at her cousin's house. She studied first in Oklahoma and then at the University of Southern Connecticut, where she received a Masters in Education. In New Haven she lived with other foreign students and cooked a lot of Persian food. If she had questions about a recipe, she'd call or write home for help. Once a week, Najmieh made a big dinner for a group of Iranian, American, and other international students. As you can imagine, these dinners became extremely popular.

In 1975, Najmieh returned to Iran with her graduate degree. In her mom's eyes she had now earned the right to indulge her passion for cooking. She found a full time job, and during her spare time, learned all she could from her mother, who was a wonderful cook. Her mom taught her how to make traditional Persian dishes, shop for the best ingredients, create balanced meals, and use herbs for their medicinal and healing powers. As Najmieh says, "My mother was an excellent herbalist, who had raised a large, healthy family, mostly without modern drugs, but with plenty of home remedies."

Najmieh loved learning about Iranian traditions, symbolism, and history. Older relatives and friends of her parents began teaching her their secret recipes and special preparation techniques. She kept a diary and recorded all the recipes she learned. She also recorded her observations of the changes she saw taking place in her country: changes that lead up to the overthrow of the Shah of Iran, the revolution, and the change in government that was accompanied by the rise to power of religious fundamentalists.

Unfortunately, under Iran's new government, women's rights took a large step backwards. The government interfered with their personal lives, forcing them to cover themselves in public and limiting their careers. For someone like Najmieh, who believed in the separation of church and state like we have in America, this was especially diffucult. By this time, Najmieh had married and decided to leave her native country. She described a cold late-December afternoon as "the saddest day in my life. Three months pregnant, I went to my old house to say goodbye to my mother and father. They were both crying. They knew how much I loved Iran, how much I appreciated my culture and traditions, and how much I wanted to be a part of it."

She took refuge in the south of France; and to her great relief, twenty days later her husband made it safely to France to join her. There, Najmieh

Pomegranates

Pomegranates have been grown in Iran for at least 4000 years. They are considered the fruit of heaven and are thought to have been the "real apple" in the Garden of Eden.

Roses

Rose water and rose petals are used to make drinks and flavor food and pastries. In addition, rose petals are used to make jam, and rose water freshens the air and colors women's makeup.

decided to take French cooking lessons. To her surprise, many of the French cooks she met were interested in learning more about Persian food, so she shared her knowledge. They loved her cooking with its different herb and spice blends. Soon Najmieh and her husband made friends not only with the chefs in her area, but also with the local doctor, artist, writer, photographer, butcher, and baker.

Najmieh started to make a scrapbook for her son and gathered informaton about Persian ceremonies and traditions. One of her neighbors convinced her to turn it into a cookbook. With the help of her new French friends, the book became a reality. As she says, "the publisher said we needed some photographs, and pretty soon the whole village was involved in helping me with every aspect of putting together a Persian cookbook in French". She named the book *Ma Cuisine d'Iran* (*My Cooking of Iran*).

In 1983 Najmieh emigrated to the United States, along with her husband, her first son, and a second son (on the way). Three years later she published her second cookbook entitled *Food of Life: Ancient Persian and Modern Iranian Cooking and Ceremonies.* It's an introduction to Persian culture that includes recipes, photos, ceremonies, stories, poetry, and art. In 1994 she introduced *New Food of Life*, an updated version.

Today, twenty-four years after leaving Iran, Najmieh is working on her sixth cookbook. As she says, "I have not spent a day when some aspect of cooking has not been a part of my life." In addition to writing cookbooks, Najmieh teaches Persian cooking in the Washington, D.C. area and gives lectures all around the country.

Rice is a staple of Persian cooking. For thousands of years many different types of rice have been grown in the area of northern Iran that surrounds the Caspian Sea. There is an abundance of rice dishes that range from simple to very elaborate with lots of ingredients mixed in. Two rice dishes in particular bring back fond childhood memories: rice with tart cherries, and rice with fava beans.

In the summertime, when the tart cherries were in season, Najmieh's family would bring wooden crateloads home, with the leaves still on. They'd wash the cherries and dump them into wicker baskets. Najmieh and her sisters had the job of removing the pits so they could be made into jam. As Najmieh says, "only half became jam." She and her sisters would hang the double-stemmed cherries over their ears to make earrings, they'd pin clusters on their clothes to make pins, and they'd rub the juice on their lips to make lipstick. In between, they ate a lot too. When the jam was finished, it was used to sweeten tea, spread on bread, or mix with yogurt to make a dessert.

Rice with fava beans (like large, light green lima beans) was made with a lot of fresh herbs and was traditionally served around the Persian New Year, a two week celebration that starts the first day of spring. Since spring marks the rebirth of nature, it's viewed in Iran as the start of a new year. It was a custom in Najmieh's family that two weeks before the New Year, an old woman from a village near the Caspian Sea would travel for many miles and appear in her garden, bringing a basket of wonderful spring treasures. The basket contained violets (her mother's favorite flower), narcissus, a delicate looking daffodil with a beautiful fragrance that perfumed their house, Seville oranges with leaves attached which represented the earth, and smoked whitefish that was later eaten with the herbed rice.

Some important ingredients in Persian cooking are pomegranates, roses, and cardamom. Eating pomegranates is thought to rid a person of envy and hatred. Each pomegranate has hundreds of seeds, each of which is surrounded by a little sac of juice. The seeds can be eaten plain, used as an ingredient, or squeezed to make juice. The juice is sometimes boiled down to make a paste that is another cooking ingredient.

Cardamom was brought to Iran from India. Each cardamom pod contains tiny seeds. They're known as "seeds of paradise" because of their wonderful taste and aroma. You can freshen your breath by sucking on the pods.

Below are some of Najmieh and her sons' favorite childhood recipes. Included are a simple, delicious, rice dish made yellow by saffron, sweet and sour stuffed chicken with dried fruits, shish kabob which is fun to skewer, and paradise custard, a dessert made with rosewater and cardamom seeds.

SHISH KABAB
Meat and Vegetable Skewers

(makes 6 servings)

It's best to start the kababs in the morning, as they have to marinate for at least eight hours. Kids will have fun "threading" the kababs with the meat and colorful vegetables.

....

2 pounds lamb, veal, beef or chicken,
  cut in two-inch cubes
4 green peppers, seeds and ribs
  removed, cut into 1 ½-inch squares
6 large tomatoes, quartered
12 cloves garlic, peeled
12 pearl onions, or 3 large ones
  peeled and cut into 2-inch cubes
12 white button mushrooms
12 bay leaves

MARINADE
1 large onion, peeled and sliced
1 cup red wine vinegar
½ cup olive oil
1 teaspoon freshly ground pepper
1 tablespoon salt
1 cup fresh oregano, chopped,
  or 1 ½ tablespoons dried oregano

FOR COOKING AND GARNISH
12 bamboo skewers soaked in water for 2 hours
1 cup plain yogurt
1 package (12 ounces) of lavash bread
Bunch of fresh scallions
Bunch of fresh basil

....

1. Combine all the marinade ingredients in a large, shallow, glass baking dish.

2. Thread each piece of meat onto the bamboo skewers, alternating them with pieces of green pepper, tomato, garlic, onions, mushrooms and bay leaves. Place the skewers in the marinade. Tilt the baking dish and with a spoon, baste all the skewers with the marinade. Cover the dish and marinate the kababs in the refrigerator for at least eight hours.

3. Heat the grill about 30 minutes in advance so the fire is good and hot.

4. When the grill is hot, place the skewers on the grill. Cook for 3 to 5 minutes on each side, turning frequently and basting with the remaining marinade.

5. Serve with lavash bread, yogurt, and fresh scallions and basil.

ADAPTED FROM NAJMIEH BATMANGLIJ

SWEET AND SOUR STUFFED CHICKEN

(makes 4-6 servings)

2 Cornish game hens
  or 2 small frying chickens
2 ½ teaspoons salt
1 tablespoon oil
1 large onion, peeled and thinly
  sliced
2 cloves garlic
1 cup pitted prunes, finely chopped
1 apple, cored and finely chopped

1 cup dried apricots, finely chopped
½ cup raisins
¼ teaspoon pepper
1 teaspoon cinnamon
¼ teaspoon ground saffron,
  dissolved in 2 tablespoons
  hot water
1 teaspoon sugar
½ cup orange juice

1. Preheat oven to 350°.

2. Clean and rinse the hens or chickens in cold water and rub with ½ teaspoon of salt.

3. Heat the oil in a non-stick skillet and brown the onion and garlic. Add all the chopped fruit and raisins, the remaining 2 teaspoons salt, the pepper, cinnamon, saffron water, and sugar. Mix well and let cool.

4. Stuff the hens or chickens with the fruit mixture and truss the cavities shut.

5. Place the stuffed birds in a greased ovenproof dish or roasting pan and pour in the orange juice. Cover and bake for 1½ hours, basting with the pan juices until the birds are golden brown and the meat separates easily from the bone.

ADAPTED FROM NAJMIEH BATMANGLIJ

CHELOW BA POLOW PAZ
Saffron Steamed Plain Basmati Rice

(makes 6 servings)

This rice looks and tastes wonderful because it has a crunchy, golden crust on the bottom and the color is white with yellow streaks.

3 cups long grain white basmati rice
4 cups cold water
1 tablespoon salt

4 tablespoons vegetable oil or butter
¼ teaspoon ground saffron threads, dissolved in 1 tablespoon hot water

1. Cover the rice with water in a large bowl. Move the rice around with your hand and let it settle. Pour off the water which will be white because it now contains the starch from the rice. Repeat two more times until the water is no longer cloudy.

2. In a rice cooker, combine the rice, water, salt, and oil. Gently stir with a wooden spoon until the salt has dissolved. Start the rice cooker.

3. When the rice is done cooking, pour the saffron water over the rice, covering as much of the surface as you can. Then unplug the rice cooker, but keep it covered for 10 minutes more.

4. Remove the lid, hold the serving platter tightly over the pot and turn the two upside down so the rice comes out as a large molded "cake".

5. Cut the rice in wedges and serve garnished with herbs.

ADAPTED FROM NAJMIEH BATMANGLIJ

YAKH DAR BEHESHT
Paradise Custard

(makes 4 servings)

6 tablespoons cornstarch
4 cups milk
1 cup sugar
10 cardamom pods, lightly crushed
¼ cup rose water*
⅓ cups slivered unsalted almonds, toasted

1. In a saucepan, dissolve the cornstarch in the milk, and add the sugar.

2. Cook over medium heat for 5 to 10 minutes, stirring constantly until the mixture has thickened.

3. Add the cardamom seeds and rose water. Stir constantly with a wire whisk to prevent sticking and lumping. Cook until the mixture reaches the consistency of a pudding. (It will thicken a little more as it cools.) Remove from heat.

4. Transfer the custard to a serving dish. Garnish with toasted almonds.

5. Chill the custard in the refrigerator for at least ½ hour and serve it cold.

* Available in Middle Eastern markets

ADAPTED FROM NAJMIEH BATMANGLIJ

Hava Volman

Israel

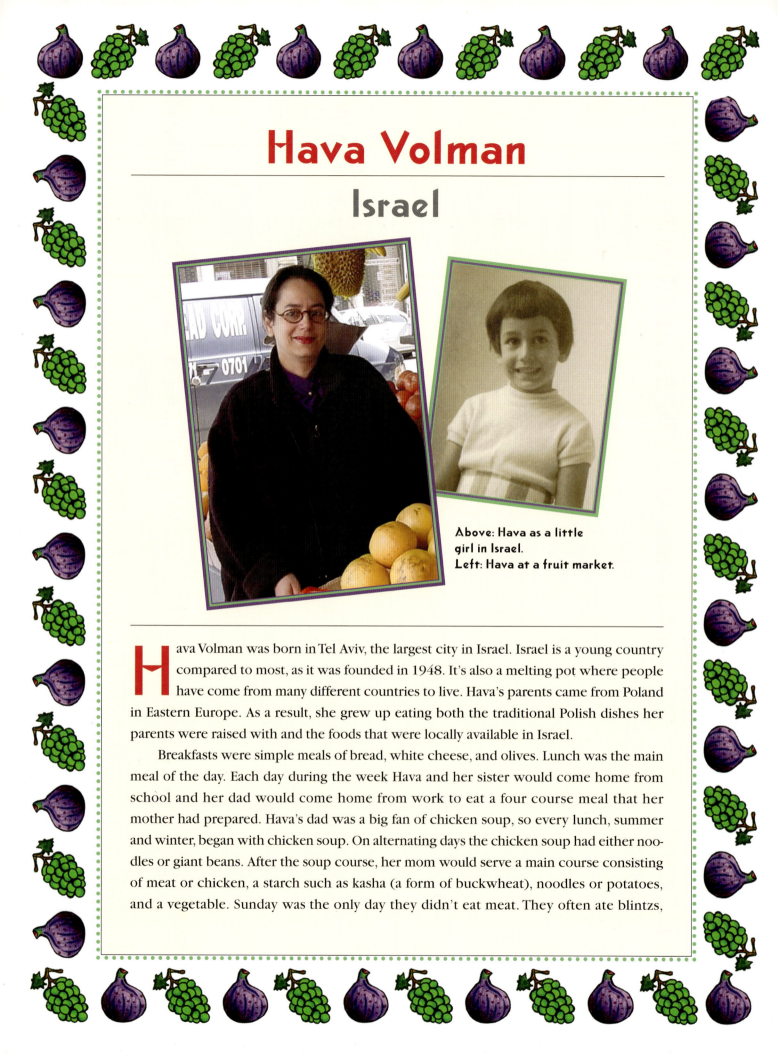

Above: Hava as a little girl in Israel.
Left: Hava at a fruit market.

Hava Volman was born in Tel Aviv, the largest city in Israel. Israel is a young country compared to most, as it was founded in 1948. It's also a melting pot where people have come from many different countries to live. Hava's parents came from Poland in Eastern Europe. As a result, she grew up eating both the traditional Polish dishes her parents were raised with and the foods that were locally available in Israel.

Breakfasts were simple meals of bread, white cheese, and olives. Lunch was the main meal of the day. Each day during the week Hava and her sister would come home from school and her dad would come home from work to eat a four course meal that her mother had prepared. Hava's dad was a big fan of chicken soup, so every lunch, summer and winter, began with chicken soup. On alternating days the chicken soup had either noodles or giant beans. After the soup course, her mom would serve a main course consisting of meat or chicken, a starch such as kasha (a form of buckwheat), noodles or potatoes, and a vegetable. Sunday was the only day they didn't eat meat. They often ate blintzs, which are thin pancakes rolled around a sweet, cheese filling, then browned in butter, and topped with sour cream or fruit sauce.

Fruit, in some form, was customary for dessert: in winter it was usually stewed, dried fruit called compote, and in summer, fresh fruit salad. On Shabbat, the Sabbath day of rest, Hava's mom made chocolate or white cake. During the week-long Jewish holiday of Passover, when regular flour and leavened cakes were not allowed, the favorite dessert was a delicious kind of layer cake made with matzohs (a large, flat, square-shaped cracker), chocolate ganache frosting, and crumbled up halvah, a very popular, sweet, sesame paste candy. For the Jewish New Year in September, honey cake was a tradition. The honey symbolizes the hope for a sweet New Year.

Because they didn't have a car, Hava's mom had to take the bus to the city's large, open-air market where she'd buy whatever foods were fresh and in season. The whole family always looked forward to the first fruits of each season. The fruits that Hava and her family enjoyed most were loquats, strawberries, clementines, and her very favorite, pomegranates. Each pomegranate has 613 seeds. Pomegranates have special significance because there were 613 good deeds mentioned in the Jewish bible called the Torah. Another treat was the fresh grape juice that her mother made by crushing the recently harvested grapes and straining their sweet liquid.

One of Hava's fondest childhood food memories was eating corn on the cob at the beach in Israel. There vendors had enormous pots filled with corn that boiled, it seemed, for hours. Even now when Hava eats corn on the cob, it reminds her of summers at the beach in Israel. Another favorite snack was bourekas, a flaky dough stuffed with leftovers such as mushrooms or

Israeli Irrigation

Israel has a warm, dry, desert climate similar to California's. Fruits and vegetables flourish there, provided they get sufficient fresh water. Because Israel borders the Mediterranean Sea, which is a large salt water body, Israeli's have learned how to remove the salt from the water so it can be used for irrigation. This irrigation has turned their desert into a "Garden of Eden".

mashed potatoes, baked in the oven until golden brown.

When Hava was a child, she dreamed of becoming a famous painter. In Israel, every girl has to serve in the army. After spending the requisite two years in the service, Hava studied painting at the Israeli Institute of Art. Following graduation, she started her own fashion business making men's clothes. This proved to be a difficult way to earn a living. In rethinking her career, she decided to become a chef instead. That meant going back to school: this time to cooking school. Like many good cooking schools all over the world, Hava first had to study classic French cooking. Soon after graduation, she met her husband and moved to New York where she became a caterer.

For a number of years Hava was the private chef to the Israeli ambassador to the United Nations. She's catered many special events for the Israeli consulate and other clients. Her specialty is Mediterranean cooking with lots of vegetable and grain dishes.

Perhaps the most popular food in all of Israel is falafel: round fritters made from ground

chickpeas that are fried, then stuffed into pita bread with shredded lettuce and chopped tomatoes, and topped with a creamy sesame sauce called tahini. It's considered street food because vendors sell it from their carts in cities all over the country. Schnitzel, a European import, is also very popular. Unlike Eastern Europe where the Schnitzel is often made from veal, in Israel chicken cutlets are primarily used. The cutlets are pounded very thin, breaded and pan-fried.

FALAFEL
Chickpea Fritters

(makes 4 servings)

1 cup dried chickpeas, soaked
    for 24 hours in water to
    cover
1 onion, finely chopped
3 cloves of garlic, minced
¼ cup fresh parsley,
    finely chopped
¼ cup fresh cilantro,
    finely chopped
1 ½ teaspoons salt
2 teaspoons ground cumin
1 teaspoon ground coriander
¼ teaspoon ground
    cardamom
1 teaspoon baking powder
¼ teaspoon black pepper
2 tablespoons of water
Canola oil for frying

FOR THE "SANDWICH"
4 pita (pocket) breads, cut in
    half and warmed briefly in
    the microwave just before
    serving
1 cup chopped tomatoes
1 ½ cups shredded lettuce
Tahini sauce

1. Drain the chickpeas to remove all the water.

2. Grind the chickpeas in a food processor until very fine.

3. In a bowl, add the onion, garlic, parsley, cilantro, and spices to the ground chickpeas. Mix well. Add the two tablespoons of water and set aside for 1 hour.

4. In a deep pot, heat 3 inches of canola oil until it reaches 350°. Fry the falafel (about six at a time to prevent crowding), until golden brown (3-4 minutes).

5. Transfer with a slotted spoon to paper towels to drain.

6. To eat, place several falafel in a pita pocket half, sprinkle with chopped tomatoes and shredded lettuce, and pour one or two tablespoons tahini sauce over it.

TAHINI SAUCE
1 cup tahini (sesame seed paste sold in glass jars)
Juice of ½ lemon
¼ cup water
½ teaspoon salt
¼ teaspoon pepper

1. Mix the ingredients together in a bowl to make a creamy sauce.

ADAPTED FROM HAVA VOLMAN

SCHNITZEL
Breaded Chicken Cutlets

(makes 4 servings)

4 chicken breasts (boneless & skinless), pounded flat
2 large eggs, beaten
2 tablespoons mustard
½ teaspoon salt
¼ teaspoon pepper
½ cup flour
1 cup bread crumbs
Oil for frying

1. Mix beaten eggs with mustard, salt, and pepper.

2. Coat the chicken breast with flour.

3. Dip chicken in the egg mixture.

4. Cover each cutlet with the bread crumbs.

5. Heat about 1 tablespoon of oil in a large frying pan. Fry each chicken breast on both sides until golden brown and cooked through; about 4-5 minutes per side.

6. Transfer chicken to a preheated 350°oven for 10 minutes.

ADAPTED FROM HAVA VOLMAN

HONEY CAKE

(makes 2 4"x8" loaves)

While honey cake can be eaten any time of the year, it is customarily eaten during the Jewish New Year in September. The honey symbolizes the wish for a sweet new year. These make wonderful gifts.

4 eggs
1 cup sugar
½ cup vegetable oil
1 cup honey
1 teaspoon grated orange rind
1 cup fresh orange juice

2 ½ cups flour
3 teaspoons baking powder
½ teaspoon baking soda
½ teaspoon salt
1 ½ teaspoons cinnamon
1 cup chopped walnuts or pecans

1. Preheat oven to 350°.

2. Grease and flour two 4"x8" loaf pans.

3. Beat the eggs, sugar, vegetable oil, and honey in an electric mixer for about 4 minutes.

4. Add the orange juice and grated orange rind.

5. Combine the remaining dry ingredients and add them to the liquid mixture.

6. Bake for at least 1 hour. Test for doneness by inserting a toothpick or knife. If it comes out clean, the cakes are done. Cool before removing from pans.

ADAPTED FROM HAVA VOLMAN

ISRAELI FRUIT SALAD

(makes 4–6 servings)

2 large navel oranges
1 pint strawberries
⅓ cup raisins
1 ripe banana

1. With a serrated knife, cut away the outside peel of the orange. Using the orange membranes as a guide, remove the individual orange sections. Place in a medium-size serving bowl.

2. Wash and dry the strawberries. Cut them in half. Add to the orange sections.

3. Add the raisins.

4. Just before serving, slice the banana and toss with the other fruit.

ADAPTED FROM HAVA VOLMAN

Hebrew/English Translations

anavim	grapes	marak-of	chicken soup
te'anim	figs	salat	salad
d'vash	honey	yay'in	wine
uga	cake	egozim	nuts
perot	fruit	itriyot	noodles

AFRICA

Colette Rossant

Egypt

Yeworkwoha "Workye" Ephrem

Ethiopia

Kitty Morse

Morocco

Pierre Thiam

Senegal

Mark Henegan

South Africa

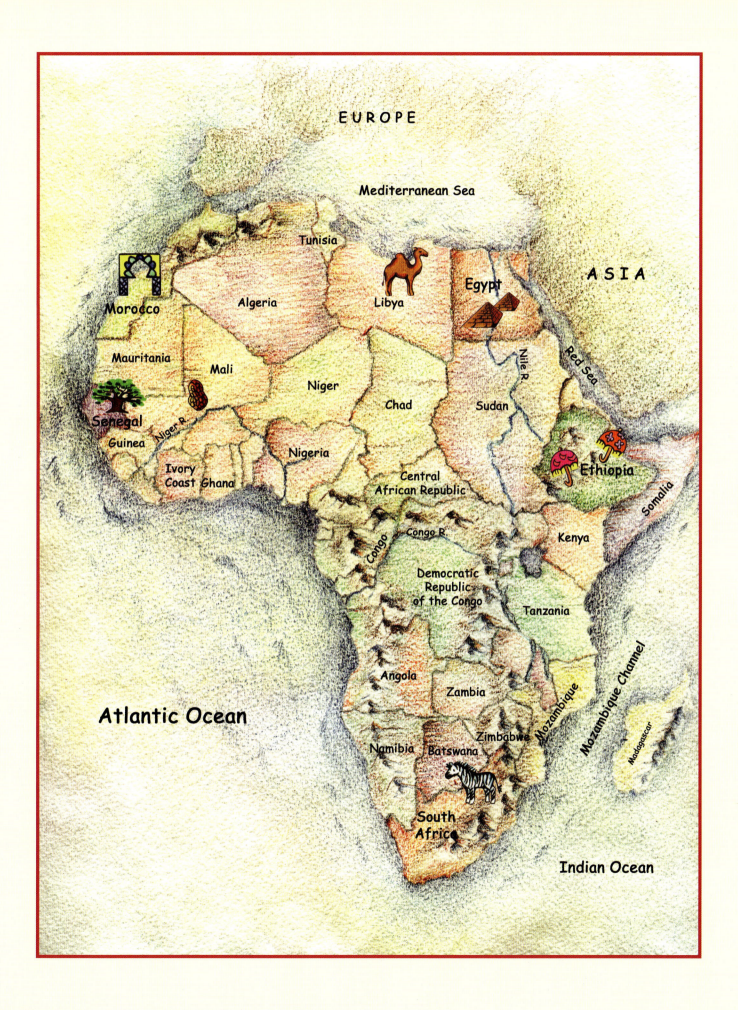

EUROPE

Mediterranean Sea

ASIA

Tunisia

Libya

Egypt

Morocco

Algeria

Mauritania

Mali

Niger

Chad

Sudan

Nile R.

Red Sea

Senegal

Niger R.

Guinea

Ivory
Coast Ghana

Nigeria

Ethiopia

Somalia

Central
African Republic

Congo

Congo R.

Kenya

Democratic
Republic
of the Congo

Tanzania

Angola

Zambia

Mozambique

Mozambique Channel

Madagascar

Atlantic Ocean

Zimbabwe

Namibia Batswana

South
Africa

Indian Ocean

Colette Rossant

Egypt

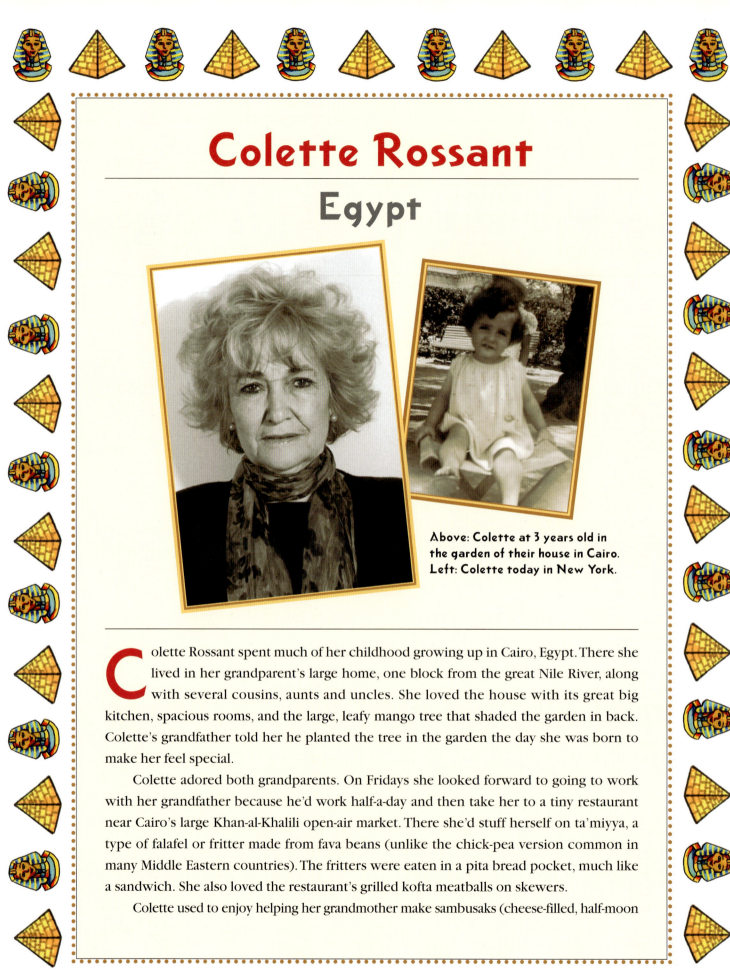

Above: Colette at 3 years old in the garden of their house in Cairo.
Left: Colette today in New York.

Colette Rossant spent much of her childhood growing up in Cairo, Egypt. There she lived in her grandparent's large home, one block from the great Nile River, along with several cousins, aunts and uncles. She loved the house with its great big kitchen, spacious rooms, and the large, leafy mango tree that shaded the garden in back. Colette's grandfather told her he planted the tree in the garden the day she was born to make her feel special.

Colette adored both grandparents. On Fridays she looked forward to going to work with her grandfather because he'd work half-a-day and then take her to a tiny restaurant near Cairo's large Khan-al-Khalili open-air market. There she'd stuff herself on ta'miyya, a type of falafel or fritter made from fava beans (unlike the chick-pea version common in many Middle Eastern countries). The fritters were eaten in a pita bread pocket, much like a sandwich. She also loved the restaurant's grilled kofta meatballs on skewers.

Colette used to enjoy helping her grandmother make sambusaks (cheese-filled, half-moon shaped turnovers), while her grandmother sang songs in Arabic. The recipe, which was hundreds of years old, never varied. Colette liked mixing and kneading the dough, rolling it out, cutting the circles, depositing the fillings, and folding and sealing them. The best part of all was eating the flaky, golden sambusaks. They were always served when company came to the house, including at her grandparents' poker games.

Ahmet was the family's very kind and wonderful cook, whom Colette adored. She would often sneak into the kitchen (where she was not usually allowed because it was considered unladylike), hop onto a stool, and watch Ahmet work his magic. Ahmet's son, Abdullah, became Colette's best friend. While Ahmet went food shopping every day, once a week Abdullah, would accompany Colette and her grandmother to the open-air market.

The market overflowed with vendors selling every type of fresh food imaginable. Colette's grandmother would buy fresh fish and chicken; meats, such as lamb or goat; fruits, like watermelons and mangoes; vegetables, such as eggplant and okra; nuts, like pistachios and walnuts; seeds, such as sesame, melon or sunflower; and dried fruits, like apricots, prunes or raisins. At the end of the day, Abdullah's arms would be very tired; and her grandmother's car would be extremely full!

Ahmet often cooked a dish called ful medames, a fava bean stew, for the household staff. He always saved some for Colette, who was not supposed to eat it. Colette loved ful medames for two reasons: the taste was delicious, and eating it made her feel closer to Ahmet and the other servants, and more a part of their world.

When Colette was twenty-two, she married an American named James Rossant and soon

Pyramids of Egypt

The ancient pyramids of Egypt served as tombs for the Egyptian royal family. The largest, the Pyramid of Khufu, was built around 2600 B.C. It was made of approximately 2.5 million enormous limestone blocks, each weighing on average 5,000 pounds.

King Tut

Tutankhamun became King in 1343 B.C. when he was only 9 years old. He died at the age of 18. Beautiful treasures were discovered in his tomb. Many are now on display at the Egyptian Museum in Cairo.

after, the couple moved to the United States. She became a professor of French literature at Hofstra University in Long Island, New York and proceeded to raise four wonderful children. Colette always loved cooking with her kids. When she came home from teaching between 4:00 and 5:00 every day, cooking was a way for the family to be together. Her kids wanted "real" cooking jobs, and so she trained them to cook "real foods" at a very young age.

One of her children developed a learning disability and had difficulty making friends. To encourage other children to come and play, Colette created a secret cooking school at her house on Saturday mornings. Each Saturday they would prepare two dishes: one to eat at her house and one to take home to their families.

The classes became so popular, that other parents who had heard about them started calling

and asking if their kids could attend. It was suggested that Colette open a larger and more formalized cooking school for children on Saturdays, and she agreed it was a good idea. To qualify for the school, the children had to be tall enough to be able to see the inside of the pot on the stove when standing flat on their feet (not on their tiptoes). She called the school "Z Cooking School" because with her French accent, the way she said "the" sounded like "Z".

One Saturday, the *New York Times* newspaper devoted an entire page to Colette's cooking school; and the next thing she knew, she had a children's TV cooking show on PBS called *Colette Z Cooking*. On each show there were eight different guests: four girls and four boys. The kids made "grown-up" foods, like goose for Christmas, the Egyptian dish chicken with leeks that her grandmother used to make, or a dessert of baked prunes stuffed with walnuts that was her aunt's specialty. Colette's TV show ran for several years.

Since the cooking show, Colette has written several cookbooks and traveled extensively to Japan and China, becoming an expert on both types of cooking. She's done specials for PBS, and written for *Vogue, Saveur,* and other magazines and newspapers. A few years ago Colette wrote a beautiful book about her childhood entitled *Memories of a Lost Egypt... A Memoir with Recipes*. Colette has just introduced a wonderful sequel entitled *Return to Paris*. What follows are the recipes for some of Colette's favorite childhood dishes.

SAMBUSAKS
Cheese-Filled Turnovers

(makes 20)

These are fun to make and the dough is a pleasure to work with.

PASTRY

½ cup melted butter
½ cup vegetable oil
½ cup hot water

A pinch of salt
3 cups of flour

1. Combine the melted butter, vegetable oil, hot water, and salt in a bowl.

2. Stir in two cups of flour and mix to incorporate. Turn the dough onto a floured board and add one more cup of flour. Knead the dough until it holds together; it will be soft, but not sticky.

3. Shape into a ball, wrap in plastic, and refrigerate for at least 30 minutes.

FILLING

11 ounces crumbled feta cheese
2 tablespoons grated Parmesan
    cheese

2 eggs
4 teaspoons baking powder
A pinch of pepper

1. Place all the filling ingredients in a food processor and pulse until light and creamy.

ASSEMBLY

Dough
Filling
2 eggs beaten

1. Preheat oven to 375°

2. Divide the dough into 20 balls.

3. Flatten each ball and roll it into a 4-inch round on a floured surface.

4. Place a heaping tablespoon of filling in the center of each round. Brush the edges with water. Fold over, and press the edges with a fork to seal.

As you finish, place on a greased baking sheet.

5. Brush the top of each sambusak with the beaten egg.

6. Bake until golden brown, about 35 minutes. Serve warm.

ADAPTED FROM COLETTE ROSSANT

KOBEIBA
Lamb and Beef Meatballs

(makes about 4 dozen "good size" meatballs)

Lamb and bulgur make these meatballs different and delicious.

BEEF MIXTURE

1 pound (16 ounces) bulgur
2 pounds of ground round
2 medium onions, finely chopped
¼ cup finely chopped chicken fat or
    2 tablespoons olive oil

2 tablespoons pine nuts
1 teaspoon salt
½ teaspoon pepper

1. Cover the bulgur with water and soak for 20 minutes. Drain off any excess water.

2. Combine the bulgur, beef, chopped onions, chicken fat, pine nuts, and salt and pepper in a bowl. Mix it well.

LAMB MIXTURE

2 pounds of ground lamb	**½ teaspoon salt**
2 medium onions, grated	**¼ teaspoon pepper**
2 tablespoons lemon juice	

Combine the lamb, grated onion, lemon juice, salt, and pepper in a bowl and mix well.

TO ASSEMBLE

1. Wet your hands.

2. Take a piece of the beef mixture about the size of a walnut. Place it in the palm of your hand and pat it into a large, flat circle. Place a similar size portion of the lamb mixture in the center. Close your hand to envelop the lamb in the outer beef layer. Shape into a ball. Repeat until you have used all the meat. Any lamb you have left over you can make into a "lamburger".

3. Heat 2 tablespoons of oil in a large skillet. Fry the kobeiba until golden brown and cooked through. Drain on paper towels. They go well with rice.

ADAPTED FROM COLETTE ROSSANT

ROAST CHICKEN ON A BED OF LEEKS

(makes 4–6 servings)

1 whole 5-pound chicken	**2 pounds leeks**
2 tablespoons olive oil	**2 tablespoons butter**
1 tablespoon lemon juice	**3 cups chicken broth,**
2 tablespoons fresh tarragon	**plus ½ cup more**
Salt and pepper to taste	

1. Preheat oven to 375°.

2. Mix together the olive oil, lemon juice, tarragon, and salt and pepper.

3. Rub the chicken inside and out with this mixture.

4. Remove the outer leaves from two pounds of leeks and wash them well. Finely chop two of the leeks and slide them under as much of the skin as you can.

5. Cut the remaining leeks into 1-inch pieces, place them in a roasting pan, sprinkle the leeks with salt and pepper and dot with the two tablespoons of butter.

6. Place the chicken on top of the leeks, add the chicken broth, and roast in the oven for 1 hour and 30 minutes or until golden brown and cooked through. Check from time and add water if the leeks are drying out.

7. Carve the chicken into serving pieces and place on a platter.

8. Stir the leeks on the bottom of the pan, and add up to ½ cup more of chicken stock to make a sauce to pour over the chicken.

ADAPTED FROM COLETTE ROSSANT

PRUNES STUFFED WITH WALNUTS IN A LIGHT CINNAMON SAUCE

(makes 8 servings)

This is one of the simplest and most delicious recipes in the book. The prunes will last for several weeks in the refrigerator (if they're not eaten by then!).

2 cups dried large prunes, pitted
2 cups hot tea
1 cup of walnuts halves (approximately)
½ cup sugar
¼ teaspoon cinnamon
Whipped cream

1. Soak the prunes in the hot tea for two hours.

2. Drain the prunes, reserving the liquid.

3. Stuff a walnut half into each prune. If the prunes are small, you'll have to use smaller walnut pieces. Place the prunes in a serving dish.

4. Pour the tea into a saucepan, add the sugar and cinnamon, and bring to a boil. Lower the heat and simmer for 10 minutes.

5. Pour the hot tea mixture over the prunes and refrigerate for at least 2 hours.

6. Serve with whipped cream.

ADAPTED FROM COLETTE ROSSANT

Yeworkwoha Ephrem (Nickname "Workye")

Ethiopia

Above: Workye at age 2.
Left: A picture of workye in her national dress.

Workye Ephrem illustrates the adage "If at first you don't succeed, try, try again" better than almost anyone I know. Workye came to New York from Ethiopia, in eastern Africa, with her young children and sister in 1979, shortly after the Emperor Haile Selassie was overthrown. Both sisters always loved cooking, having learned by watching their grandmother. To support themselves they decided to open the first Ethiopian restaurant in New York City. Unfortunately, the restaurant did not have enough customers and was forced to close after only one year.

Workye then took a job at the United Nations in Manhattan, where she worked for 18 years until her children were grown. At that point she decided it was time to try opening an Ethiopian restaurant again, since her kids were grown and she could now give the business her full attention. In 1998 Workye opened a restaurant called Ghenet "Where Angels Eat" in

Soho, New York. By this time, New Yorkers had become more adventurous in their eating and were ready for African food. Happily, Workye's restaurant has became very successful.

For years Workye cooked for her own children and taught them how to prepare food for themselves. She knows which foods Ethiopian children like to eat and which foods American kids enjoy when they come to her restaurant. The most common and most popular Ethiopian food of all is injera bread. It's a special flatbread, somewhat similar to a tortilla, with a sourdough flavor and a somewhat "spongy" texture. It's made from teff, a form of millet that's the smallest and oldest grain on earth. The grain is ground into flour, mixed with water, and allowed to ferment for three or four days. Then the batter is poured onto a very large, circular griddle, as much as two feet wide in diameter. It looks like a cross between a giant tortilla press and a French crêpe griddle. As the injera cooks, bubbles appear on the surface, giving the bread its spongy texture. The common way to eat injera bread is by tearing off a piece and wrapping it around stew, lentils, or the popular bean dip, shiro aletcha. Then you pop the "package" you've created into your mouth.

Shiro aletcha is made from a special mixture of soybeans, chickpeas, kidney beans, and herbs such as thyme, basil, garlic, and onions. The beans, which have been sun dried, are ground together and then boiled with water until the mixture becomes a thick paste or dip. It's high in protein and extremely nutritious. Rich, poor, young, and old, all love Shiro aletcha.

Lamb is the most popular form of meat in Ethiopia. In winter time the lamb stew called beg aletcha is a favorite with kids. Aletcha means mild. That's because many stews in Ethiopia are made with the fiery hot spice mixture called berberé, and those stews are often too spicy for children. Because of the small pieces of meat in the dish and the delicious sauce, kids love beg aletcha; and it goes well with injera bread which absorbs the gravy. Like poor people's food all over the world, most Ethiopian dishes are cooked long and slow to make the meat softer and blend the flavors.

Since meat is a treat, there are many vegetarian dishes in Ethiopia. One of Workye's favorites as a child was yeatkelt wett, a mixture of cabbage, onions, carrots, and potatoes sautéed with mild spices. It's satisfying, delicious, and a great dish for vegetarians.

Ethiopian desserts are simple, often consisting of sweet, ripe, tropical fruits such as pineapple, banana, and papaya. Kids also enjoy sucking on the stalks of fresh sugar cane for the sweet juice inside, or dipping whole-wheat buns in honey, a common ingredient in Ethiopian cooking.

Maskal

One of the most widely celebrated and most colorful festivals in Ethiopia is the Christian holiday Maskal, in celebration of the finding of the true cross, in late September. Christianity is the dominant religion in Ethiopia. In every town, priests and dignitaries march through the streets in a procession carrying beautiful, colorful umbrellas that are decorated and fringed with gold.

YESHIRO ALETCHA
Bean Dip

(makes 4 servings)

This bean dip is very nutritious because it's high in protein. It's also versatile: you can dip pieces of injera bread in it, spread it on toast, serve it as a dip for vegetables or chips, or you can thin it slightly and serve it as a sauce over rice. The special powder that's used is already spiced. It can be purchased by mail order by contacting Workye's website: ghenet.com, or by calling the restaurant at (212)343-1888.

1 cup shiro aletcha powder (spices included in the mix)
3 cups of water

3 tablespoons vegetable oil
¼ teaspoon salt, or more to taste

1. Bring the water to a boil in a medium saucepan and then add the vegetable oil.

2. Remove the pot from the fire and sprinkle the shiro aletcha powder over the water. Stir it with a whisk, making sure there are no lumps.

3. Return the pot to the fire and keep on whisking until it gets to the consistency of a béchamel sauce.

4. Lower the heat, cover the pot, and cook it for about 10 minutes more, until it has the thickness of sour cream. Check for salt, and let it cool if serving as a dip. If serving as a sauce over rice, don't cook it quite as long, and serve it hot.

ADAPTED FROM WORKYE EPHREM

YEATELT WETT
Winter Vegetable Medley

(makes 4 servings)

1 medium red onion,
   cut in ¾-inch pieces
2 carrots, peeled and cut
   in ¾-inch pieces
1 large potato,
   cut in ½-inch pieces
¼ of a small green cabbage,
   cut in ¾-inch pieces
2 tablespoons vegetable oil

1 cup water
1 teaspoon minced fresh garlic
1 teaspoon minced ginger
¼ teaspoon of turmeric
½ teaspoon salt
¼ teaspoon pepper
1 plum tomato (optional),
   cut in small pieces

1. Heat the oil in a medium saucepan. Add the onion and sauté until it becomes translucent. Add the minced garlic, ginger, and turmeric and continue to cook over medium heat until it starts to stick to the pot.

2. Add the carrots and enough water so the vegetables don't stick. Stir the vegetables, cover, and cook for about 5 minutes more.

3. Add the cabbage and tomato, salt, and pepper and cook approximately 5 minutes more, until cooked through. Add a little more water if necessary. There should be a little sauce, but the vegetables should not be watery.

4. Add the potatoes and a little bit of water so they don't stick. Cover the potatoes with a lid and cook for about 10-15 minutes, or until the potatoes are tender when pierced with a fork.

ADAPTED FROM WORKYE EPHREM

YEBEG ALETCHA
Lamb Stew

(makes 4-6 servings)

Kids in Ethiopia like this dish best when it is soupy. They add small pieces of injera bread to absorb the delicious flavor of the gravy. For a thicker gravy and a dish that's more stew-like, use half the water.

2 pounds (32 ounces) leg of lamb,
   cut in small pieces and washed
4 medium red onions, chopped fine
4 tablespoons vegetable oil
2 teaspoons minced garlic
2 teaspoons minced ginger

2-4 cups of water (see
   step 2 below)
1 teaspoon salt
½ teaspoon turmeric
2 tablespoons chopped fresh
   basil (optional)

1. In a large pot sauté the onion, garlic, ginger, and turmeric in the oil until they become translucent.

2. Add the leg of lamb and 4 cups of water if making the "soupy" version, and 2 cups of water if making the more "stew-like" version.

3. Cover and simmer over low heat until the meat is cooked, about one hour.

4. Remove from heat, check to see if it needs more salt, and sprinkle with fresh basil.

5. Serve in bowls, accompanied by injera or pita-type bread.

ADAPTED FROM WORKYE EPHREM

ETHIOPIAN FRUIT SALAD

(makes 6 servings)

1 ripe mango, peeled and
   cut in pieces
1 small, ripe papaya, peeled
   and cut in pieces

1 navel orange, peel removed
   and cut in sections
1 ½ cups seedless grapes
1 banana, sliced

Combine all the cut up fruit. Add the banana at the last minute.

ADAPTED FROM WORKYE EPHREM

Ethiopian/English Translations

sega	beef	shinkurt	onion
gomen	collard greens	aletcha	mild stew
doro	chicken	wet	stew
dinich	potato	selatta	salad
birtukan	orange	mouz	banana

Kitty Morse

Morocco

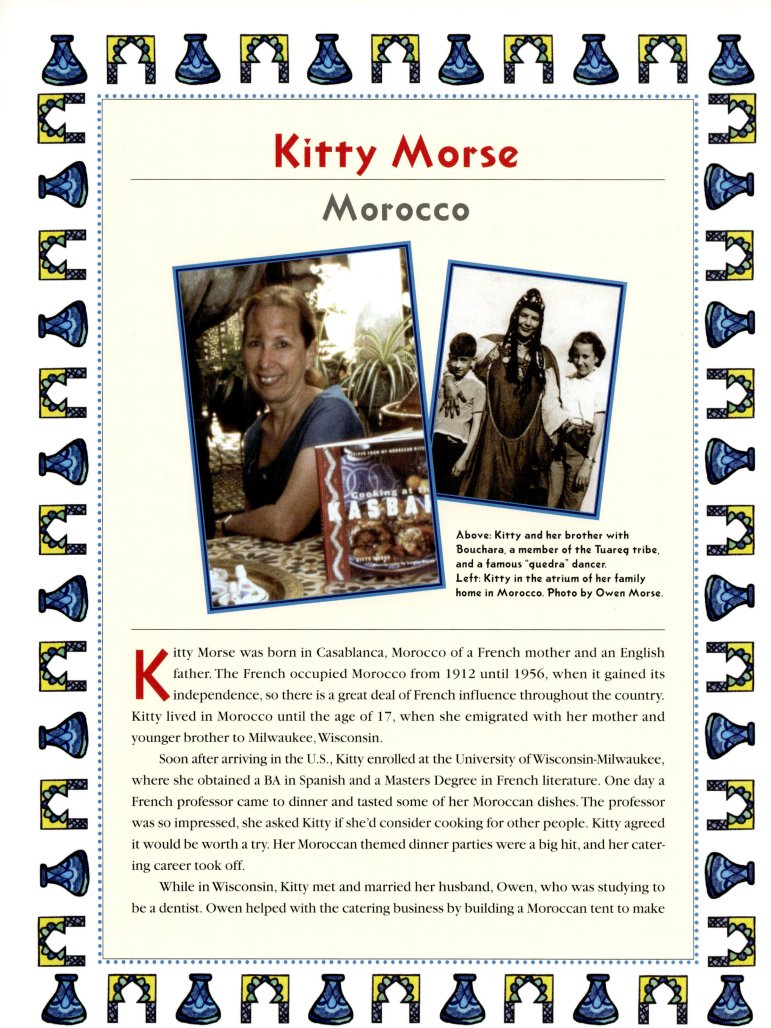

Above: Kitty and her brother with Bouchara, a member of the Tuareg tribe, and a famous "guedra" dancer.
Left: Kitty in the atrium of her family home in Morocco. Photo by Owen Morse.

Kitty Morse was born in Casablanca, Morocco of a French mother and an English father. The French occupied Morocco from 1912 until 1956, when it gained its independence, so there is a great deal of French influence throughout the country. Kitty lived in Morocco until the age of 17, when she emigrated with her mother and younger brother to Milwaukee, Wisconsin.

Soon after arriving in the U.S., Kitty enrolled at the University of Wisconsin-Milwaukee, where she obtained a BA in Spanish and a Masters Degree in French literature. One day a French professor came to dinner and tasted some of her Moroccan dishes. The professor was so impressed, she asked Kitty if she'd consider cooking for other people. Kitty agreed it would be worth a try. Her Moroccan themed dinner parties were a big hit, and her catering career took off.

While in Wisconsin, Kitty met and married her husband, Owen, who was studying to be a dentist. Owen helped with the catering business by building a Moroccan tent to make

Kitty's parties more colorful and festive. On the day of a party, the two would empty their client's living room of furniture and set up the tent. They created an authentic Moroccan atmosphere by lining the floor with Moroccan rugs, placing low round tables inside the tent, and surrounding them with fluffy pillows for their guests to sit on. They often hired a belly dancer, and Kitty even designed Moroccan style invitations. Sometimes, to complete the theme, the hostess would ask her guests to come dressed in Moroccan costumes. Because of the fun atmosphere and wonderful seven course meals Kitty prepared, her business grew through word of mouth.

After Owen's graduation from dental school, he joined the United States Navy. The Navy sent them to Morocco for two years which made Kitty extremely happy! It gave her the opportunity to be closer to her dad, and also to gather more recipes from family and friends in Morocco.

When Kitty and Owen returned to California, she thought it would be fun to have a cooking show on television. One day she walked into her local cable TV station in the San Diego area (cable TV was in its infancy then) and said to the producer, "I'd like to do a cooking show and I think I can do a good job." The producer agreed to give her a try and soon, *Food, Etc.* went on the air.

When her weekly show ended a year later, Kitty decided to write a cookbook. She tested many of the recipes in her kitchen in California, and also in Morocco when she went to visit her father. Because she wanted the book to be beautiful, she asked twelve of Morocco's leading painters to contribute their artwork. *Come with me to the Kasbah: a Cook's Tour of Morocco* was published in Casablanca in 1989. (A Kasbah is an ancient walled city.) Kitty has written eight other cookbooks since then.

Tagine Dish

A tagine dish is a unique earthenware cooking vessel with a cone-shaped lid that's often beautifully decorated. Many Moroccans eat the tagine stew out of this communal dish. They sop up the sauce with small morsels of bread.

In 1983, Kitty was asked to take a group of people from America on a tour of her native country. Since that time, she's led over 18 tours to Morocco. The groups travel all over the country, visit local markets and taste regional dishes. Kitty also gives a cooking class for her guests at her dad's home, a restored Pasha's (governor's) residence in the ancient town of Azemmour, one hour south of Casablanca.

Kitty has been a guest speaker on Moroccan food and culture at the Smithsonian Institute in Washington, D.C., and she teaches cooking at professional cooking schools around the country. She also writes articles for newspapers and magazines.

When Kitty was young, she often accompanied her mother or grandmother to the beautiful Marché Central (Central Market) in Casablanca. Each stall sold something different. Her mother might have to go to five different vendors to buy five different ingredients. What a surprise it was when she walked into a supermarket on her first trip to America and found thousands of items under one roof!

Growing up, Kitty always looked forward to visiting her French grandmother. One of her favorite meals was her grandmother's roast chicken with tarragon (a fragrant herb that's

Horseshoe Arch

The distinctive Islamic horseshoe arch decorates many of the doorways of structures all over Morocco. Beautiful, colorful, geometric patterns often adorn the building walls that surround the arches.

popular in French cooking), accompanied by creamy, puréed potatoes.

Kitty also adored couscous, Morocco's national dish. Couscous is to Moroccans what rice is to the Chinese. In Morocco, families traditionally eat couscous on Friday, the Muslim day of rest. Couscous is made from durum wheat semolina. The tiny granules are steamed in a special pot called a "couscoussier" in French. To serve couscous, the steamed granules are mounded on a large platter and topped with vegetables and meat. The platter is placed in the center of the table so everyone can eat out of it using their fingers, as is customary in many Moroccan homes. Moroccans use only the first three fingers of their right hand: the thumb, pointer, and index fingers. They roll the couscous into little balls, and then swiftly pop them into their mouth with a flick of the thumb.

Couscous can be prepared in many different ways. Kitty's favorite was a sweet couscous mixed with raisins and fried almonds called seffa, which is served on special occasions. Almond paste, used in confections and pastries, was a festive treat enjoyed during a variety of holidays.

Another of Kitty's favorite dishes was a stew called a tagine. There are hundreds of variations of this one-dish meal. To make a tagine, you combine meat, chicken, or fish, with vegetables, and often fresh or dried fruits, as well as spices. Moroccan cooks place the ingredients in a special, conical-shaped tagine dish.

Instead of soda or coffee, Kitty preferred mint tea, the national drink of Morocco. This special tea is made with Chinese green tea, a generous amount of fresh spearmint leaves, and lots of sugar. It is supposed to be syrupy and sweet! Here are a few recipes to help you put on your own Moroccan party, using some of Kitty's favorite childhood dishes.

SALAD OF TOMATOES AND CUCUMBERS

(makes 4 servings)

1 large cucumber, peeled
   and finely diced
2 ripe tomatoes, chopped
½ green pepper, seeded
   and finely diced
1 tablespoon minced cilantro leaves

2 tablespoons olive oil
2 teaspoons fresh lemon juice
Salt and freshly ground pepper
   to taste

1. In a serving bowl, combine the cucumber, tomatoes, peppers, cilantro, olive oil, lemon juice, salt, and pepper.

2. Serve at room temperature.

ADAPTED FROM KITTY MORSE

SWEET COUSCOUS

(makes 4 servings)

4 tablespoons butter
1 cup slivered almonds
1 ⅓ cups water
½ teaspoon salt
½ cup (about 3 ounces) raisins

1 cup couscous
3 tablespoons granulated sugar
¼ cup ground cinnamon
¼ cup confectioner's sugar

1. In a medium skillet, heat 3 tablespoons of the butter over medium-high heat. Fry the almonds, stirring occasionally, until golden brown, about 5 to 6 minutes. Set aside.

2. In a medium sauce pan over medium heat, bring the water, salt, raisins, and remaining butter to a boil. Add the couscous in a stream. Stir once. Remove from the heat. Cover and let stand until the couscous is tender, 12 to 15 minutes. Transfer the couscous to a bowl. Stir in the granulated sugar and fluff with a fork.

3. Heap the couscous into a conical mound in the center of a serving platter. Decorate the mound from the peak to the base, with alternating "spokes" of almonds, cinnamon, and confectioner's sugar. Serve warm with several saucers of sugar and cinnamon, so that more can be added to taste.

ADAPTED FROM KITTY MORSE

DATES FILLED WITH ALMOND PASTE

(makes about 30)

Serve this traditional dessert with a glass of mint tea. They're fun and easy to prepare. Stuffed dates make a great gift, as well! You'll have to start these the day before you intend to serve them, to give the almond paste time to soften. You'll find almond paste in the baking section of supermarkets.

7 ounces pure almond paste
Finely grated rind of 1 lemon
30 large pitted dates
Granulated sugar, for coating

1. The day before you plan to serve the dates, place the almond paste in a sealed container or plastic bag along with a slice of fresh bread, and let it stand overnight. This will soften the almond paste so it will be malleable.

2. With your hands, combine the almond paste with the lemon zest until the mixture is smooth.

3. Mold a heaping teaspoon of the paste into a spindle shape, and stuff each date. Squeeze the sides so the paste bulges out slightly at the top.

4. Place the sugar in a saucer. Roll the date in the sugar to coat. Continue until all the dates are filled. They will keep for up to a month in an airtight container in the refrigerator.

ADAPTED FROM KITTY MORSE

MINT TEA

(makes 5 cups)

2 teaspoons Chinese green tea
5 cups boiling water
½ cup granulated sugar
1 bunch fresh spearmint (common backyard mint),
  rinsed under running water

1. Place the tea and the boiling water in a teapot. Let steep for 2 minutes.

2. Add the sugar and mint and let stand for 2-3 minutes.

3. Serve immediately.

ADAPTED FROM KITTY MORSE

Arabic/English Translations

a'tai	tea	guirga	walnut
nah'na	mint	l'looz	almond
matisha	tomato	t'mer	date
l'mekla	meal	souk	market
moussem	celebration	tobsil	dish (plate)

Pierre Thiam

Senegal

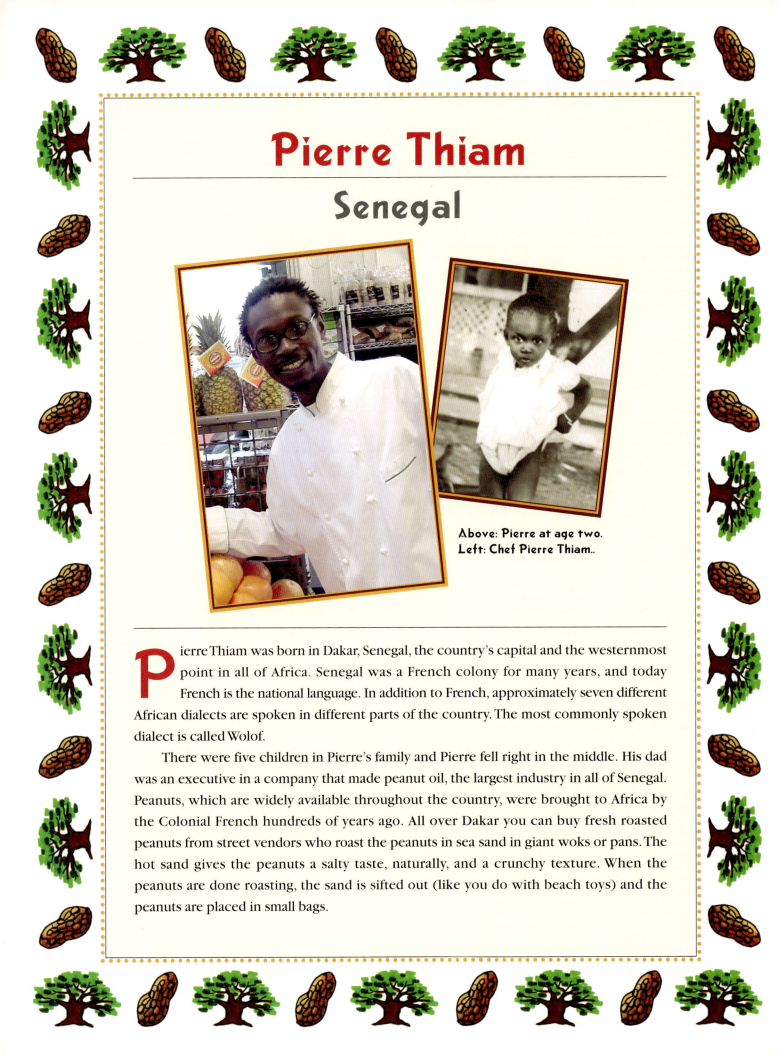

Above: Pierre at age two.
Left: Chef Pierre Thiam..

Pierre Thiam was born in Dakar, Senegal, the country's capital and the westernmost point in all of Africa. Senegal was a French colony for many years, and today French is the national language. In addition to French, approximately seven different African dialects are spoken in different parts of the country. The most commonly spoken dialect is called Wolof.

There were five children in Pierre's family and Pierre fell right in the middle. His dad was an executive in a company that made peanut oil, the largest industry in all of Senegal. Peanuts, which are widely available throughout the country, were brought to Africa by the Colonial French hundreds of years ago. All over Dakar you can buy fresh roasted peanuts from street vendors who roast the peanuts in sea sand in giant woks or pans. The hot sand gives the peanuts a salty taste, naturally, and a crunchy texture. When the peanuts are done roasting, the sand is sifted out (like you do with beach toys) and the peanuts are placed in small bags.

Another popular snack in Senegal is akara or black-eyed pea fritters. Black-eyed peas got their name because they have a black spot in the middle of each pea that looks like an eye. The peas, which often come dried, are first soaked for hours to soften them. Then they're mashed into a thick paste with a little salt and dropped into hot oil where they fry up into crunchy, little balls that look like donut holes. They're sold from carts on street corners all over West Africa, accompanied by a tomato, onion dipping sauce.

It seems that every event in Senegal is an occasion for celebration. When an old person dies, there is an elaborate feast to celebrate the person's entire life's accomplishments. A very well-known Senegalese poem talks about how the souls of one's ancestors remain with you even after they die. The poem says you can hear their voices in the wind or in the water if you just listen. It reminds me of the way Simba's father spoke to him from the heavens in the Disney movie, *The Lion King*.

Another special occasion is the baby naming ceremony where a dish called Lakh is traditionally served. It's a sweet, hot cereal made with millet (a small, round, yellow grain), raisins, sour cream, milk, sugar, and vanilla. For birthdays, a very popular dessert called Thiakry is customary. It's made with couscous (a type of wheat in grain form), yogurt, pineapple, sugar, and other fruits.

In Dakar, most households eat both French and Senegalese dishes. Breakfast consists of long, narrow, French breads called baguettes served with butter and jam, as well as coffee or tea. Lunch is most often Senegalese, with dishes like Mafé, a stew made with vegetables and chicken or lamb in a peanut butter and tomato based sauce, or the national dish called Tiébou Dienn that's made of fish stuffed with herbs and

Baobab Tree

The fruit of the baobab tree, Senegal's national tree, is called monkey bread because monkeys love to hang from the trees' branches. There are compartments within the outer shell that protect the sweet and juicy fruit inside.

Peanuts

When peanuts are fresh and just harvested, they're made into a snack by boiling them in their pods. The peanuts are eaten by squeezing them out of their shells and popping them into your mouth.

spices served over delicious tomato rice. Dinners consist of either Senegalese or French dishes.

For dessert, kids love to eat the fruit of the Baobab tree, Senegal's national tree. The fruit is sometimes combined with milk and sugar to make a special drink. Another dessert is mangos lightly poached in a sweet ginger and vanilla flavored syrup. The mangos in syrup taste great plain, or served over vanilla ice cream.

In Senegal, it's common for people to celebrate each other's holidays. Christians and Muslims invite each other to their homes to share in their feasts and their customs.

Pierre remembers first becoming interested in cooking when he was only five years old. His mother had a set of French cookbooks, and while the other kids would play outside, he would spend hours sitting in the corner of his living room looking through the pictures of food. In Senegal, Pierre grew up with French, West African

and even Vietnamese cooking. The only man he saw cooking as a child was his half-Vietnamese, half-Senegalese uncle, who loved to cook Vietnamese food. Years ago Senegal was a French colony and the Senegalese people were considered French citizens. As a result, many Senegalese men were sent to Vietnam to fight in the French army. Some like Pierre's uncle were born and raised in Vietnam by Vietnamese mothers, and then moved back with them to Senegal when the war started in the 60's.

Since it was considered a woman's place to be in the kitchen in Senegal, and a man didn't really have the option of being a chef as a career, Pierre studied the other subjects that interested him most: chemistry, physics and math. After two years in college in Senegal, Pierre decided to study business at New York University. To help pay for his expenses, he took a job working in a restaurant kitchen and found he really liked the work. He trained in a variety of restaurants around New York City until he developed his own cooking style.

Today Pierre has his own catering company in New York City called Sage and he recently opened a new modern, Senegalese restaurant in Brooklyn named Yolêlê, which means "Let's Play". He cooks food for parties and special dinners at museums, universities, and people's homes. Because of all the influences he experienced growing up in Senegal, different styles of cooking come naturally to Pierre and as a result, he prepares dishes from many different countries. When Pierre plans a menu with his clients, he can make almost any style of food they like depending on the theme of the party. In addition to catering, Pierre sometimes gives lectures and demonstrations about African cooking at the Museum of African Art in New York City, and he's recently hosted a TV program for French television featuring the foods and neighborhoods of New York City.

What follows are some of Pierre's favorite childhood dishes.

AKARA
Black-eye Pea Fritters

(makes about 40 fritters)

These remind me of falafel, but they're less spicy and they have a wonderfully crunchy exterior. They taste best when fresh and hot. The tomato onion sauce is very simple and it makes a great complement to the fritters. Because the peas need to soak a long time to soften, you should start these either the night before or the morning before you intend to make them.

FRITTERS
1 pound (16 ounces) dried black-eyed peas
2 teaspoons salt
2 cups peanut or vegetable oil

1. Soak peas over night, or all day.

2. In a blender or food processor, briefly chop the dried peas with a little water. Be careful not to over process.

3. Remove peas from food processor and place them in a large bowl of cold water. Let soak two more hours. Rub them vigorously with your hands to remove the black-eyed skins. The skins will float to the top. Skim them off.

4. Repeat two more times in fresh water until most of the peas are white.

5. Drain peas and return them to the blender or food processor and process to a paste. The mixture should be loose, but not runny.

6. Add oil to a medium-size saucepan to a depth of about 3 inches. Heat over medium heat and when hot, drop level tablespoon-size portions into the oil. Don't cook more than about 6 at a time, so as not to crowd them. Fry until the akara turn golden brown. Drain on paper towels. (A wonderful tool for making falafel (Israel) and these akara is a tablespoon-size, squeezable, ice cream scoop.)

7. Serve with tomato onion sauce.

TOMATO ONION SAUCE

One medium onion, finely chopped
3 tablespoons peanut or vegetable oil
¼ cup tomato paste

1 teaspoon chili powder
Water (about 1 ¼ cups)
Salt and pepper to taste

1. Heat 3 tablespoons of oil in a medium-size pan. Add the onion and cook until slightly brown.

2. Add tomato paste and chili powder and gradually dilute with enough water to achieve the consistency of tomato sauce.

3. Season with salt and pepper to taste.

ADAPTED FROM PIERRE THIAM

MAFÉ
Chicken and Vegetable Stew in Peanut Butter Tomato Sauce

(makes 4 servings)

¼ cup peanut or vegetable oil
½ cup peanut butter or "tigadege" (roasted peanut paste)
3-pound chicken cut in eighths
1 large onion, chopped
¼ cup tomato paste
1 large tomato, chopped
1 teaspoon salt

½ pound potato (one large one)

1 small cabbage, cut in ½-inch pieces (or 6 Brussel sprouts)

½ pound carrots, peeled and cut into small chunks

1 small butternut squash, peeled and cut into ½-inch pieces
   (or 6 patty pans, cut in half)

1 scotch bonnet pepper, whole (optional)

3 tablespoons Thai or Vietnamese fish sauce

1. In a large pot, heat oil until hot and brown chicken pieces on all sides. Remove chicken temporarily.

2. In the same frying pan, add the onions and stir until soft and slightly brown. Add the tomato paste and salt, and stir well.

3. Add all the prepared vegetables and fish sauce to the pot. Return the chicken to the pot and add just enough water to cover. Bring to a boil, stir, and reduce heat to medium. Simmer for approximately 30 minutes. Check the vegetables to avoid overcooking, removing them in a bowl as they are done.

4. When all the vegetables are cooked and removed from the stew, add the peanut butter or "tigadege", 1 tablespoon at a time to make sure it is well dissolved in the broth. Add the scotch bonnet pepper (if using) and simmer until broth thickens, about 20 to 30 minutes.

5. Return all the vegetables to the pot and simmer 5 minutes more.

6. Serve over white rice.

ADAPTED FROM PIERRE THIAM

THIACRI
Sweet Couscous with Yogurt, Pineapple, and Raisins

(makes 4-6 servings)

This makes a wonderful breakfast, a light lunch, or a satisfying dessert.

¾ cup couscous (millet or wheat)

1 tablespoon butter, cut in small pieces

1 cup crushed pineapple or pineapple chunks, drained, from a 20 ounce can (save the juice for the liquid below)

Drained pineapple juice plus enough water to make 1 cup liquid

¼ cup honey (more if you like)

1 ½ cups (12 ounces) plain yogurt

⅓ cup raisins, soaked in warm water until plump

Mint leaves for garnish

1. Bring the pineapple juice and water mixture to a boil. Remove from heat and add the couscous and butter. Mix until the butter is melted. Cover and let sit until all the liquid is absorbed. Stir with a fork to separate the grains. Let cool.

2. Sweeten yogurt with honey and add the raisins and pineapple.

3. Fold the yogurt mixture into the couscous and garnish with mint.

ADAPTED FROM PIERRE THIAM

MANGOS IN GINGER AND VANILLA SYRUP

(makes 4-6 servings)

3 large mangos
1 cup of water
1 cup sugar
1 vanilla bean (or 1 teaspoon vanilla extract)
1-inch piece of fresh ginger, peeled and sliced

1. Peel and slice the mangoes into ⅓ inch slices.

2. Put water, sugar, and ginger in a saucepan and bring to a boil.

3. If you're using a vanilla bean, split it open lengthwise and with a small knife, scrape the soft center into the syrup along with the long outer pod.

4. Reduce heat to low and add the mango slices. Let simmer for 5 minutes if the mangos are ripe, and 10 minutes if they're not ripe. When done, remove the mangos with a slotted spoon and arrange them in a shallow serving bowl.

5. Raise the heat beneath the saucepan and reduce the remaining liquid to a thick syrup. When thickened, remove from heat and discard the vanilla pod and ginger slices. If you're using vanilla extract, mix it in at this point. Pour syrup over mango slices.

6. Serve warm or cold. It's delicious over vanilla ice cream or plain yogurt.

ADAPTED FROM PIERRE THIAM

Mark Henegan

South Africa

Above: A picture of the
Chef childhood or school picture.
Left: A picture of the Chef
in their chef's coat.

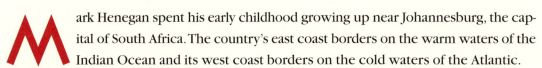

Mark Henegan spent his early childhood growing up near Johannesburg, the capital of South Africa. The country's east coast borders on the warm waters of the Indian Ocean and its west coast borders on the cold waters of the Atlantic.

In 1652 the Dutch who worked for the East India Trading Company trading European goods for Asian spices, silks, and teas, created the first white settlement in Cape Town, at the southwest tip of South Africa. The Cape of Good Hope, as it was called, was halfway between the Far East and Holland. Because the climate was good and the land was fertile, the Dutch could supply fresh food for the sailors for their long voyage back to Europe. To farm the land, slaves were brought from the East Indies (Malaysia, Java, and Sumatra) and from East Africa. The Dutch who settled the area became known as Afrikaners. Even though they were a minority, they ruled parts of the country for several hundred years.

Later the Dutch were joined by the French Huguenots who came in search of religious freedom. In 1814 when the British came and took over the Cape area, the Afrikaners moved inland where they discovered valuable gold and diamond mines. In the 1860's the British brought still more slaves to South Africa, primarily from India, to work on the sugar plantations.

Before the foreigners came, a number of large native African tribes lived in different parts of what is today South Africa. These included the Zulu, Xhosa, Sotho, Ndebele, Swazi, and Venda tribes. They still live in South Africa and are an extremely important part of the country's culture. For many years the native peoples were treated very poorly, forced to live and be educated separately from whites, and banned from owning property. In 1994 a new constitution was written, with a Bill of Fundamental Rights that provides for equal treatment of everyone, regardless of race, color, religion, or sex. Today there are at least 11 different languages spoken in South Africa and the cooking is a blend of all the different influences.

While Mark enjoyed his mother's English cooking, he preferred the foods prepared by his Zulu nanny which were tastier, spicier, more varied, and interesting. As a kid, Mark enjoyed visiting his grandmother who lived on a small plot of land nearby. He loved her chicken, which she roasted with garlic and other seasonings and stuffed with grapefruit. The chickens ran around her yard and when she was ready to cook one, she'd give thanks to god for the blessing of food and then kill and clean the chicken. All meals started with a prayer of thanks.

Eating in South Africa was very communal. The native peoples ate with their hands, sharing from a large plate in the middle of the table. A very common dish was pap, served with gravy, curry, or stew. Pap was a thick, cornmeal porridge, almost the consistency of soft play dough, only more grainy in texture. Everyone would take a little bit of the mixture, role it into a ball, and dip it into the gravy or stew to sop up the sauce. Since food was eaten with the fingers, it was very important to have clean hands. There was always a bowl of water and lemon juice on the table to wash your hands before eating.

Another favorite dish was bunny chow. Bunny chow was a hollowed out half loaf of bread placed on its end, almost like a tall, steep bowl. The bread served as a container for a variety of foods like French fries, stews, or curries. The inside bread would be scooped out, the filling placed inside, and the bread placed back on top of the filling. Small pieces of the bread would be broken off and dipped in the sauce or stew. The dish was named bunny chow because rabbits were fed in a similar way. Their feed was put into a bread "container" to keep it from getting wet on the bottom. Bread in South Africa was plentiful!

When Mark was in high school, he moved to Durban, a city on the Indian Ocean where many Indian people had settled. There his dad opened a coffee shop or café where he served English food such as sandwiches, Indian inspired curries, and dishes from his native Portugal. Here Mark was exposed to the life of a restaurant owner and he liked it. After graduating from high school, Mark had to serve in the South African Army. Because he was opposed to violence, he was placed as a cook in the army kitchen, and he enjoyed the work. After finishing his service, he was encouraged to visit America by his sister, who had come to the U.S. to take care of small children. Mark spent a number of years traveling and working in restaurants in Hawaii, California, Arizona, and New York and finally decided to settle in Brooklyn, New York.

One day a small store became available across the street from where he lived. For a long

time he'd dreamed of opening his own restaurant. He had very little money, but his sister gave him a loan. He named the restaurant Madiba, the nickname for Nelson Mandela, the leader of the new South Africa who won the Nobel Peace Prize for encouraging all the people of the country to live together in peace and harmony. Madiba means "son of Africa, father of a nation".

When it first opened, Madiba was so small, there wasn't room for a kitchen. Mark would cook the food in his apartment and bring it to the restaurant. People liked the food and fun atmosphere. Soon the space next door became available and the restaurant expanded. Today Madiba, the only South African restaurant in New York City, is very popular.

Besides the interesting, different, and delicious food, the restaurant is a lot of fun. Outside the front door is a South African Airlines, little kid airplane ride. Inside, the restaurant is decorated with objects Mark treasured from his childhood including the little suitcases he took to school, animal prints, flags of the country, and South African art. There's also a pantry where South African grocery products are sold. Customers eat at small desks and drink from mason jars. The waiters and waitresses sometimes sing and do a Zulu line dance, and on Friday nights there's South African music. Some of the cast from the Broadway show, *The Lion King,* even come to perform.

Mark has not forgotten his homeland. He helps raise money for a school for disabled children in South Africa, a children's educational fund for orphans, and for South Africa's disabled athletes in the international Achilles Sports Competitions.

What follows are some of Mark's favorite childhood dishes.

GEEL RYS
Yellow Rice

(makes 4-6 servings)

3 tablespoons vegetable oil
2 cups long grain white rice
2 sticks cinnamon
2 tablespoons brown sugar
1 ½ teaspoons salt
1 teaspoon turmeric
1 cup raisins

Heat the oil in a medium-size pot. Pour in the rice and stir to coat completely. Add remaining ingredients, bring to a boil, cover and let simmer over low heat until all the water is absorbed.

BOBOTIE
Curried Meatloaf

(makes 6 servings)

This is one of South Africa's national dishes. It's the contribution of the country's Malay people.

2 tablespoons cooking oil
2 pounds ground beef or lamb
  or a combination
1 large onion, chopped fine
  (about 1 ½ cups)
2 cloves of garlic, minced
2 tablespoons curry powder
1 teaspoon turmeric
1 tablespoon brown sugar
1 ½ teaspoon salt
½ teaspoon black pepper

1 slice white bread
1 cup milk
Juice of ½ lemon
3 eggs
½ cup dried apricots, diced
⅓ cup raisins
1 apple, peeled and finely
  chopped
¼ cup slivered almonds,
  lightly toasted

1. Preheat oven to 325°.

2. Pour milk into a small bowl. Tear bread into pieces and soak in the milk.

3. In a large frying pan, heat the oil and fry the onion and garlic until translucent. Mix in the curry powder, brown sugar, turmeric, salt and pepper and cook for two minutes.

4. In a large bowl, beat one of the eggs. Add the meat, the onion mixture, the apple, dried apricots, raisins, almonds, and lemon juice.

5. Squeeze the milk out of the bread. Reserve the milk and add the bread pieces to the meat mixture. Mix well.

6. Butter a 3-quart soufflé dish and fill it with the meat mixture, packing it down like a meatloaf.

7. Beat the remaining two eggs with the remaining milk. Pour it over the meat mixture.

8. Bake approximately one hour. The custard on top should be golden brown and the meat inside no longer pink.

ADAPTED BY MARK HENEGAN

GREEN MEALIE BREAD
Corn Pudding Loaf

(makes 4-6 servings)

3 tablespoons butter, melted
4 ½ cups corn kernels (fresh, frozen, or canned, drained)
3 eggs
3 tablespoons sugar
3 tablespoons flour
3 teaspoons double-acting baking powder
1 ½ teaspoons salt

1. Preheat oven to 375°.

2. Line a 9" x 5" loaf pan with aluminum foil and grease the foil.

3. Combine the remaining ingredients in a food processor until the corn is gritty and still has some texture.

4. Pour into the prepared loaf pan.

5. Bake for at least one hour. A toothpick inserted in the center should come out clean and the top should be golden brown.

6. Let cool in the pan for at least ½ hour.

7. To unmold, place a plate over the loaf pan, and turn upside down. Carefully remove foil and slice.

ADAPTED BY MARK HENEGAN

KOESISTERS
Braided Doughnuts with Cinnamon-and-Lemon Syrup

(makes about 48)

Koesisters were brought to South African by the Dutch or Afrikaaners who settled there. They're fun to make because you braid each one. Koesisters are incredibly delicious and addictive when they're fresh and warm.

SYRUP

3 cups sugar
1 ½ cups water
3 cinnamon sticks
2 tablespoons lemon juice

Grated rind of half a lemon
¼ teaspoon salt
¼ teaspoon cream of tartar mixed
   with 2 teaspoons water

1. Add the sugar, water, cinnamon stick, lemon juice, lemon rind, and salt to a medium-size saucepan. Cook over low heat until the sugar is dissolved.

2. Add the cream of tartar mixture and stir well. Raise the heat to medium-high and cook the liquid uncovered and undisturbed until it forms what looks like a fishing line when a small amount is dropped into ice water. Watch the mixture carefully as it will caramelize and turn brown fairly quickly. If the mixture becomes too hard and brittle, it won't be usable.

3. When ready, remove from the heat and dip the outside of the pan into a cold water bath to stop the cooking process. Remove the cinnamon sticks and allow to cool to room temperature.

DOUGHNUTS

4 cups all-purpose flour
4 teaspoons baking powder
½ teaspoon ground cinnamon
½ teaspoon ground nutmeg
½ teaspoon salt
4 tablespoons cold butter
1 ½ cups buttermilk
Vegetable oil for frying

1. Mix together the dry ingredients in a food processor.

2. Add the cold butter, cut into small pieces, and process until incorporated into the dry mix.

3. Add the buttermilk through the mixer chute and process until a dough is formed. Turn the dough onto a floured surface and knead the mixture until it's soft and malleable. Divide the dough into two balls.

4. Roll the first ball on a floured surface into a 12" x 6" rectangle. With a sharp knife or a pizza wheel, cut the rectangle in half so you have two rectangles that are 12" x 3" each. Now cut each half into 12, 1" by 3" strips. Leaving about ¼-inch joined at the top, cut each little strip so you have three "braidable" arms. Braid the little doughnut and pinch both ends tightly so they don't unravel. Braid them all and repeat with the second ball of dough.

5. Pour vegetable oil to depth of about 3 inches in a large, heavy saucepan. Heat the oil to a temperature of 375°. When the oil is hot, fry the doughnuts about 6 at a time, making sure not to crowd them. When golden brown on one side, flip them over to brown on the other. When done, remove and drain on paper towels.

6. While they're still hot, dip them in the syrup. Drain on a rack with paper towels underneath to catch the drippings.

ADAPTED BY MARK HENEGAN

EUROPE

Madeleine Kamman

France

Inez Bon

France

Holland

Hans Röckenwagner

Germany

Piero Selvaggio

Italy

Alexis Bakouros

Greece

Teresa Barrenechea

Spain

Marcus Samuelsson

Sweden

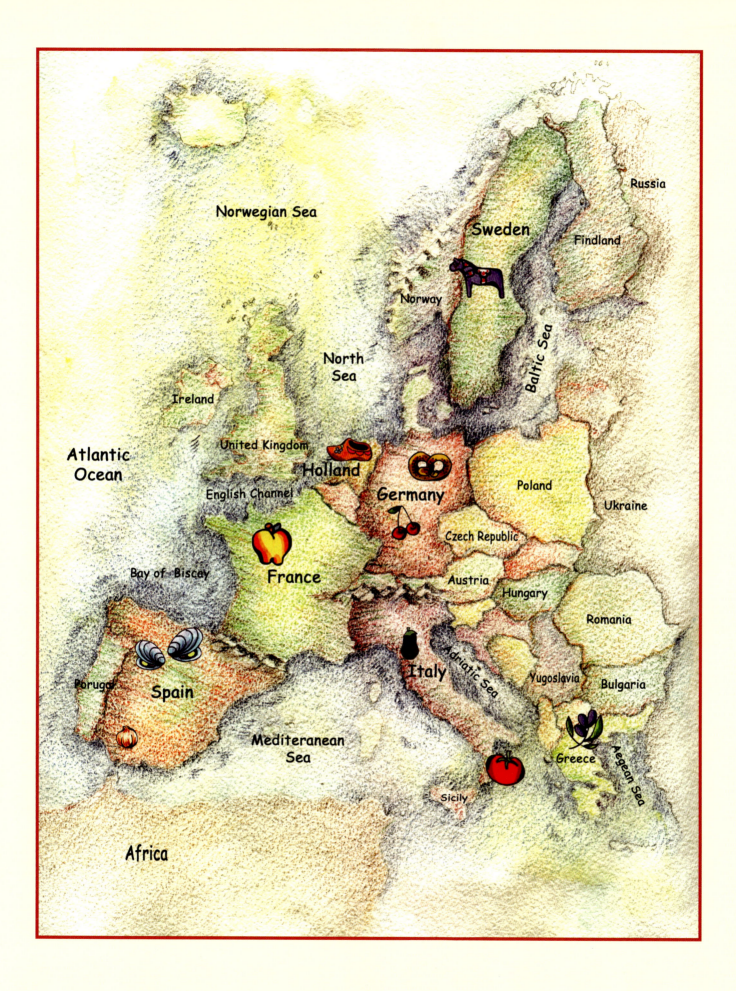

Madeleine Kamman

France

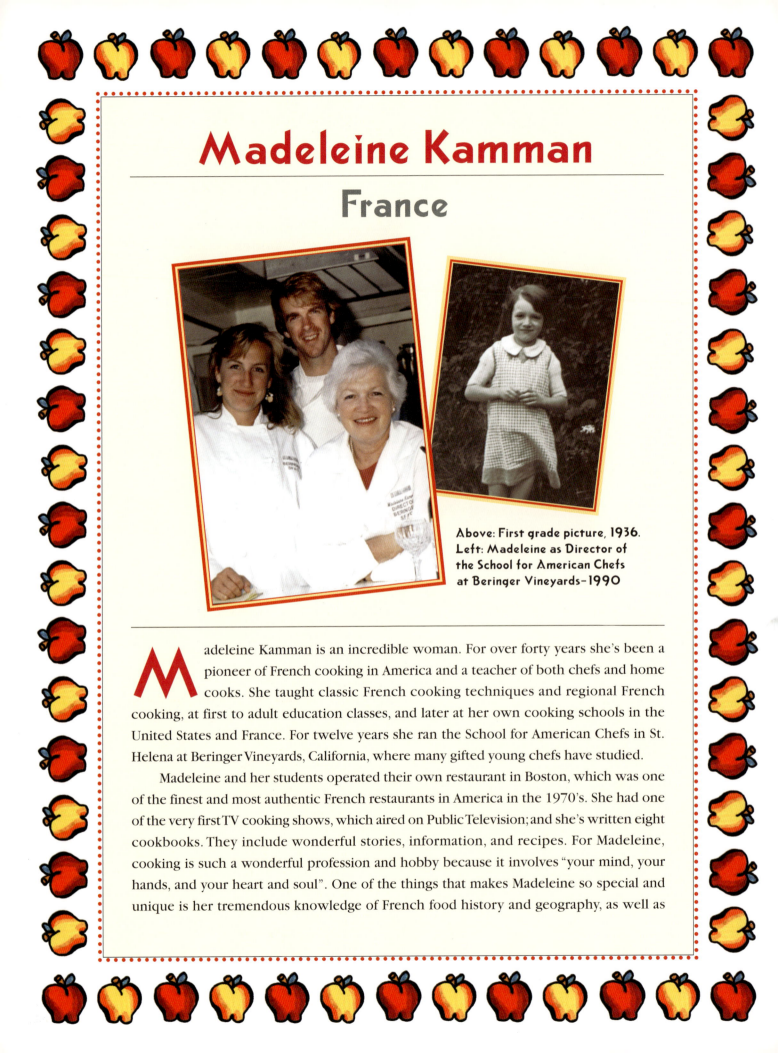

Above: First grade picture, 1936.
Left: Madeleine as Director of
the School for American Chefs
at Beringer Vineyards–1990

Madeleine Kamman is an incredible woman. For over forty years she's been a pioneer of French cooking in America and a teacher of both chefs and home cooks. She taught classic French cooking techniques and regional French cooking, at first to adult education classes, and later at her own cooking schools in the United States and France. For twelve years she ran the School for American Chefs in St. Helena at Beringer Vineyards, California, where many gifted young chefs have studied.

Madeleine and her students operated their own restaurant in Boston, which was one of the finest and most authentic French restaurants in America in the 1970's. She had one of the very first TV cooking shows, which aired on Public Television; and she's written eight cookbooks. They include wonderful stories, information, and recipes. For Madeleine, cooking is such a wonderful profession and hobby because it involves "your mind, your hands, and your heart and soul". One of the things that makes Madeleine so special and unique is her tremendous knowledge of French food history and geography, as well as food chemistry, physics, and anatomy (the structure of different parts of animals, fish, and poultry used in cooking).

Madeleine had a wonderfully rich childhood thanks to her experiences with people who loved her and taught her as she was growing up in France. Like most French children, she spent time with relatives in different parts of the country. They were all exceptional cooks who taught her a great deal about the cooking of the different regions of France.

On weekends, Madeleine's family liked to visit a friend named Henriette, who lived in the French province of Normandy, about a two-hour drive, northwest of Paris. Normandy's coast lies on the English Channel. The province is known for its rich green pastures. The cows that graze there produce milk that's made into wonderful cream, butter, and cheeses. Henriette owned two cows which she taught Madeleine how to milk. The first time Madeleine tried, the warm cow's milk missed the pail and sprayed all over her face. It didn't take long before she figured out how to do it properly.

Henriette made one of the local cheeses, the popular Camembert, from the cows' milk. To start the process, she warmed the milk slightly, and added rennet, which made the watery whey in the milk separate from the firmer curds. The curds were then placed in a mold with holes so the liquid could drain out. After a few hours, Henriette sprinkled the cheese with a special Camembert mold or bacteria that gave the cheese its unique taste. The cheese was then left to age for about six weeks. This allowed the mold to develop the white rind or skin on the outside and the smooth, creamy inside texture.

Normandy borders the English Channel and at low tide, the kids of the area often went to the

Normandy

In spring, the apple trees in Normandy are covered with blossoms that are beautiful to see and that perfume the air. In the fall, the air is fragrant with the smell of ripe apples which will soon be made into apple cider, tarts, jelly, apple butter, apple sugar, and the famous distilled spirit of Normandy, Calvados.

beach with pails to collect cockles or large mussels. They found the mussels stuck to rocks jutting out from the beach, or they would look for air holes in the sand under which the cockles would be hiding. Besides mussels, the children collected razor clams, tiny crabs, and starfish. A wide variety of fish and shrimp were also plentiful in the Channel. The seafood was made into wonderful soups, or it was broiled or sautéed, and often covered with a cream sauce. One of Madeleine's favorite dishes that Henriette made was pan-fried shrimp. To make the dish, whole shrimp were sautéed in brown butter and then combined with a simple cream sauce. As Madeleine recollects in her book *When French Women Cook,* "What a messy, delicious and happy feast that was for a bunch of loud kids".

Apples and hard apple cidre are used often in the cooking of Normandy. A side dish that Madeleine enjoyed as a kid was Brussels sprouts mixed with apples and spices and sautéed in butter.

Crêpes are an extremely popular, versatile, and fun-to-eat food that's made in Normandy and especially in Brittany, the province to the southwest of Normandy. Crêpes are about the

thinnest pancakes you can make (hence the name). They're cooked on a large, round, flat griddle using a special paddle to spread the batter as thinly as possible. At home, a large frying pan or a special crêpe pan is used instead of that griddle. After the crêpe is flipped over to cook on its second side, it's filled. In Brittany the four sides are folded in toward the middle, creating a square shape, which is then flipped over again, with the seamless side on top.

Crêpes come in two basic varieties: sweet and savory. The sweet crêpe batter is often made with sugar. In Normandy they're commonly filled with a type of apple butter called ramangerie, that's like a thick, concentrated, sweetened applesauce. If a watery applesauce is used, the crêpes will fall apart from the excess moisture.

For variety, the crêpes can also be spread with butter and sugar, or jam before folding.

The savory crêpes are often made with buckwheat flour. The filling choices are only limited by your imagination: cheese, ham, bacon, egg, cream-of-chicken and mushrooms, and spinach.

A simple but rich cookie, that children all over Normandy and Brittany love are Sablés. "Sablé" means sandy; so named because of the sandy texture of these cookies. The dough is pressed into the bottom of a round cake pan and is then scored into triangles or petticoat tail shapes and baked. This type of cookie was brought to Normandy by the Vikings hundreds of years ago.

Here for you to prepare, are the recipes for some of Madeleine's favorite childhood dishes.

CREVETTES À LA POÊLE
Pan-Fried Shrimp

(makes 4-6 servings)

2 lbs. whole, medium size shrimp (heads, tails and shells), unwashed (the sauce will cling better to the shrimp)	3 tablespoons minced shallots (optional)
	Salt and freshly ground black pepper to taste
2 tablespoons butter	⅔ cup heavy cream
	⅓ cup sour cream

1. Melt butter in a large frying pan over medium heat until it turns light brown, but doesn't burn. The brown butter gives a delicious flavor to the shrimp.

2. Sauté the shallots in the brown butter for about one minute. Add the shrimp and sauté over high heat until all the shells turn red.

Remove the pan from the heat, cover it with a lid and let it sit and steam for about three minutes. Place the cooked shrimp on a platter.

3. Add the cream and salt and pepper to taste to the pan, and cook over medium heat for about five minutes, or until the sauce is reduced by half.

4. Stir in the sour cream and then add the shrimp back into the pan to reheat and coat with the sauce.

5. Serve the shrimp with a loaf of fresh French bread. Eating the shrimp will be messy but fun because you'll have to remove the heads, tails, and shells. Use the bread to soak up any sauce left on your plate.

ADAPTED FROM MADELEINE KAMMAN

BRUSSELS SPROUTS WITH APPLES

(makes 4–6 servings)

My daughter didn't think she liked Brussels sprouts until she tried these. She immediately asked for seconds.

20 ounces Brussels sprouts, fresh or frozen
2 apples (you can try different varieties)
3 tablespoons butter
Salt and pepper to taste
¼-½ teaspoon of quatre-épices (spice mixture, below)

1. Let the Brussels sprouts thaw to room temperature. Peel and core the apples and cut them into ½-inch chunks.

2. Heat the butter in a large frying pan and sauté the apples until they turn golden brown (they'll look like home fries). Add the Brussels sprouts and toss them with the apples.

3. Sprinkle all with salt, pepper, and the quatre-épices. Cover the pan and cook over low heat until the sprouts are tender (a few minutes), stirring with a spatula to make sure they don't burn.

QUATRE-ÉPICES SPICE MIXTURE

This makes more than you will need for the Brussels sprouts recipe. It's also used in the crêpe recipe. The spice mixture will keep in a small, covered jar.

1 teaspoon ground cinnamon
2 teaspoons ground allspice
⅛ teaspoon ground cloves

½ teaspoon grated nutmeg
1 teaspoon ground coriander

Mix the spices. Store any extra in a small, enclosed container.

ADAPTED FROM MADELEINE KAMMAN

CRÊPES AU BEURRE DE POMMES

Crêpes with Appple Butter

(makes 10-12 crêpes)

1 cup sifted all-purpose flour
3 eggs
¼ teaspoon salt
¾ cup apple juice

¾ cup half-and-half cream
¼-½ teaspoon quatre-épices
    spice mixture (previous page)
¼ cup melted butter

1. Place flour in a bowl and make a well in the center. Break the eggs into the well and mix with a whisk.

2. Add the salt, then the apple juice and the half-and-half cream.

3. Add the spice mixture and the melted butter and let batter stand for 40 minutes at room temperature. This will allow the flour to be properly absorbed by the liquid and the batter will be very smooth.

4. To cook the crêpes, lightly butter a large frying pan or crêpe pan and heat until "hot". Swirl approximately ⅓ cup of batter all around the bottom of the pan, until it coats the entire bottom in an even layer. Cook for a few minutes until lightly browned on one side. Turn over with a spatula and cook another minute on the second side, until done.

5. Place on plate and spread with apple butter, butter and sugar, or jam.

6. Fold the four sides into the center to make a large square shape and flip over so the seams are on the bottom.

7. You can make your own delicious apple butter easily (see recipe below), or you can buy it already made in the grocery store.

BEURRE DE POMME (APPLE BUTTER)
16 oz. jar of cinnamon flavored apple sauce or 2 cups homemade applesauce
1 packed cup of brown sugar

Add brown sugar to applesauce in a small saucepan. Cook over low heat for approximately 45 minutes, until reduced by half, stirring often to prevent sticking. When ready, the mixture should be as thick as pudding. Store in a glass jar in the refrigerator.

ADAPTED FROM MADELEINE KAMMAN

SABLÉS NORMANDS SHORTBREAD

(makes 12 cookies)

1 cup sweet butter, plus 1 tablespoon at room temperature
½ cup sugar
¼ teaspoon salt
1 tablespoon apple juice
2 ½ cups sifted all-purpose flour

1. Preheat oven to 350°.

2. Beat the butter for about 10 minutes with an electric mixer until it becomes pale yellow and whipped. It's important for the butter to be very soft so it will incorporate all the flour.

3. Gradually add the sugar, salt, and apple juice and beat 10 minutes more.

4. Switch to a large wooden spoon to add the flour. Add the flour by pressing it gently against the side of the bowl. Grease a 10-inch spring form pan.

5. Press the dough evenly into the bottom of the pan. With a dull knife, cut the circle into four equal wedges and then cut each wedge into thirds. You'll end up with 12 triangular pieces. This "scoring" will make it easier to break the cookies into petticoat tail shaped pieces after they're baked.

6. Bake about 30 minutes, or until light brown.

ADAPTED FROM MADELEINE KAMMAN

French/ English Translations

pomme	apple	moules	muscles
crevette	shrimp	biscuit	cookie
beurre	butter	farine	flour
crème	cream	four	oven
plage	beach	verger	orchard

Hans Röckenwagner

Germany

**Above: Hans as a little boy in Germany.
Left: Hans Röckenwagner**

Hans Röckenwagner is the chef-owner of Röckenwagner, a wonderful restaurant in Santa Monica, California, where he's pioneered the combination of fresh, local California ingredients with traditional German dishes to create lighter variations of German cooking. In addition to this original style of cooking, Hans' restaurant makes wonderful fresh breads and scones that can be purchased at local farmers' markets. As a credit to his talents, several years ago Hans was asked to design and create a very special birthday cake for the 50th anniversary of the UNICEF "Celebrating Children" birthday party at the United Nations International Children's Emergency Fund headquarters in Geneva, Switzerland.

Hans grew up in the Black Forest of southern Germany, an area known for its beautiful pine tree forests as well as for cuckoo clocks. Traditional cuckoo clocks are carved out of woods obtained from the forest. The clocks are shaped like small, traditional, German-style houses from the area, and they're mounted on walls as decorations. Weights that are often shaped like pine cones, hang from the bottom. To wind the clocks, these weights are pulled. At regular 15-minute, half-hour, or one-hour intervals, a little bird pops out of the roof portion of the clock and says "cuckoo, cuckoo, cuckoo". Some of the fancier clocks play tunes and have little costumed "people" come out and spin around like they're dancing. Cuckoo clocks are known and enjoyed all over the world.

In addition to his many other impressive abilities, Hans is a skilled woodcarver. There's a beautiful and unique table with matching chairs in his restaurant that he carved himself. The table is fun and very clever because underneath each person's place setting, there are special drawers that contain individual salt and pepper shakers and can be used for storage. Guests can request this table ahead of time.

When Hans was a little boy, his father owned a butcher shop. Around the time Hans turned twelve, his father decided to open a restaurant; and Hans found himself helping out in the kitchen. The first food he was allowed to prepare was späetzle, irregularly shaped, noodle-like, mini egg dumplings. Späetzle is the most common starch side dish in southern Germany (like pasta is to Italy, or rice is to China).

Späetzle means "little sparrows" in German, because their unique shape looked like little birds. Restaurants were (and still are) measured in part, by the quality of their späetzle, so it was important that it be good. Every day Hans had to make a fifty-egg batch because it was served with almost every meal. Späetzle is made by extruding a dough made of flour, eggs, salt, and water, through the large holes of either a grater, a colander, or a special späetzle press, which looks like a giant garlic press.

Hans also liked to make Black Forest cake for the restaurant. It's still one of the most popular desserts in Germany and is a specialty of the area

Cherries

There are cherry trees all over the countryside of southern Germany. In the summer when the cherries ripen, they're made into jams or otherwise preserved to be enjoyed throughout the winter months, when fresh fruit is harder to find.

Pretzels

Pretzels are one of the most popular German snacks. Freshly baked, soft pretzels are sold on street corners in cities throughout Germany. They're often accompanied by mustard, and consumed with beer. There is an old custom that German children used to wear pretzels around their necks at New Years to bring them good luck.

where he grew up: hence the name. It's made with layers of chocolate cake, whipped cream, cherries, and cherry schnapps, a cherry flavored liquor.

Two of Hans' favorite dishes to eat as a child were goulash and German apple pancakes. Goulash is a meat stew with a delicious, rich sauce that tastes great over späetzle. It was a comfort food that was enjoyed during the colder months of fall, winter, and spring. Hans also has wonderful memories of his mom dipping sliced apple rings in a batter and pan-frying them. German apple pancakes were another special treat that could be eaten for breakfast, lunch, or a light dinner. He serves his own version of the apple pancake in his restaurant for Sunday brunch, and it's extremely popular. His version is a large, puffy pancake (the size of an entire plate), with caramelized, cinnamon-flavored

apples cooked right in it. It's hard to imagine anything more delicious! When ready to be served, the pancake is sprinkled with confectioners' sugar and topped with a little whipped cream.

BEEF GOULASH SOUP OR STEW

(makes 4 servings)

1 ½ tablespoons vegetable oil
1 ½ pounds beef skirt steak for
 the soup: (2 pounds, for the stew),
 cut into ¾ x ¾-inch chunks
½ cup finely diced yellow onion
2 cloves garlic, finely chopped
½ cup finely diced carrots
½ cup finely diced celery
½ cup diced red bell pepper
¼ cup tomato paste
1 teaspoon sweet paprika
⅓ cup all-purpose flour

1 teaspoon salt
¼ teaspoon freshly ground
 black pepper
Tabasco sauce to taste
1 teaspoon Worcestershire sauce
1 cup red wine
3 ½ cups water, for the soup:
 (1 cup water for the stew)
2 cups chicken stock
1 cup white button mushrooms
 halved and thinly sliced

1. Heat the oil in a large, heavy saucepan. Brown the beef on all sides.

2. Reduce heat to medium, add the garlic and onion, and stir for 4 to 5 minutes, or until softened.

3. Add the carrots, celery, and bell pepper, and cook for 3 minutes, stirring frequently.

4. Add the tomato paste, decrease the heat to very low, and cook, stirring continuously, for 2 minutes, scraping the bottom of the pan as you stir to keep the tomato paste from sticking.

5. Add the paprika and the flour and continue stirring and scraping the bottom of the pan for 1 ½ minutes. A stiff mixture will form. It's important to keep stirring so the flour taste cooks away without the mixture burning.

6. Add the salt, pepper, Tabasco sauce, Worcestershire, and red wine. Stir to mix well, and bring to a simmer. Let the liquid reduce by two-thirds, then add the water, stock, and mushrooms, and bring to a slow simmer.

7. Partially cover the pan and reduce the liquid by about one-third. The meat should be very tender (almost falling apart), and the soup should be very thick. Taste and adjust the seasonings if necessary.

8. Serve in shallow bowls.

9. If you prefer stew instead of soup, proceed as above, but only use 1 cup of water, and don't cook quite as long. Stir occasionally, until a thick, gravy consistency is achieved.

10. If you make the stew and have leftovers, it can be turned into soup the next day by adding a little water.

ADAPTED FROM HANS RÖCKENWAGNER

SPÄETZLE
Noodle-Like Dumplings

(makes 6 servings)

3 cups all-purpose flour
1 teaspoon salt
6 large eggs
4 tablespoons water
2 tablespoons unsalted butter
Salt and freshly ground pepper to taste
3 tablespoons snipped chives or green onion tops, cut on the diagonal

1. In a large mixing bowl, combine the flour and salt and make a well in the center.

2. In a small mixing bowl, whisk eggs with the water. Then pour into the well.

3. With a wooden spoon, stir the egg mixture, gradually incorporating the flour, until you have a thick, wet, dough. Continue mixing the dough, lifting it up as you stir to incorporate air and make it a little bubbly. It should be the consistency of biscuit dough: thick enough to cling to the spoon and then drop off.

4. Bring a large pot of salted water to a rapid boil.

5. Form the späetzle by pushing the dough through a special späetzle press, the holes of a colander with large holes, or a perforated pie pan using the back of a large wooden spoon. Scrape the outside of the colander when the extruded dough is approximately 1 inch in length. If the dough seems too stiff, add more water. The softer the dough, the lighter the späetzle will be.

6. Add the späetzle to the boiling water. When they rise to the surface, give them a gentle stir and cook for about 20 seconds. Drain briefly in a clean colander before tossing with the butter, salt, pepper, and chives. Serve immediately.

7. If spätzle is not served immediately, remove it from the boiling water, rinse it with cold water. Then drain and toss with 2 teaspoons of vegetable oil. When ready to serve, heat the butter, salt, pepper, and chives in a large nonstick frying pan, add the spätzle and toss to coat well.

ADAPTED FROM HANS RÖCKENWAGNER

GERMAN APPLE PANCAKE

(makes 4 servings)

You can make 1 large pancake, or 3 smaller ones. A critical element in making the larger pancake is the 12-inch, non-stick, oven proof skillet. If your pan is too small, the pancake will be too thick and will not cook properly. The non-stick surface insures the caramelized apples won't stick to the pan.

PANCAKE BATTER
7 large eggs
**1 tablespoon pure vanilla
   extract**
¾ cup granulated sugar
½ cup all-purpose flour
½ teaspoon salt

APPLES
2 tablespoons unsalted butter
**3 medium-size apples, peeled if
   desired, and sliced**
1 ½ teaspoons ground cinnamon
1 ½ tablespoons granulated sugar

GARNISH
1 tablespoon confectioner's sugar
¼ cup crème fraîche (optional)
1 cup strawberries (optional)

1. In a blender or food processor, combine the eggs, vanilla, and sugar, and blend for about 15 seconds, or until combined.

2. Add the flour and baking powder and blend for 60 seconds more, or until very smooth. Set aside.

3. Melt the butter in a 12-inch nonstick, oven proof skillet over medium heat. Add the apples and sauté 4 to 5 minutes, or until softened.

4. Sprinkle the cinnamon and sugar evenly over the apples, and stir 2 minutes, or until apples are glazed and slightly translucent at the edges.

5. Preheat the broiler to medium-high heat.

6. Distribute apples evenly in the skillet and pour batter over them. Cook over medium heat until the bottom seems quite firm, 6-8 minutes. If making smaller pancakes, use an 8-inch pan, ⅓ the apples, and ⅓ the batter for each.

7. Transfer pan to the broiler and cook for several minutes, watching carefully, until pancake is firm throughout and golden on top.

8. If serving the large pancake, cut it into 4 wedges. Transfer, to serving plates, apple side up. Sprinkle with confectioner's sugar, place a dollop of the crème fraîche on top, and garnish with the strawberries.

ADAPTED FROM HANS RÖCKENWAGNER

BAVARIAN SOFT PRETZELS

(makes large 10 pretzels)

This recipe takes a while to make since you prepare it in stages. It's worth the time and effort.

2 envelopes dry yeast
(¼ ounce each)
1 ¼ cups warm water
3 ¾ cups bread flour
2 teaspoons salt
¼ cup unsalted butter, softened

3 tablespoons baking soda
2 quarts water
1 large egg yolk, lightly beaten
with 2 teaspoons water
Coarse salt to taste

1. In a small bowl, whisk together the yeast and ¼ cup of warm water.

2. In the bowl of a heavy-duty electric mixer fitted with a dough hook, add the remaining 1 cup of warm water, the bread flour, yeast mixture, salt, and butter.

3. Mix at slow speed for 3 minutes, making sure mixture blends evenly. Increase mixer speed to high. Continue mixing 8 minutes more, or until dough is firm and elastic. (If dough is too firm for mixer to handle, finish kneading by hand.)

4. Turn the ball of dough onto a lightly floured work surface and let rest for 5 minutes, loosely covered with a kitchen towel. Line 2 baking sheets that can fit in your freezer with parchment paper, and set aside.

5. Cut the dough into 10 pieces. Roll each piece into a 5-inch long cylinder about 1 inch in diameter. Roll each ball into a long rope (about 2 feet) with the ends much thinner than the center portion.

6. Twist the two ends together twice about 4 inches from the ends. Form a circle with the twisted part in the center and the tips facing down. Attach tips to the lower portion of the circle, separating them and pressing them onto the dough, about 3 inches apart. You should have

a pretzel shape. Place on the prepared baking sheet. Repeat with remaining ropes.

7. When the pretzel dough is shaped, let it sit in a very warm, moist place to rise until almost doubled in size, about 30-50 minutes.

8. Freeze the pretzel dough, uncovered on the baking sheets for at least 2 hours, and up to 24 hours; dough should be frozen solid.

9. Before removing pretzels from the freezer, combine the baking soda and water in a large saucepan and bring to a simmer.

10. Preheat the oven to 425°.

11. Remove pan from freezer and, using a large, flat skimmer, dip each frozen pretzel in the simmering water for about 3 seconds, letting the excess water drain before returning it to the baking sheet.

12. Brush pretzels with the egg yolk and water mixture. Then sprinkle with coarse salt.

13. Immediately place in the hot oven. Bake for 10 minutes. Then lower the oven temperature to 375°, and bake 5 to 8 minutes more.

14. Once cool, the pretzels can be kept in an airtight container for 1 day.

ADAPTED FROM HANS RÖCKENWAGNER

Alexis Bakouros

Greece

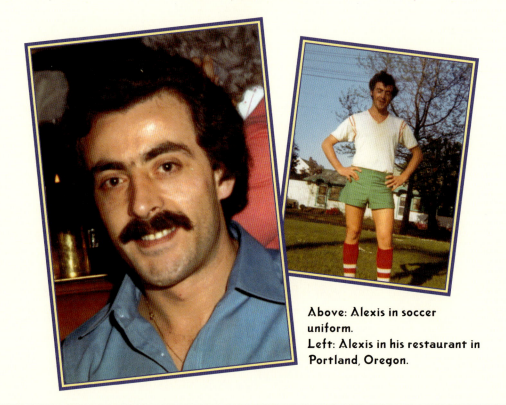

Above: Alexis in soccer uniform.
Left: Alexis in his restaurant in Portland, Oregon.

When Alexis Bakouros was growing up in Greece, all the kids in the neighborhood would come over to his house to eat because his mother was widely known as the best cook in his village of Filiatra. Alexis was raised in a farming family near Kalamata, Greece, the country's "olive capital". There, olive trees grow almost everywhere. In addition to olives, his family grew fruits and vegetables such as watermelons, cucumbers, zucchini, and potatoes. Everyone in the family helped out. At meal times they were ravenous from all the hard work and his mom kept them happy and satisfied with her delicious meals.

Alexis's mom learned to cook when she was eleven years old. That year her mother died and she suddenly found herself the oldest cook in her family. She knew that her family was depending on her, so she went around to her neighbors and asked them to share their recipes with her. Then she went back home and taught herself how to cook. Over time she experimented on her own and improved upon each recipe. Eventually she stopped measuring the ingredients, as she could tell by her hands and eyes just how much to add.

Alexis's favorite dishes when growing up were hilopittes, little square shaped homemade egg noodles with tomato sauce, and Pastitsio, a delicious baked casserole with macaroni, tomato-meat sauce, and a custard topping. In winter, when it was cold, he loved his mother's Avgolemono Soup (chicken soup with egg and lemon). It's the most popular soup in Greece. Another favorite was Spanikopita, made with the very thin, very flaky, many layered phyllo dough that Greece is known for. The phyllo is baked till golden brown with a mixture inside of spinach, eggs, and Greek Feta cheese made from sheep's milk. Spanikopita is delicious and it's nutritious because of the spinach, eggs, and cheese.

For dessert everyone loved Alexis's mom's Galaktoboureko and Baklava, both made with crispy layers of phyllo dough. The Baklava was made with a chopped walnut and almond filling, and the Galaktoboureko with a wonderful custard baked inside. A sweet syrup, lightly flavored with cinnamon, cloves, honey, and lemon was poured over both. It was fun to help his mom make foods with phyllo dough because each layer had to be brushed with butter.

Alexis came to America when he was fifteen years old. His aunt had married a man in Portland, Oregon; and she liked America so much, she encouraged her brother, Alexis's dad, to send his family to the United States where she thought they'd have a better life and an easier time earning a living. Alexis's aunt turned out to be right. After the family moved to Portland, as a result of hard work and good business sense, they thrived and prospered.

When Alexis married, his wife was so impressed by his mother's cooking that she resolved to learn how to prepare all her recipes. His wife became such an exceptional cook that she and her sister decided to open a Greek restaurant in Portland, where at the time, there were none. They named the restaurant Alexis. The food was so terrific, different, and interesting, that two months after opening, there was a line of people waiting to get in each night.

Besides the tasty, authentic Greek food, the restaurant was a "taverna" just like in Greece. Tavernas are places where Greeks go out to have fun. In Greece people never drink without also eating, as the food prevents them from getting really drunk: they just have a good time. Tavernas are known for festive music and dancing, and Alexis has replicated this joyful atmosphere in his restaurant. When customers go there to celebrate their birthdays, the waiters all sing "happy birthday" in Greek. In keeping with a fun-loving custom, some time during the evening, a waiter will intentionally break a plate or glass.

The restaurant also serves a dramatic and mouth-watering appetizer called Saganaki. The waiters pour the grape liquor, ouzo, over Greek Kaseri cheese and light it on fire in the kitchen. It's carried to the table in a special dish while still flaming. The specially trained waiters extinguish the flame by squeezing lemon juice over it. The heat gives the cheese a light crust on the outside, and it's soft and melted inside.

Alexis's restaurant is also famous for its fried calamari, or squid, that looks like fried onion rings. Some say it's the best fried squid in America. Years ago Alexis brought squid to Oregon for the first time. It was viewed as a bit strange at first, but it's now extremely popular.

Since the restaurant opened, Alexis's brother not only learned to cook, he's become the executive chef. This left Alexis with time to pursue

his other food business ideas. Because the food in his restaurant became so well liked, he was asked to supply grocery and specialty food stores around the western United States with fresh and frozen Greek dishes, as well as pita pocket bread for deli departments. He also started an importing business that sells Greek specialties such as olive oil, olives, Feta cheese, roasted peppers, and pepperoncini (pickled peppers) to food stores in many western states.

What follows are Alexis's mom's recipes for his favorite childhood dishes. Note that most packages of phyllo dough weigh 16 ounces and contain about 28 paper thin sheets.

PASTITSIO
Macaroni and Baked Meat Custard

(makes 8 servings)

1 lb. long macaroni
1 large onion chopped
2 cloves garlic
3 tablespoons extra virgin
  olive oil
2 lbs. ground lean beef
2 cups tomato purée
⅓ cup chopped fresh parsley
1 teaspoon salt

¼ teaspoon ground nutmeg
½ teaspoon cinnamon
4 tablespoons flour
4 tablespoons butter
4 cups whole milk
4 egg yolks
½ teaspoon salt
1 ½ cups grated cheese (Greek
  Mitzithra or Parmesan)

1. Cook the macaroni in boiling, salted water until tender. Drain and rinse under cold water. Empty drained macaroni into a large mixing bowl.

2. Heat oil in a skillet and sauté onion and garlic, until wilted, about 5 minutes. Add ground beef and cook, stirring for about 10 minutes. Then add tomato purée and seasonings and cook for about 10 more minutes. Add this mixture to the pasta and combine well.

3. Preheat oven to 350°.

4. Grease a 10 x 15-inch baking pan. Pour the macaroni and meat mixture into the baking pan and spread it evenly.

5. Melt butter in a medium saucepan over medium heat. Add flour and stir for one minute. Gradually add the milk, stirring continuously so it will be smooth. When it starts to thicken, remove from heat and beat in egg yolks, one at a time. Return to stove, lower heat, and cook two more minutes, stirring continuously.

6. Pour white sauce over macaroni and meat, spreading it evenly.

7. Sprinkle the cheese evenly over the top.

8. Bake for 45 minutes or until golden brown.

9. When done, remove from oven and let stand for 15 minutes to firm up before serving.

ADAPTED FROM ALEXIS BAKOUROS

SPANIKOPITA
Greek Spinach Pie

(makes 8 servings)

This is always a great party dish.

20 sheets phyllo dough
2 pounds fresh spinach,
   chopped, or 2 10-ounce packages
1 tablespoon salt
1 small onion, chopped
½ cup parsley, chopped
½ cup dill, chopped
½ pound feta cheese, crumbled
4 eggs, lightly beaten
2 tablespoons olive oil
3 tablespoons farina
1 stick of butter

1. If using fresh spinach, chop it in a food processor, not too fine. Empty it into a colander. Sprinkle salt over the spinach and let it sit for 15 minutes.

2. Press the excess water from the spinach and empty it into a large mixing bowl.

3. Add the onion, parsley, dill, crumbled feta cheese, olive oil, and farina to the spinach, and mix well. If using frozen spinach, let it thaw and add 1 ½ teaspoons salt. (You will not be using the 1 tablespoons salt that was required for the fresh spinach in step 1.)

4. Butter a large, 10" x 15" baking pan. Lay one sheet of phyllo dough in the bottom of the pan.

5. Melt the butter and lightly brush the sheet of phyllo all over. Place another sheet on top. Brush again until you have a stack of 10 sheets.

6. Pour the spinach mixture over the stack of buttered phyllo and spread it evenly.

7. Preheat oven to 350º.

8. Place another phyllo sheet on top of the spinach layer. Brush it with melted butter and repeat until you've used up the remaining 10 sheets. If you'd like, you can score the top layer of phyllo into individual size portions prior to baking.

9. Bake for 45 minutes, or until the top is golden brown.

10. Cut into squares, through to the bottom, while still warm.

ADAPTED FROM ALEXIS BAKOUROS

BAKLAVA
Nut Pastry in Syrup

(makes 24 servings)

1 cup almonds, finely chopped
2 cups walnuts, finely chopped
¼ cup sugar
1 teaspoon ground cinnamon
½ teaspoon ground cloves
1 pound phyllo dough (28 sheets)
8 ounces (2 sticks) butter
1 container of whole cloves (optional)

1. Thaw the frozen phyllo dough.

2. Mix the nuts, sugar, and spices together in a large mixing bowl.

3. Butter a large, 10" x 15" baking pan. Lay one sheet of phyllo dough in bottom of pan.

4. Melt the butter.

5. Lightly brush the sheet of phyllo with butter all over. Place another sheet on top. Brush again until you have a stack of 9 sheets.

6. Pour half the nut mixture over the stack of buttered phyllo dough and spread it evenly.

7. Place another sheet on top of the nut layer.

Brush the phyllo dough with melted butter and repeat until you have layered 9 sheets.

8. Spread remaining nut mixture over the phyllo.

9. Preheat oven to 350°.

10. Top with remaining 10 sheets of phyllo, brushing each sheet, including the top one, with butter. Score the baklava into diamond shapes, cutting to the bottom of the pan. For a nice touch you can put a whole clove in the center of each diamond.

11. Bake for 45 minutes until the top is golden brown.

SYRUP FOR BAKLAVA
2 cups sugar
2 cups water
1 cinnamon stick

4 cloves
4 tablespoons honey
Rind of 1 lemon

1. Place all the ingredients in a pot, stir to dissolve the sugar, and boil for 15 minutes. Remove the spices and lemon rind.

2. Pour syrup over the entire pan of baked Baklava while it's still warm. Let cool.

ADAPTED FROM ALEXIS BAKOUROS

GALAKTOBOUREKO OR BOUGATSA

Milk Custard Baked in Phyllo

(makes 24 servings)

Both are as warm, delicious, and as comforting as comfort food gets! Galaktoboureko is soaked in the same syrup as the baklava, while the Bougatsa is sprinkled with confectioner's sugar and cinnamon.

FILLING INGREDIENTS:
3 cups milk
⅔ cup sugar
½ cup farina
½ teaspoon salt
4 eggs
1 teaspoon vanilla extract

FOR BOUGATSA
1 tablespoon ground cinnamon
1 cup confectioner's sugar

PHYLLO CRUST INGREDIENTS
14 sheets phyllo dough
1 tablespoons ground cinnamon
½ cup sugar
6 tablespoons butter

1. Bring milk to a boil. When boiling, add farina and mix well. Continue stirring for 5 more minutes, or until mixture starts to thicken.

2. Remove from heat and whisk in the sugar, the vanilla, and then the eggs, one at a time. Set aside to cool.

3. In a small bowl, combine 1 tablespoon cinnamon and the sugar.

4. Melt the butter and set aside.

5. Butter a large, 10" x 15" baking pan. Lay one sheet of phyllo dough in the bottom of the pan.

6. Lightly brush the sheet of phyllo with butter all over. Sprinkle with 2 teaspoons of the cinnamon sugar mixture. Repeat until you have stacked 7 sheets.

7. Pour the farina custard mixture over the stack of phyllo and spread it evenly.

8. Preheat oven to 350°.

9. Place a sheet of phyllo over the custard. Brush it with melted butter and sprinkle with 2 teaspoons of the cinnamon sugar. Repeat until you've used up the second set of 7 sheets. Brush the top layer with butter and then score the top set of sheets into 2-inch squares, cutting through only to the custard.

10. Bake for 45 minutes until the top is golden brown.

11. For Galaktoboureka, top with the baklava syrup recipe, while still warm.

12. For Bougatsa, omit the syrup. Combine the confectioner's sugar and cinnamon and sprinkle all over the top while still warm.

13. Cut into squares, through to the bottom, while still warm.

ADAPTED FROM ALEXIS BAKOUROS

Inez Bon

Holland

Above: Inez as a little girl in Holland.
Left: Inez at her restaurant in New York City.

Inez Bon grew up in Velsen, Holland, about twenty minutes outside of Amsterdam, on the North Sea. She majored in art history in college and hoped to work in a museum one day. To support herself in the interim, she tried to get a job as a waitress in a café in Amsterdam. She was told, however, that without any previous experience, she couldn't wait on customers: she could only be a dishwasher. Inez took the job anyway, worked her way up to waitress, later to manager, and she eventually bought the restaurant. Today the restaurant is a modern café that serves breakfast, lunch, dinner, and late night snacks. The food is interesting, creative, somewhat experimental, and not too expensive. It attracts a lively crowd and is always busy.

While Inez was happy with the success of her restaurant in Amsterdam, she had always loved New York City and had dreamed of opening a restaurant there. In January 2001, she opened her Dutch restaurant, one of the only Dutch restaurants in the United States, near New York University in Greenwich Village, Manhattan. The restaurant is called NL for

Netherlands, the Dutch name for Holland. It serves traditional Dutch foods with unique twists.

Traditional Dutch foods include pea soup with smoked sausage and bacon, pickled herring (a small fish that comes from the North Sea), smoked eel (a long, snake-like fish), hearty stews, one pan dishes with mashed potatoes, and pancakes. Many of the ingredients are dried, smoked, or preserved so they can be used throughout the long, cold, Dutch winters. Because for hundreds of years Indonesia was a Dutch colony, many Indonesian dishes such as satays (grilled meat skewers with peanut sauce) and rijsttafel or rice table (yellow rice with lots of little dishes to sample) are still common in Holland today.

Some of Inez's favorite childhood food memories include visits each year from Sinterklaas on December 5th. Sinterklaas is a bishop with a long white beard, who comes by boat from Spain with his helpers known as Pieten. Sinterklaas rides his white horse over the rooftops of Holland, and his helpers drop presents and candies through the chimneys of the houses of boys and girls who have been good during the year. Sometimes the helpers have to climb down the chimneys to deliver the gifts.

Each night during the week before Sinterklaas's visit, children put one of their shoes in front of the fireplace with bread and hay or a carrot for Sinterklaas's horse. On several of the mornings the children receive a little gift, but the big presents come on December 5th. Dutch settlers brought this custom with them to America, and the colonists adopted the tradition. They changed Sinterklaas's name to Santa Claus, and his visit was moved to Christmas Eve.

During the first four days of December, children in Holland go with their parents to the

Klompen

Because the land in Holland was often wet, the Dutch cleverly invented wooden shoes that didn't get soaked like other shoes. They were called klompen, perhaps because of the klomp, klomp noise they make! The colors and designs of wooden shoes vary based on the part of the Holland where they're made. Today many farmers and gardeners still wear them.

nearest town with a harbor or beach to see a reenactment of Sinterklaas and his helpers arriving by boat and then docking and coming ashore to ride his white horse through the city streets. This reenactment makes the story of Sinterklaas come alive for young Dutch children.

On the evening of the December 5th celebration, a family friend dressed as Sinterklaas, comes knocking at the door with Piet, his helper. Sinterklaas sits down in a chair, opens his book, and tells who's been bad or good during the year. Treats are served, including special chocolates for which the Dutch are famous, that come in different letters depending on the child's first or last name, as well as a pastry called Boterletters or "butter letters". Butter letters are made with a flaky pastry dough and an almond filling. They're made into the shapes of the letters "S" for Sinterklaas and "M" for mother.

Speculaas, which are crispy cookies made with almonds and spices, and cut into different shapes, are also served that night. They're sometimes known as St. Nick cookies and can be pressed into molds with the design of St. Nicholas. The cookies are based on a very old

Dutch Flowers

The Dutch are known for the wide variety of tulips, daffodils, hyacinths, and other colorful flowers that grow there. They export flower bulbs all over the world, so people almost everywhere can enjoy them.

In Spring, the Dutch go to see the glorious flower fields which are planted in bands of brilliant color. They bring home flower garlands to wear and even to decorate their cars.

recipe. Because the Dutch were known throughout history as great sailors and traders, they brought spices back to Holland from the Far East. Speculaas cookies use many of those spices (traditionally seven), including cinnamon, nutmeg, cloves, allspice, ground ginger, anise, and salt.

Two other delicious sweets that are eaten between Christmas and New Years are apple fritters and oliebollen (literally "oil balls"). Oliebollen are round doughnuts that contain raisins and candied orange rind or lemon peel. Apples are the most popular fruit in Holland. Children of all ages enjoy apple fritters: apple rings that are dipped in batter, fried, and dusted with powdered sugar. Between Christmas and New Years, there are carts decorated with colored lights on the street corners of Dutch cities and towns, where the oliebollen and apple fritters are continually being made. At twelve midnight on New Year's Eve, Dutch families (who are allowed to have their own fireworks in Holland) go outside to light them and then return home to celebrate with champagne for the adults and rich, creamy hot chocolate for the kids.

Another fond food memory for Inez was of poffertjes: the little, puffy, round pancakes that are traditionally served with butter and powdered sugar sprinkled on top. These pancakes are commonly eaten at fairs and birthday parties, or as an afternoon snack with tea. They can also be filled with a small piece of fruit, or topped with chocolate sauce or jam. Poffertjes are made in a special pan with lots of round, deep cavities that give them their unique, puffy shape. Knitting needles or toothpicks are used to turn the poffertjes in the pans. At NL they're served both as a dessert after dinner, and at the restaurant's weekend brunch.

Lastly, Inez and children all over Holland, even today, relish shrimp and veal croquettes, because of their creamy, flavorful interior and crisp outer coating. The shrimp croquettes originated in Belgium and migrated to Holland, where they've become very popular.

What follows are the recipes for some of Inez's favorite childhood dishes.

Holland

PEA SOUP

(makes 6–8 servings)

This soup takes 3-4 hours to cook, so start it early in the afternoon for that evening's supper.

3 quarts water
3 cups dried split peas
2 pounds pork butt,
   shoulder, or ham hocks
4 to 6 potatoes, diced
3 stalks celery
4 leeks

1 large onion
1 teaspoon thyme
1 tablespoon salt
½ teaspoon pepper
1 12-ounce package smoked
   sausage links (or hot dogs)

1. Rinse and drain the split peas. Put them in a pot and cover with water. Soak the peas overnight.

2. Drain the split peas. Put them in a large pot with 3 quarts of fresh water. Bring to a boil.

3. Add the pork and simmer, over medium-low heat, covered, for 1½-2 hours. Remove meat from pot, discard any bones, cut meat into very small pieces, and return it to the pot.

4. Peel the potatoes and cut them into small pieces. Dice the celery, and slice the onions. Slice the leeks the long way and separate the layers. Wash leeks well and then cut them into thin slices. Add all the vegetables to the soup.

5. Cut smoked sausage links or hot dogs into small pieces and add to the soup, along with the thyme, salt, and pepper.

6. Simmer, covered, for 1½- 2 more hours over medium-low heat or until vegetables are tender and the soup is almost a purée.

7. Before serving, skim off any fat from the top.

ADAPTED FROM INEZ BON

Dutch/English Translations

rÿst .... rice
patat friet .... french fries
kaneel .... cinnamon
ei .... egg
minuut .... minute

lepel .... spoon
vork .... fork
mes .... knife
kip .... chicken
suiker .... sugar

SHRIMP CROQUETTES

(makes about 12 croquettes, or 4-6 servings)

3 tablespoons butter
3 tablespoons flour
1 cup milk
1 tablespoon minced parsley
2 tablespoons finely minced onion
2 cups tiny cooked shrimp
   (preferably) or chopped,
   larger shrimp

2 teaspoons lemon juice
¼ teaspoon of sage
1 teaspoon salt
¼ teaspoon pepper
1 egg
1 tablespoon water
2 cups of bread crumbs.
Vegetable oil for frying

1. Melt butter in a saucepan over low heat. Stir in the flour with a spoon (it will look like a thick paste), and stir another 1-2 minutes, until it starts to turn light brown.. Gradually add the milk and stir continuously for several minutes until it becomes a little thicker than pudding. It's important that it be fairly thick so the croquettes will hold their shape.

2. Add the parsley, onion, shrimp, lemon juice, and seasonings, and mix well.

3. Take approximately 2 tablespoons of the mixture and roll it into a cylinder shape.

4. Beat the egg and water and put it in a shallow bowl. Put the bread crumbs in another shallow bowl.

5. Roll the cylinders in the bread crumbs, then in the egg mixture, and then in the crumbs again. Refrigerate the cylinders for several hours.

6. Pour oil into a frying pan up to a depth of 1 inch, or use a deep-fry cooker according to its directions. When oil is very hot (about 385°), fry the croquettes until golden brown. Drain on paper towels.

ADAPTED FROM INEZ BON

DUTCH APPLE FRITTERS

(makes about 3 dozen fried apple slices)

6 large cooking apples
1 cup flour
¼ cup sugar
2 teaspoons baking powder
¼ teaspoon salt

1 large egg, beaten
½ cup milk
Oil for deep frying
Powdered sugar

1. Peel apples and remove the cores. Slice into ⅓-inch thick slices.

2. Combine the flour, baking powder, sugar, and salt.

3. Add the beaten egg and milk to the flour mixture, and mix well to remove any lumps.

4. Pour cooking oil into a large frying pan to a depth of ½ inch. Heat the oil. Then dip the apple slices into the batter and deep-fry until golden on one side. Flip and fry until golden brown on the other side. Drain on paper towels.

5. Sprinkle the fried apples with confectioner's sugar.

ADAPTED FROM INEZ BON

POFFERTJES
Mini-Pancakes

(makes 4 servings)

Poffertjes are a cross between a donut and a pancake. In Holland they're made using a special poffertjes pan that has numerous round indentations in the bottom, thereby producing the rounded, puffy shape. In Denmark a similar dessert called Aebelskiver is also made using this pan. It's known as an aebelskiver or monk's pan and it can be purchased in cooking stores. The pans come in various sizes and the smaller ones are not expensive. If you don't have the special pan, you can make these just as you would silver dollar pancakes. They're the lightest, fluffiest pancakes I've ever had.

2 cups flour
2 tablespoons sugar
1 teaspoon salt
1 teaspoon baking soda
2 cups buttermilk
3 large eggs, separated

Apple or banana slices, optional
Vegetable oil
Butter
Powdered sugar, jam, or chocolate
   syrup

1. Mix the flour, sugar, baking soda, and salt.

2. Add the buttermilk and egg yolks with a wire whisk, mixing well until the batter is lump-free.

3. Beat the egg whites until soft peaks form. Fold the egg whites into the batter.

4. Grease a frying pan, or if using the aebelskiver pan, pour a little oil into each cavity. It's important that the cavities are sufficiently greased or the pancakes will be hard to turn. Use about 1 tablespoon of batter for each pancake. The aebelskiver pan cavities should each be about two-thirds full. If you want, at this point you can put a small piece of apple, banana, or other fruit into the center of the batter. When brown on one side, flip and brown on the other. If using the aebelskiver pan, use a toothpick or fork prong to turn the pancakes.

5. To serve, spread with butter and sprinkle with powdered sugar. You can also squeeze a little lemon juice on them, spread them with a little jam, or top with chocolate syrup.

ADAPTED FROM INEZ BON

Piero Selvaggio

Italy

Above: Piero, age two, in Sicily.
Left: Piero in the Garden at VALENTINO.

Piero Selvaggio's **VALENTINO** Restaurant in Los Angeles, California, is considered by many food experts to be the best Italian restaurant in the United States. Considering all the Italian restaurants in America, that's quite an accomplishment! Piero is also one of the most respected wine experts in the country. For the past nine years has passed on many of his favorite recipes to radio listeners in the Los Angeles area. He loves sharing his knowledge about food and wine with others.

Piero grew up in Sicily, a large island across from the "toe" of the Italian "boot". Sicily has twenty-five centuries of history. It was conquered many times by many different peoples. Over the centuries Sicily was occupied by the Phoenicians, the Greeks, the Carthaginians, the Romans, the Byzantines, the Arabs, the Normans, the French, the Spanish, and the Austro-Hungarians. The Arabs had probably the greatest influence on the cooking of Sicily. They brought with them almonds and pistachio nuts, sugar cane, honey, sesame seeds, cinnamon, and chocolate.

Sicily was a busy port, and traders from around the world were always passing through, bringing spices and other exotic ingredients. Because Sicily is surrounded by the Ionic and Mediterranean Seas, fish and shellfish are plentiful. The first Italian pasta was made in Sicily, and pastry making was invented there because it was one of the first places to grow and grind wheat. The Arabs discovered that by pounding the wheat and mixing it with water, it could be stretched and cut into shapes to make fresh pasta. When it was dried in the sun, it could be kept unspoiled for a long time. That was how dried pasta was invented.

During his childhood, Piero learned about Italian cooking from his mother (Mama Lina), grand-mother, and other family members. No one used a cookbook. Recipes were simply taught at the stove, from one generation to the next. There was no refrigeration in those days. Meals were made from whatever Piero's mother bought fresh at the market and butcher that day. His mother kept a pantry with homemade tomato sauce and sun dried tomatoes, olives, pasta, garlic, and onions. There were always enough ingredients in the pantry to create a meal.

Piero's childhood memories center around food and wine and family meals at the table. His mother made hearty food with simple ingredients such as pasta, eggplant, and anything with ricotta. As he says in his book, *The VALENTINO Cookbook*, "Growing up, I was starting to connect food with happiness." The main meal of the day was eaten at lunchtime. It would start with antipasti: a colorful plate of vegetables, olives, sliced hard sausages or salami, and cheese. There was usually pasta, meat, fish or chicken, and vegetables. Rich desserts were rarely eaten. Meals more typically ended with fresh or dried fruit.

Sicily

Sicily is sometimes known as the garden of Europe. The climate is like California, and fruits and vegetables grow there in abundance. Blood oranges (named because they are red inside), lemons, peaches, figs, tomatoes, peppers, eggplants, artichokes, garlic, onions, olives, and pasta are staples of the local kitchens.

The first time Piero ate in a restaurant was when he was sixteen, and his family drove to a town an hour and a half away to apply for documents to travel to the United States. It wasn't a fancy restaurant; but it was exciting to have a choice of what to eat, to have everyone, including his mother, be served by a waiter, and for the food to be so good. Piero ordered pasta, still one of his favorite foods today. Both the experiences of eating in a restaurant and moving to America changed his life.

Piero and his family moved from Italy to Brooklyn, New York. His first job in America was washing pots and pans on the breakfast shift in the cafeteria at New York University. His first American restaurant meal was a hamburger with ketchup, French fries, and a Coca-Cola. Piero had an uncle who lived in California and was a waiter at Chazen's restaurant in Beverly Hills, where many movie stars dined. That sounded exciting, so Piero decided to join his uncle in California, where he got a job as a busboy and room service waiter at the Beverly Hills Hotel. Later he enrolled in college and majored in languages.

When Piero was twenty-four, a friend asked him to open a restaurant together, and he agreed to give it a try. They named it VALENTINO after the

famous Italian movie star Rudolph Valentino. Little by little, Piero took trips to Italy to learn how to improve the quality of the food and wine he served; and he also gradually improved the restaurant's décor and ambience. Today VALENTINO is a wonderful restaurant, serving authentic Italian dishes from all over Italy. It's a favorite spot for celebrating happy occasions.

Some of Piero's most memorable childhood dishes include a comforting chicken soup his mother made with tiny meatballs and shredded egg noodles, fried rice croquettes filled with meat and cheese, eggplant parmesan with layers of hard-cooked eggs, and sausage, and cannoli, one of the most popular of all Italian desserts. Cannoli are fried, crisp, hollow tubes of dough with a lightly sweetened, creamy, ricotta cheese filling that often includes little chunks of candied fruit, chopped chocolate, and pistachio nuts.

MAMA LINA'S CHICKEN BROTH WITH NOODLES & TINY MEATBALLS

(makes 8 servings)

CHICKEN BROTH
5 pounds chicken bones, including wings, backs, feet, and necks
3 quarts (12 cups) water
1 large onion, roughly chopped
1 carrot, roughly chopped
1 celery stalk, roughly chopped
1 head garlic, cut horizontally in half
2 bay leaves
6 sprigs Italian parsley
4 sprigs fresh thyme
4 whole white peppercorns
Salt to taste

1. Place the bones and chicken parts in a large stockpot and cover with the water. Bring to a boil over high heat and skim off the foam that accumulates on the surface. Add the remaining ingredients.

2. Turn the heat down to medium-low and simmer gently, uncovered, for about 3 ½ hours.

3. Using a large colander, strain the bones and vegetables, pressing out the liquid. For a very clear broth, strain through a cheesecloth, once more.

4. Refrigerate and skim off any fat that rises to the top. If you don't plan to use the stock within a few days, freeze in airtight containers. If you plan to make the rice croquettes, set aside two cups of the broth.

THE TINY MEATBALLS

3 tablespoons stale bread, crust removed

2 tablespoons milk

8 ounces lean ground beef

4 ounces imported prosciutto, diced (optional)

3 tablespoons Parmesan cheese, grated

1 large egg

1 tablespoon fresh marjoram, finely chopped (or 1 teaspoon dried)

1 tablespoon fresh basil, finely chopped (or 1 teaspoon dried)

1 tablespoon fresh chives, finely chopped

Salt and pepper, to taste

3 tablespoons all-purpose flour, for dredging, or more if needed

5 tablespoons olive oil

8 ounces fine egg noodles

1. Place the ground beef and prosciutto in a food processor and process to a paste. Transfer to a large bowl.

2. To the meat mixture in the bowl, add the bread, Parmesan cheese, egg, marjoram, basil, chives, and salt and pepper. Mix well.

3. Form into small ½-inch balls. Roll the meatballs in flour until lightly coated.

4. In a large skillet, heat the olive oil over medium heat and brown the meatballs on all sides. Cook for about 10 minutes and transfer them to a paper towel to drain.

5. A few minutes before you are ready to add the meatballs to the broth, add the egg noodles to the simmering broth and cook until soft, but not "mushy".

6. Add the meatballs while the noodles are cooking. Heat them for approximately 15 minutes.

7. Ladle into individual bowls.

ADAPTED FROM
THE VALENTINO COOKBOOK

Italian/English Translations

formaggio	cheese	minestra	soup
pomodoro	tomato	uovo	egg
melanzana	eggplant	fritto	fried
peperone	bell pepper	grazie	thank you
brodo	broth	prego	you're welcome

MELANZANE RIPIENE
Eggplant Stuffed with Egg, Sausage, and Cheese

(makes 6 servings)

This is a wonderful, versatile dish, and the individual size servings look great. You can make it with or without the sausage or tomato sauce. All the variations work well, and you can try making a few each way.

BREAD CRUMBS (2 CUPS)
1 cup freshly grated, day old Italian bread
½ cup grated cheese (Romano or Pecorino)
2 garlic cloves, finely chopped
½ cup Italian parsley, finely chopped
Pinch of salt

1. Combine everything above together, and mix well. Set aside

2 cups bread crumbs from above
2 ½ pounds medium size eggplant, peeled and sliced lengthwise in ¼-inch thick slices (the eggplant shouldn't be too wide or the slices won't fit neatly into the ramekins)
1 cup extra virgin olive oil
6 large eggs
2 tablespoons milk
10 tablespoons grated cheese (Romano or Parmesan)
½ pound Provolone cheese, sliced thick
2 sweet sausages, pan-fried and also sliced thick (optional)
½ cup tomato sauce (optional)

1. Beat 3 of the eggs and the milk, and pour into a shallow bowl.

2. Place the bread crumbs on a plate.

3. Dip the eggplant in the egg, and then coat the slices with the bread crumbs. Repeat to coat all the slices.

4. Heat half the oil in a large frying pan and place over medium heat. In batches, add the eggplant slices and cook, turning once (about 2 minutes on each side). Sprinkle with salt and lay on paper towels to absorb any excess oil. Add more oil as needed, to cook the remaining slices.

5. Hard boil the remaining 3 eggs (about 20 minutes). Allow eggs to cool. Peel and slice them thick.

6. Preheat the oven to 350°.

7. Lightly brush 6 individual 3½-inch wide ramekins with olive oil.

8. Place a slice of the fried eggplant in each. Sprinkle each with about 1½ tablespoons of the Romano or Parmesan. Next, evenly divide the egg slices and layer them in the ramekins. If you're using the sausage, add it now. If you're using tomato sauce, spread about 1½ tablespoons in each as the next layer. The slices of Provolone may be wider than the ramekin. If so, find a cup or mug the diameter of the ramekin. Lay it over the cheese and cut around it to create a cheese circle that will fit in nicely. Lastly, top with a slice of the fried eggplant.

9. Place the ramekins on a cookie sheet and bake for 40 minutes, or until everything is cooked and melted. Let it rest for 10 minutes.

10. To serve, run a dinner knife around the edge of each ramekin and invert it on a plate. It will look like a little round cake or timbale.

ADAPTED FROM
THE VALENTINO COOKBOOK

LE ARANCINE DI MAMMA LINA
Mamma Lina's Rice Croquettes

(makes 6 servings)

These rice croquettes are shaped like little oranges. Arancine means "little oranges" in Italian. They are crunchy on the outside, with melted cheese and meat inside.

2 cups of chicken stock (see recipe above)
1 tablespoon onion, chopped
8 ounces Arborio rice
2 tablespoons olive oil
2 tablespoons Parmesan cheese, grated
3 large eggs
1 small onion, chopped
¼ cup (2 ounces) butter
4 ounces ground veal or pork
1 ½ cups tomato sauce
3 tablespoons frozen peas
Salt and pepper, to taste

1 large egg, hard-boiled and chopped
4 ounces mozzarella cheese, cut in ¼-inch cubes
⅔ cup flour
1 cup bread crumbs
1 quart (4 cups) peanut oil

1. Heat the broth. Set aside.

2. In a heavy saucepan, toast the tablespoon of onion and the rice over medium-high heat. When the rice begins to crackle, add the olive oil, a pinch of salt, and 1 cup of warm broth. Cook as you would make risotto, by adding broth, a little at a time, stirring constantly, until absorbed and the rice is al dente (creamy, but still a little chewy). The risotto should not be too wet or too loose or the croquettes will not hold together. Remove from the heat and let cool.

3. Combine the Parmesan cheese with the cooled rice and one of the eggs, beaten. Set aside.

4. In a small skillet over medium heat, sauté the remaining onion in the butter. Add the ground meat and cook until it's browned. Add the tomato sauce, simmer for 15 minutes, and add the peas. Season with salt and pepper to taste. The sauce should be a little "dry": not too runny.

5. Beat the remaining 2 eggs and pour them into a shallow bowl. Place the flour on a plate. Place the bread crumbs on another plate.

6. To assemble, dust your hands with flour and place about 1 ½ tablespoonsof the risotto in the palm of your hand. Make a deep, wide indentation. Place 1 heaping teaspoon of the meat mixture in the center, along with a little mozzarella cheese and hard-boiled egg. Close your palm and form a round shape, adding more rice if necessary to completely cover the insides.

7. Roll each croquettes in the flour. Then dip it in the beaten egg. Lastly, coat it with the bread crumbs. The process is a bit messy and the croquettes will be a little fragile.

8. Heat the oil in a deep saucepan or electric fryer to about 350˚. Fry each rice croquette until golden brown. Drain on paper towels.

ADAPTED FROM
THE VALENTINO COOKBOOK

CANNOLI
Fried Pastry Tubes with Ricotta Cheese Filling

(makes approximately 20 cannoli)

These are wonderfully delicious. You'll have to start the recipe the night before to allow the ricotta cheese to drain so it's not too moist. This will prevent the cannoli from becoming soggy. You will need to buy metal cannoli tubes. The cannoli shells can be made ahead of time, but don't fill them until ready to serve, so they remain crisp.

SHELLS

½ cup all-purpose flour
1 tablespoon granulated sugar
Pinch of salt

1 tablespoon plus 1 teaspoon olive oil
½ cup Marsala wine or red wine
2 quarts vegetable oil for deep frying

1. Put the flour, sugar, and salt in the bowl of an electric mixer.

2. On low speed, using the paddle attachment, pour in the olive oil and wine, and mix until the dough comes together to form a ball. Wrap dough in plastic and refrigerate for at least 2 hours.

3. Remove cannoli dough from refrigerator 30 minutes before frying.

4. Divide the dough into 4 pieces, dust lightly with flour, and if you have a pasta machine, roll it through the machine set at its widest position. Decrease the width of the rollers with each pass through, until you reach the lowest setting. Repeat with the remaining dough. If you don't have a pasta machine, you can roll the dough by hand. Roll it as thinly as you can on a lightly floured surface. It will be hard to get the dough as thin as the pasta machine can, so you'll have fewer cannoli. They will still be delicious.

5. Cut the dough into 5-inch circles with a large, circular cookie cutter or a fine edged bowl.

6. Wrap each dough circle around a cannoli tube. Moisten the edges with water, as you would an envelope. Slightly overlap the ends and press them firmly to seal.

7. In a large heavy-duty saucepan, heat the vegetable oil to 375° degrees.

8. Add about 4 cannoli at a time and fry until golden brown. Remove the cannoli with tongs. Let cool. When cool enough to handle, carefully grasp the cannoli shell and pull out the metal tube. Drain on a paper towel.

9. Allow the cannoli shells to cool before filling.

FILLING

½ cup granulated sugar
1 pound fresh ricotta cheese (about 2 cups), drained in a sieve overnight
1 tablespoon vanilla extract
2-3 tablespoons candied orange peel, finely chopped (optional)
3 ounces bittersweet chocolate, finely chopped
½ cup shelled pistachios, finely chopped
Powdered sugar, for dusting

1. Combine the sugar, ricotta cheese, and vanilla in a mixing bowl. Beat with a wire whisk until smooth. Then add the chopped chocolate and candied orange peel.

2. Place the filling in a pastry bag fitted with a large tip and squeeze the filling into each end of the cannoli shells. Sprinkle the chopped pistachios on both ends and dust with the powdered sugar. Serve immediately.

**ADAPTED FROM
THE VALENTINO COOKBOOK**

Teresa Barrenechea

Spain

Above: Teresa as a little girl in Spain.
Left: Teresa at her restaurant Marichu in New York City.

Teresa Barrenechea grew up in the Basque region of northern Spain in the city of Bilbao. The Basque region borders on France to the east and the Bay of Biscay in the Atlantic Ocean to the north. People there speak a unique language called Euskera that's neither French, nor Spanish. It's still a mystery how the language developed.

Food is a very important part of life in this area of Spain. People love to talk about restaurants and recipes, their next meal, and their last meal. Food is always on their minds. Teresa recently found a diary she'd written when she was ten years old about a trip she'd taken with a friend. She found it funny to read because so much of what she had written were her opinions of the meals she'd eaten.

Teresa grew up in a large family with seven siblings. They spent summers in a small coastal fishing village where they caught and ate loads of seafood. Her friends and family loved to go out on the water in little fishing boats. They'd leave at four in the morning to catch tuna and to watch the schools of silvery fish called bonito leap out of the water. At times Teresa would wander off to the beach to collect seaweed (which she would eat), live crabs, and tiny shrimp called quisquillas.

One of her favorite types of shellfish were the very expensive gooseneck barnacles called percebes that clung to the rocks. Her brother would hunt for them at low tide and sell them to earn extra money for school. Another favorite dish was arroz con chirlas, or rice with clams; and today Teresa's 15-year-old son enjoys preparing it.

Around Christmas time, Teresa loved to eat baby eels which were in season. Because they were very expensive, they were considered a real treat. They're small, skinny fish, the length of a finger, and they look a bit like spaghetti. The baby eels were delicious cooked in a sizzling, garlic sauce. Another Christmas special was snails. Teresa said that if she had to pick one dish that most reminded her of her mother, it would have been snails in the special sauce she made with vegetables, minced ham, and sausage. In her parents' house it was the custom for men to be served first, and then the women. One Christmas, to Teresa's great disappointment, by the time her brothers had helped themselves, there were no snails left for her.

Eating in Spain is very different from the way most Americans eat. In Spain most people still come home for a leisurely lunch of several courses. Shops and schools close at noon for a few hours each day. When children return from school around 5:00, they usually have a merienda or snack which often consists of bocadillos or sandwiches that have rolls as the bread. A very popular bocadillo filling is a Spanish tortilla de patata (a thick potato and onion omelet) that's cut into wedges. Many adults like to meet friends for a small glass of wine on their way home after work, and they eat lots of little hors d'oeuvres

Rice with Clams

While Teresa's older brothers were off fishing in the ocean, her little brothers would stay behind and dig for clams on the beach. Teresa's mother made their favorite dish called rice with clams, in honor of her little boys, so they would feel special too!

called pinchos or tapas at the bars. Dinner is eaten very late: as late as 10:00 in the evening.

Teresa's path to opening a restaurant was an interesting one. She has a Masters degree in Philosophy and Anglo-German Philology. That's the study of how the English and German languages developed and changed over the centuries. She came to New York City for a job as Spain's press attaché to the United Nations where she was responsible for communicating the news from the United Nations back to the press organizations in Spain. She was disappointed when she was unable to find authentic Spanish food in New York and so she decided to open a Spanish restaurant. Since she'd always loved food and cooking for large groups of people, she thought she'd enjoy owning her own restaurant.

In preparation, Teresa went back to Spain to train with several chefs. Then she worked to convert her home cooking into recipes that could be followed by chefs in a restaurant kitchen. Twelve years ago she opened Marichu (which means little Maria), in New York City. It was named after her mother who taught her most of what she knows about cooking. The restaurant's food has been described as the most authentic Spanish food in America. It's the food Teresa

grew up with. She doesn't try to experiment with inventions or new variations on traditional foods because she feels strongly that recipes which have survived for centuries by being handed down from generation to generation, deserve respect and shouldn't be tampered with.

What follows are the recipes for some of Teresa's favorite childhood dishes, including the rice with clams and garlic that her mother used to make using the fresh clams her brothers would gather by the beach. You'll also find an onion soup with bread and melted cheese, the traditional potato and onion omelet, and a very comforting crustless custard tart that the city of Bilbao is known for. Happy eating!

ONION SOUP BASQUE-STYLE

(MAKES 6 SERVINGS)

¼ cup olive oil
1 tablespoon unsalted butter
4 medium Spanish onions, sliced
6 cups homemade or canned beef or chicken broth
Salt to taste
12 thin slices French bread, lightly toasted
1 cup grated aged Idiazabal or Gruyère cheese

1. In a large pot, heat the oil and butter. Sauté the onions over medium heat for about 20 minutes, or until soft and light golden brown.

2. Add the broth, bring it to a simmer, and cook the soup for about 10 minutes longer, until it's hot and the liquid is infused with the onions. Season the soup to taste with salt.

3. Place two slices of bread in the bottom of each of 6 shallow soup plates. Sprinkle each with 2 heaping tablespoons of cheese.

4. Ladle the hot soup over the bread and cheese, and serve immediately.

ADAPTED FROM TERESA BARRENECHEA

TORTILLA DE PATATA
Potato and Onion Omelet

(makes 20 tapas hors d'oeuvres or enough filling for 6–8 sandwiches)

A slice of this tortilla, served with a salad, also makes a nice lunch or light supper. It's the type of recipe that can be made on the spur of the moment because it's quick, and the ingredients are usually on hand.

1 cup olive oil
½ medium onion, coarsely chopped
3 medium potatoes (about 1 pound), cut into small pieces
½ teaspoon salt
4 large eggs, beaten

1. In a large skillet, heat the olive oil over medium-high heat. Add the onion and sauté for about 5 minutes, or until light golden. Add the potatoes, reduce heat to medium, and cook about 15 minutes longer, stirring, until the potatoes are tender.

2. Raise heat to medium-high, and cook the potatoes 1 to 2 minutes longer, until they're light brown, crisp outside, and soft inside. Using a slotted spoon, remove the potatoes and onions and drain them on paper towels or in a colander. Remove all but 1½ teaspoons of the oil. Save the remaining oil.

3. In a bowl, combine the beaten eggs, potatoes, onions, and salt, and mix well.

4. Heat the skillet over high heat, tipping the pan to coat it with the oil. When very hot, pour in the egg mixture, and spread it evenly with a spatula. Cook omelet for about 1 minute over high heat and then reduce the temperature to medium. Cook for several minutes more, until the eggs begin to set around the edges.

5. Place a large round plate that is wider than the pan on top of the pan and invert it so the wet part of the omelet is touching the plate.

6. Add another 1½ teaspoons of the reserved oil to the pan. When the oil is hot, slide the omelet into the pan so the wet part is now touching the pan.

7. Raise heat to high and cook about 1 minute. Lower heat to medium and cook another 3 minutes, or until the omelet is set. Add salt to taste.

8. To serve as hors d'oeuvres, cut the omelet into 20 small squares. For sandwiches, or lunch or dinner, cut it into wedges.

ADAPTED FROM TERESA BARRENECHEA

ARROZ CON CHIRLAS
Rice with Clams

(makes 4 servings)

This is a simple dish that's rich in flavor and extremely satisfying. You'll find yourself preparing it often.

20 Manila, littleneck, or cherrystone clams, well scrubbed
4 cups water
¼ cup olive oil
2 garlic cloves, minced
2 cups medium-grain rice
2 tablespoons flat-leaf parsley, chopped
¾ teaspoon salt

1. Put the clams in a bowl or pot, and cover them with lightly salted, cold water. Using your hands, swish the clams in the water, and then let them sit in the water for about 30 minutes. Drain and rinse them well.

2. In a large saucepan, combine the clams and 4 cups water, and bring to a boil over medium-high heat. Cook clams for about 5 minutes, stirring them with a spoon until they open. Discard any that do not open. Add enough water to the cooking liquid to total 4 cups. Strain and reserve.

3. In a pot, heat the oil over medium heat, and cook the garlic for 3 minutes, stirring until it's softened. Before garlic starts to brown, add the rice and stir to mix it well.

4. Add the reserved liquid and salt, and bring to a boil. Add the clams and parsley. Reduce the heat and cover the pot. Simmer for about 20 minutes, or until the rice is cooked and most of the liquid is absorbed.

5. Serve in shallow bowls.

ADAPTED FROM TERESA BARRENECHEA

CUSTARD TART BILBAO STYLE WITH STRAWBERRY COULIS

(makes two 8-inch pies or one 9-inch pie and two small custard cups)

2 cups whole milk
1 cup unbleached all-purpose flour
3 large eggs, separated
1 cup sugar
¼ cup (½ stick) unsalted butter, melted and slightly cooled
1 14-ounce package frozen, sweetened strawberries thawed

1. Preheat oven to 350°. Lightly butter the pie plates and custard cups.

2. In a blender or food processor fitted with a metal blade, combine the milk, flour egg yolks, and sugar. Blend just until the contents are mixed. Transfer them to a bowl.

3. In a separate bowl, whisk the egg whites with a wire whisk until they start to form soft peaks.

4. Gently fold the egg whites and melted butter into the milk mixture until the whites are almost completely incorporated.

5. Pour the mixture into the pie plates and bake for 45 minutes to 1 hour, or until the custard is golden brown and a toothpick inserted near the center comes out clean. Cool until lukewarm.

6. To make the strawberry coulis, simply purée the frozen strawberries with their juice in a food processor or blender.

7. To serve, spread several tablespoons of the strawberry coulis onto each dessert plate and top with a slice of the custard tart.

ADAPTED FROM TERESA BARRENECHEA

Spanish/English Translations

playa	beach	chico	boy
cebolla	onion	sopa	soup
ajo	garlic	recetas	recipes
mariscos	seafood	oceano	ocean
fresa	strawberry	queso	cheese

Marcus Samuelsson

Sweden

Above: Marcus baking cookies in his grandmother's kitchen.
Left: Chef Marcus Samuelsson.

Marcus Samuelsson is an extremely nice, energetic, and interesting person. He was born in Ethiopia. At the age of three he was orphaned when his parents sadly died of tuberculosis. Marcus and his sister were adopted by a kind, Swedish family; and they moved to western Sweden to a town on the North Sea called Gothenburg.

Marcus's grandmother was a big influence in his life. She was a wonderful cook, and she began teaching him how to cook when he was six years old. They started by making traditional Swedish foods, cookies, and fresh bread. His grandmother, who he called mormor (the Swedish word for grandmother), showed him how to search for wild mushrooms and berries in the woods. This is a common activity in Sweden. The Swedes pickle the vegetables and preserve the fruits that ripened in summer, so they can be enjoyed during the colder winter months.

Both saltwater fish and seafood from the North Sea, and freshwater fish from nearby rivers are plentiful in Gothenburg. The fish are cured or preserved with vinegar, salt, and sugar during the summer for use throughout the year. Marcus's mormor often cooked from her pantry as though she didn't have a refrigerator. Typically foods were brought in fresh and cooked right away, or the preserved foods from the pantry shelf were used.

Marcus's grandmother was a careful cook and nothing was wasted. If chicken was served one night for dinner, the next night they would have chicken soup with chicken dumplings. There was a pattern to dinners every week. Tuesdays the Samuelsson family ate herring, a fish that's plentiful and prepared in many different ways in Scandinavia; Thursday was split pea soup night with Swedish pancakes for dessert; Fridays, hash brown potatoes were served; and Sunday was steak or Swedish meatball night.

On special occasions, Marcus's family would either make a smorgasboard at home or go to a smorgasboard in a restaurant. A smorgasboard is a bountiful buffet that can have as many as sixty different dishes on it. It's nearly impossible to taste everything, though it's fun to try. At Christmas time, Marcus and his family would bake holiday favorites such as gingersnap cookies and almond cookie ring cake. The cookie ring cake was made of approximately fifteen circle shaped cookies, each one slightly smaller than the next, stacked from large to small. Sometimes they were stacked around a champagne bottle, and they were decorated with Swedish flags.

When Swedish teens turn sixteen, they're expected to choose a profession. Marcus, who had loved to cook nearly his whole life, decided he would train to be a great chef. When he was still a teenager, he apprenticed at a local bakery and at several local restaurants. He also attended

Dala Horses

Dala horses are Sweden's national symbol. They originated in the 18th Century in the Dalarna region of Sweden. The horses were hand carved from scraps of wood that came from the pine forests of the area. Because they're carved by hand, no two are exactly alike. In the 19th Century it became customary to paint flowers on the horse's saddle. While the traditional color was red, today the horses come in blue and black as well.

a professional cooking school called the Culinary Institute of Gothenburg.

After Marcus graduated, he went to work at a grand old hotel in Interlaken, at the base of the tallest mountains in Switzerland. There they spoke French, German, and English, but not his native Swedish. Not only did he survive, he thrived. After that, Marcus apprenticed at the most famous pastry shop in all of Europe near Salzburg, Austria, the home of Mozart and *The Sound of Music*.

Marcus's next adventure was cooking on an extremely luxurious cruise ship that traveled all around the world. That was a great education because he learned about the different cooking ingredients and dishes that were native to many different countries. Marcus accomplished all this by the time he was twenty-one. At the age of twenty-four he took a full time job in New York City at Aquavit Restaurant where today he is the head chef and part owner.

Marcus won many awards for his exceptional cooking and he's just completed his new

book *Aquavit: The New Scandanavian Cooking.*

Marcus is someone who had a dream to be the best chef he could be. He studied hard and tried to learn everything he could from talented cooks and bakers in Sweden and other countries. Today, aside from being a chef, Marcus works with UNICEF (the United Nations International Children's Emergency Fund) to support children's health programs in poor countries; and he teaches inner city youth how to train for jobs in the restaurant and food industries. Marcus is widely admired, and respected.

What follows are some of Marcus's favorite childhood dishes that he still enjoys today, including the coconut cookie recipe you can see him making in his childhood photo.

SWEDISH MEATBALLS

(makes 4 servings)

½ cup white bread crumbs
¾ cup heavy cream or half-and-half
1 cup ground beef
½ cup ground veal
½ cup ground pork
½ yellow onion, finely chopped
1 large egg, beaten
½ teaspoon salt
¼ teaspoon white pepper
3 tablespoons butter

1. Soak bread crumbs in the cream until soaked through. Set aside.

2. Brown the onion in 1 tablespoon of butter in a 10-inch skillet, and set aside.

3. In a large bowl, combine the browned onion and bread crumbs and cream with the egg and ground meats. Stir with a spoon, adding a little water as needed to create a firm, yet smooth consistency. Season with salt and pepper.

4. Shape the meatballs by rolling two tablespoons of the meat mixture into a ball. The balls will be soft.

5. Melt remaining 2 tablespoons of butter in the skillet. Add the meatballs and brown on all sides. Remove from the skillet with a slotted spoon and drain on paper towels to remove any excess grease.

6. Serve with lingonberries and pan gravy. Lingonberries are sold at Ikea and some gourmet food stores. The closest substitute would be whole berry cranberry sauce.

ADAPTED FROM MARCUS SAMUELSSON

JANSSON'S TEMPTATION

Potato, Onion and Anchovy Casserole

(makes 4–6 servings)

2 large Idaho potatoes (about 16 ounces each), thinly sliced
4 tablespoons butter
1 medium red onion, thinly sliced
1 medium Spanish onion, thinly sliced
2 cans of anchovy fillets, drained of oil and chopped
2 cups heavy cream or half-and-half
2 tablespoons bread crumbs
1 tablespoon butter

1. Preheat oven to 375°.

2. Brush the inside of a 9 x 13-inch baking dish with 1 tablespoon of the butter.

3. Take out two large frying pans. Melt 1½ tablespoons of butter in each. Separately sauté the red and yellow onions until golden colored.

4. Spread half the potato slices over the bottom of the pan. Top with sautéed red onion. Sprinkle with half the chopped anchovies.

5. Top with the remaining potato slices, followed by the sautéed Spanish onion, and then the remaining anchovies.

6. Pour cream evenly over the potato and onions, and sprinkle with the bread crumbs. Cover with aluminum foil

7. Bake for about 30 minutes. Remove the foil and bake another 20-30 minutes, until the potatoes are tender when pricked with a knife and the top is golden brown.

ADAPTED FROM MARCUS SAMUELSSON

 Magical Melting Pot

AQUAVIT'S GINGERSNAP COOKIES

(makes 4 dozen)

These cookies are slightly chewy, with a wonderfully, spicy flavor.

½ cup sugar, plus sugar for coating the cookies.
½ cup light brown sugar
2 sticks unsalted butter
1 egg
⅓ cup molasses
2 teaspoons ground ginger
½ teaspoon ground cardamom
½ teaspoon ground cloves
2 teaspoons baking soda
½ teaspoon salt
½ teaspoon white pepper
2 ½ cups all purpose flour
1 cup coarsely chopped, candied orange peel

1. Preheat oven to 350°.

2. In a medium bowl, cream together brown and white sugar and butter until light and fluffy. Add egg and molasses, and incorporate well.

3. Sift together the dry ingredients and add to the creamed mixture. Mix well. Gently mix in the candied orange peel.

4. Cover the dough and refrigerate for 2 hours or longer.

5. Place about ½ cup of white sugar on a plate. Shape dough in 1-inch balls and roll each in sugar until well coated. Place 2 inches apart on an ungreased cookie sheet.

6. Bake for 8-10 minutes, or until golden brown. Let cool slightly before removing from the cookie sheet.

ADAPTED FROM MARCUS SAMUELSSON

COCONUT COOKIES

(makes about 2 dozen cookies)

These are extremely quick and easy to make.

8 ounces coconut flakes
2 tablespoons butter, melted
2 large eggs, beaten
¾ cups sugar

1. Preheat oven to 325°.

2. In a small bowl, combine the coconut flakes and melted butter.

3. In a large bowl, beat the eggs and mix in the sugar. Beat until light and fluffy.

4. Add the coconut mixture to the egg mixture.

5. Drop by the level tablespoonful onto a greased cookie sheet and bake for approximately 12-14 minutes, or until golden brown.

ADAPTED FROM MARCUS SAMUELSSON

Swedish/English Translations

potato	potatis	fish	fisk
onion	lök	meatball	köttbulle
cream	grädde	cookie	smäkaka; kex
berry	bär	spice	krydda
mushroom	svamp	dessert	dessert

Alvina Kwong

Illustrator

Above: Alvina, age 2.
Left: Alvina with her sketch pad.

A lvina Kwong was born and raised in Hawaii until age 8, when her family moved to southern California. Family and friends say she's been drawing since she could hold a pencil. From the time she was very little, Alvina carried a sketchbook with her wherever she went. She tried to capture with her pencil and sketchbook everything beautiful she saw that she wanted to remember…from the shimmery blue ocean with the sun shining through the clouds, to horses running across the sandy beach.

As Alvina says "I was just a little kid with no camera to capture the things I thought were beautiful, and I had no money to buy books full of pretty pictures of horses. So I borrowed books from the library and imagined pretty little horses running across my head. I used these images and put them on paper as realistically as I could, so I could keep them forever."

While she was growing up, Alvina took lots of art classes, including ceramics, drawing, and painting. In high school she was in the Advanced Placement Studio Art Program. Today Alvina majors in Illustration at Brigham Young University's Visual Arts Department. Her goal is to illustrate anything: from books to advertisements. She believes that everyone has a dream, and that their dream will come true eventually, as long as they work hard and never give up. This is the first book Alvina has illustrated.

MORE INFORMATION ABOUT THE CHEFS

Alexis Bakouros
Alexis Restaurant
Alexis Foods
215 W. Burnside St.
Portland, Oregon
Phone: (503) 224-8577
Website: www.alexisfoods.com

Teresa Barrenechea
Marichu Restaurant
342 East 46th St.
New York, New York
Website: www.marichu.com
Phone: (212) 370-1866
Cookbooks: *The Basque Table*
   (Harvard Common Press)
The Cuisines of Spain (Ten Speed
   Press)

Najmieh Batmanglij
Website: www.najmieh.com
Cookbooks:
*New Food of Life: Ancient Persian and
   Modern Iranian Cooking and
   Ceremonies*
A Taste of Persia
Silk Road Cooking
*Persian Cooking for a Healthy
   Kitchen*

Inez Bon
NL Restaurant
169 Sullivan St.
New York, New York
Phone: (212) 387-8801
Website: www.nl.nv.com

Ella Brennan
Commanders Palace Restaurant
1403 Washington Ave.
New Orleans, Louisiana
Phone: (504) 896-7600
Website: commanderspalace.com
Cookbook: *Commander's Kitchen*,
   2002

Jorge Chan
El Rocoto Restaurant
1356-1358 West Artesia Blvd.
Gardena California
Phone: (310) 768-8768
Website: www.elrocoto.com

Sam Choy
Website: www.samchoy.com
Restaurant and cookbook information
   are available on Sam's website

Marion Cunningham
Cookbooks: *Lost Recipes*, Fall 2003
The Supper Book, 2002
*Learning to Cook with Marion
   Cunningham*, 1999
The Fannie Farmer Baking Book,
   1996
The Fannie Farmer Cookbook, 1996
Cooking with Children, 1995
The Breakfast Book, 1987

Norma Jean Darden
Miss Mamie
366 West 110th St. at Columbus Avenue
New York, New York
Phone: (212) 865-6744
Miss Maude
547 Lenox Ave. (bet. 137th & 138th Sts.)
New York, New York
Phone: (212) 690-3100
Website: spoonbreadinc.com
Cookbook: *Spoonbread and
   Strawberry Wine: Recipes and
   Remembrances from a Black
   Family*,
Doubleday

Dimitri Dimitrov
Diaghilev Restaurant
1020 N. San Vicente Blvd.
West Hollywood, California
Phone: (310) 854-1111

Workye Ephrem
Ghenet Restaurant
284 Mulberry St.
New York, New York
Phone: (212) 343-1888

José Fonseca
Delícia Brazil Restaurant
322 West 11th St.
New York, New York
Phone: (212) 242-2002
Some Brazilian products available by
   phone.

Mark Henegan
Madiba Restaurant
195 DeKalb Ave.
Brooklyn, New York
Phone: (718) 855-9190
Websites: www.madibaweb.com
   www.i-shebeen.com,
Cookbook: *I-Shebeen Cuisine*

Madeleine Kamman
Cookbooks:
In Madeleine's Kitchen, 1984
The Making of a Cook, 1999

Thomas Keller
The French Laundry Restaurant
6640 Washington, St.
Yountville, California
Phone: (707) 994-8979
Book: *The French Laundry Cookbook*,
   IACP Cookbook Award 2000

Zarela Martinez
Zarela Restaurant
953 Second Avenue
New York, New York
Phone: (212) 644-6740
Website: www.zarela.com
Cookbooks:
Zarela's Veracruz, Houghton Mifflin,
   2001
The Food and Life of Oaxaca,
   Macmillan, 1998
Food From My Heart, Macmillan, 1992

Nobu Matsuhisa
Website: www.nobumatsuhisa.com
Restaurant information available on the
   website
Cookbook: *Nobu the Cookbook*

Kitty Morse
Website: www.kittymorse.com
Cookbooks:
*The Scent of Orange Blossoms:
   Sephardic Cuisine from* Morocco,
   co-authored with Danielle Mamane,
   (Ten Speed Press, 2001)
*Couscous: Fresh and Flavorful
   Contemporary Recipes*, (Chronicle
   Books, July 2000)
*Cooking at the Kasbah: Recipes from
   my Moroccan Kitchen* (Chronicle
   Books, 1998)
*A Biblical Feast: Foods from the Holy
   Land for Today* (Ten Speed Press,
   1998)
The Vegetarian Table: North Africa
   (Chronicle Books, 1996)
*Edible Flowers: A Kitchen Companion
   with Recipes* (Ten Speed Press,
   1995)
Edible Flowers poster (Ten Speed
   Press, 1995)
365 Ways to Cook Vegetarian (Second
   edition, Barnes and Noble, 2002)
The California Farm Cookbook
   (Pelican Publishing, 1994)

Shoba Narayan
Komala Vilas Restaurant
Sunnyvale, California
Websites: www.shobanarayan.com,
   www.komalavilas.com
Book: *Monsoon Diary*, Random House
   (April 2003)

Patrick O'Connell
The Inn at Little Washington
Middle and Main Streets
Washington, Virginia
Phone: (540) 675-3800
Cookbook: *The Inn at Little
    Washington, A Consuming Passion*

Samuel Oh
Ham Hung Restaurant
809 South Ardmore St.
Los Angeles, California
Phone: (213) 381-1520

Loretta Barrett Oden
Corn Dance Café at Fire Lake
1905 Gordon Cooper Dr.
Shawnee, Oklahoma
Phone: (405) 395-9050
Website: www.corndancecafe.com
Cookbook: *Seasoned with Spirit—A
    Native Cook's Journey*, Fall 2004

Guillermo Pernot
¡Pasión! Restaurant
211 S. 15th St.
Philadelphia, Pennsylvania
Phone: (215) 875-9895
Website: www.pasionrestaurant.com
Cookbook: *¡Ceviche!* (available through
    the website)

Douglas Rodriguez
Alma de Cuba Restaurant
1623 Walnut St.
Philadelphia, Pennsylvania
Phone: (215) 988-1799
Of Latin America (OLA)
304 East 48th St.
New York, New York
(212) 759-0590
Deseo
The Westin Kierland Resort
6902 E. Greenway Parkway
Scottsdale, Arizona
www.chefdouglasrodriguez.com
Cookbooks:
Nuevo Latino
The Great Ceviche Book
Latin Flavors on the Grill
Latin Ladles

Hans Röckenwagner
Röckenwagner Restaurant
2435 Main St.
Santa Monica, California
Phone: (310) 399-6504
Website: www.rockenwagner.com
Cookbook: *Röckenwagner*

Colette Rossant
Cookbooks:
Memories of a Lost Egypt, (Clarkson
    Potter)
Return to Paris (Atria Books)

Marcus Samuelsson
Aquavit Restaurant
13 West 54th St.
New York, New York
Phone: (212) 307-7311
Website: www.aquavit.org
Cookbook: *Aquavit and the New
    Scandinavian Cuisine*

Piero Selvaggio
Valentino Restaurant
3115 Pico Blvd.
Santa Monica, California
Phone: (310) 829-4313
Cookbook: *The VALENTINO Cookbook*

Pierre Thiam
Sage Catering
Brooklyn, New York
Phone: (718) 398-8900
Yolêlê Restaurant
1108 Fulton St.
Brooklyn, New York
Email: food4zsoul@aol.com

Mechel Thompson
Maroons Restaurant
244 West 16th St.
New York, New York
Phone: (212) 206-8640
Website: maroonsnyc.com

Ming Tsai
Blue Ginger Restaurant
583 Washington St.
Wellesley, Massachusetts
Phone: (701) 283-5790
Website: www.ming.com
Cookbook:
*Blue Ginger East: Meets West Cooking
    with Ming Tsai*, Clarkson Potter,
    November 1999
Simply Ming, Fall 2003

Alice Waters
Chez Panisse Restaurant
1517 Shattuck Ave.
Berkeley, California
Phone: (510) 548-5072
Website: www.chezpanisse.com
Books: *Chez Panisse Fruit,* by Alice
    Waters and the cooks of Chez
    Panisse in collaboration with Alan
    Tangren and Fritz Streiff, Harper
    Collins, 2002.
Chez Panisse Café Cookbook, by Alice
    Waters and the cooks of Chez
    Panisse in collaboration with David
    Tanis and Fritz Streif, Harper Collins,
    1999.

Alan Wong
Alan Wong's Restaurant
1857 S. King St.
Honolulu, Hawaii
Phone: (808) 949-2526
Website: www.alanwongs.com
Book: *Alan Wong's New Wave Luau*

Su-Mei Yu
Saffron Thai Grilled Chicken Restaurant
3731 India St.
SanDiego California
Phone: (619) 574-0177
Saffron Noodles and Saté Restaurant
3737 India Street
San Diego, California
Phone: (619) 574-7737
Website: www.sumeiyu.com
Cookbooks:
*Cracking the Coconut—Classic Thai
    Home Cooking*, 2000
Asian Grilling, 2002

RECIPE INDEX